Praise for Jason O'Toole

"Indisputably Ireland's most talented and prolific interviewer."

—*Irish Daily Mail*

"I love the style of interviews and the way Jason O'Toole poses the questions. It's more like radio on paper."

—Broadcaster Niall Boylan, winner of the *Best Schedule Talk Show in the World* at the New York Radio Awards 2017 and 2019

"O'Toole is Ireland's best interviewer."

— *Irish Mail on Sunday*

"O'Toole specialises in in-your-face interviews."

—*Sunday Independent*

"O'Toole's skill is getting access to important figures and being a good listener."

—*Metro*

"O'Toole is one of our frontline interviewers, handling a plethora of headline making tête-à-têtes."

— Niall Stokes, *Hot Press*

"The finest interviewer of his generation."

— *Gill & MacMillan*

"Jason O'Toole is the journalistic equivalent of a hangman. Cleverly giving some of his notorious subjects just enough rope to do the job themselves."

— *Evening Herald*

HOLLY WOOD IRISH

An anthology of interviews with Irish movie stars

Jason O'Toole

BEARMANORMEDIA.COM

Hollywood Irish

Published in the USA by:
4700 Millenia Blvd.
Suite 175 PMB 90497
Orlando, FL 32839
www.bearmanormedia.com

Printed in the United States of America

ISBN 978-1-62933-418-9 (paperback)
978-1-62933-419-6 (hardcover)

Book and cover design by Darlene & Dan Swanson • www.van-garde.com

About the author

Born in Dublin, Jason O'Toole is a columnist with the *Irish Sunday Mirror* and writes about music for the *Irish Daily Mirror*. He is a best-selling author of several non-fiction titles and his journalism has appeared in dozens of publication, such as *The Sunday Times, Daily Mail, Irish Independent, Irish Mail on Sunday, Empire, Playboy, Hot Press*, and Italy's *La Republica and Panorama*. He resides in Madrid.

Also by the same author

Brian Cowen: The Path to Power

Crime Ink

Katie Taylor: Journey to Olympic Gold

The Last Days of Katy French

The End of the Party (with Bruce Arnold)

Memory Man (with Jimmy Magee)

Different Class (with Jimmy Magee)

Off The Edge (editor)

For Eva, mi media naranja.

To quote Jack Lemmon's character from

her favourite movie, *The Apartment,*

"I used to live like Robinson Crusoe;

I mean, shipwrecked among 8 million people.

And then one day I saw a footprint in

the sand, and there you were."

Contents

“What Freud said about the Irish is,

we’re the only people who are

impervious to psychoanalysis.”

— Matt Damon, The Departed

Introduction

This is not a collection of brief interviews with stars cobbled together from press junkets in which they talk ad nauseam with a journalist—as stipulated in their movie contract—about their latest role for an allocated 15 minutes. Instead, these particular in-depth interviews were set-up directly with the actors themselves, without any interference from publicists or movie studios.

Reflecting back on it all, as I was compiling this anthology, I still can't believe that I managed to cajole such big Irish names in Hollywood, or those with connections to the auld sod—such as Martin Sheen, Maureen O'Hara, Gabriel Byrne, Saoirse Ronan, Jonathan Rhys Meyers, Brenda Fricker, John Boorman, and Patrick Bergin—to agree to do these deeply personal interviews about their lives and careers.

You could say all these interviews came about by sheer luck. As a journalist colleague of mine, Valerie Hanley, likes to say, "You make your own luck in this game." By this, I think she meant you've got to be a hard grafter. And I certainly worked my socks off with building up a large network of contacts to get access to Irish celebrities.

I arranged the vast majority of the interviews in this anthology through a friend of a friend, or by writing directly to the star, either by email or snail mail. A fellow author mentioned that he grew up with Gabriel Byrne and he got me his personal email address; my local barman introduced me to Patrick Bergin; the actor Vincent Smith arranged interviews for me with his close friends, David Kelly and Niall Tóibín; while another friend, Fr. Shay Cullen introduced me to Martin Sheen; a work colleague gave me Kate O'Toole's email address; and so on. He didn't know me from Adam, but I once got a hold of Paul Ronan's mobile number and he kindly helped organise an interview with his daughter, Saoirse.

It even once transpired that the guy sitting next to me in the office, who was there on work experience, just so happened to be Jonathan Rhys Meyers' kid brother. Coincidentally, Jonathan was in town at the time and the brother brought me down to his hotel to get an interview. Talk about the luck of the Irish on that occasion.

Nine times out of ten, my sales pitch worked and they'd be generous enough to give me at an hour or two of their time, sometimes longer, like with Martin Sheen, with whom I was lucky enough to spend an entire weekend. Most times I was able to get back to them via email or phone with follow-up questions.

One editor in London told me that my tactics would never have worked over in England. It definitely made it easier that Ireland is a small country—to such an extent that you can easily come across the likes of Gabriel Byrne walking down the street, or bump into Patrick Bergin enjoying the *craic* in a bar. No, I'm not referring to an illegal substance here: *craic* is Irish for fun. Sometimes I'd walk out of a bar with a celebrity's email or phone number and the promise of an interview. On one occasion, I met a famous TV sports broadcaster named Jimmy Magee this way and we ended up co-writing two bestsellers together.

It also helped that I wasn't writing for the gutter press and I had a reputation for conducting fair and balanced interviews. The majority of these interviews were written as the main interview for the influential magazine *Hot Press*, which is often described as the Irish version of *Rolling Stone* and for my weekly two-page feature slot called 'The Jason O'Toole Interview', in the *Irish Daily Mail* and its sister paper, the *Irish Mail on Sunday*, which I did for five years, between 2009 and 2014.

Sigmund Freud once claimed that the Irish are "one race of people for whom psychoanalysis is of no use whatsoever", as Matt Damon famously paraphrased in *The Departed*. But we Irish can be a remarkably candid race—as is evident in this anthology. Brenda Fricker holds the honour of being the first—and so far only—Irish woman to win an Oscar for acting. Yet her life has been far from all sweetness and light. She opened up to me about her battle with depression and countless suicide attempts. While Jonathan Rhys Meyers, David Kelly, Martin Sheen, Peter Sheridan, and the Olivier Award winning actor Alan Devlin were all candid about their issues with the demon drink.

Even Martin Sheen astonished me by admitting, "I am proud of just a handful of films. I would say 90% of it was basically trash. I did it for the money, and most of the stuff I did was a great source of embarrassment to me." It's far from the typical sound bite you'll usually pick up at a press junket.

I'm not taking any credit for these confessions—I simply asked the questions that everybody else would've too, if given the opportunity. It's the subjects themselves who deserve praise for their refreshing candour.

For Jason — it was
good to meet you — Good
Luck + may Marianne
love you always — Love
from me too! —
Maureen
O'Hara

CHAPTER ONE:

A private audience with the Queen of Technicolor, Maureen O'Hara

Entering the hotel, the elderly lady, who was aided by a walking cane and her personal assistant, was still instantly recognizable from her halcyon days as 'The Queen of Technicolor'.

She had just turned 90-years-old when we met for what transpired to be her last ever in-depth interview, conducted in her beloved Ireland. Time had been kind to Maureen O'Hara, who still oozed charisma. There was a twinkle in those piercing green eyes and she could instantly disarm you with her legendary beguiling smile.

Still possessing a full head of those famous fiery red locks, Maureen had also retained her famous delightful feistiness and an incredibly sharp mind, coupled with an even quicker tongue—which she became famous for in those memorable onscreen verbal duels with John Wayne. Maureen was still more than capable of delivering killer one-liners with perfect timing, as I was soon to discover.

"You know what they say about old age? Old age is a terrible thing, particularly when it strikes you when you're so young," she said, when we met in Glengarriff, West Cork.

As she rested her cane beside the armchair in the residents' lounge in Casey's Hotel, I reminded Maureen that she once stated that as a little girl she dreamt of growing into a "wonderfully, eccentric, tough, cantankerous, and sometimes mean old lazy who thumps her cane loudly" to get what she wanted and to express herself.

Maureen smiled. "I'm doing it right now. And I'm going to do it. Oh, God!" she said, jokingly thumping her cane against the floor and then waving it about dramatically in the air. "And today in this world—and the world since the beginning of time—a woman has to be tough."

There were only two stipulations for the granting of my rare interview with Maureen O'Hara—one was that I wasn't to broach the subject of her first two marriages, which I didn't particularly mind because they'd already been relatively well documented in her autobiography. Secondly—and perhaps even more intriguingly—I wasn't to ask anything "too personal", as her assistant advised, about her close friendship with John Wayne. The actress was obviously fearful of having to address questions about the persistent rumours of a love affair between them. (After her death in October 2015, John Wayne's son revealed that his father was in love with Maureen O'Hara.)

Respecting these stipulations, I simply asked her, "You had special bonds with many special actors and directors, but it appears that the closest was with John Wayne?"

Maureen's eyes lit up at the mention of John Wayne's name and nodded enthusiastically. "Oh, yeah," she told me.

I then asked, "Why was this friendship so special?"

"Well, he was a wonderful person. And a wonderful person to work with. We were proud of our work and proud of ourselves. And he had a wonderful family and wonderful kids and a wonderful wife and they were all there for each other, supporting each other," she stated. "And you were a member of a gang and it was wonderful. And a gang that you knew if there was ever a problem or trouble that [they would] support you—that they'd be there."

It was perhaps surprising to discover that this Hollywood legend, who has starred in some of cinemas most memorable all-time classics—such as *The Quiet Man* (1952), *Miracle on 34th Street* (1947), *How Green Was My Valley* (1941), and *The Hunchback of Notre Dame* (1939)—actually resided for the last couple of decades of her life in this remote, picturesque village in West Cork.

After making the western *McLintock!* (1963) with John Wayne, Maureen stunned Hollywood by deciding to retire from acting to be with her husband, the late Irish-American Brigadier General Charles F. Blair, who tragically died in a plane crash in 1978.

The couple set up home in West Cork after falling in love with the area.

"We drove down to Glengarriff—where I had never been before—and we saw this house," she recounted. "Charlie looked out at it and he said, 'Oh, my God! This is a perfect place to land a seaplane. We're going to buy the house'. I said, 'Wait a minute! Let's look at the house first before we decide on the basis of a seaplane'. And we fell in love with house and we bought the house. And, yes, we did land the seaplane."

It was her glowing memories of their blissful times together in West Cork, which prompted O'Hara after her husband's death, to spend her retirement years in that little village, while occasionally dividing her time between homes in the US and the Caribbean.

I was taken aback when O'Hara told me that she never once dreamt about becoming a famous actress.

"I wanted to be an opera singer. And I wanted to write beautiful poetry. I always intended to do great things. I didn't do all of the things I wanted to do," she said. "My older sister Peg won a scholarship as a soprano and gave it up to be a nun. So, in the family we had all of that."

Growing up, her father owned shares in one of the most successful soccer teams in Ireland, Shamrock Rovers. This connection cemented her lifelong love of soccer, a subject that she frequently turned to during our time together. "Of course, I wanted to play soccer," Maureen told me, adding that her "TV is well used for the games". Maureen loved the game so much that she hoped there would be "soccer games in heaven". I like to imagine her now in heaven—if it exists—sitting in an armchair and watching her beloved Shamrock Rovers or the Irish national side playing a game on TV.

Born Maureen FitzSimons on August 17, 1920, she grew up at number 13 Churchtown Road, Milltown, Dublin, as the second oldest of six children in a respectable, but what she described as an "eccentric" family.

"I was born in Ranelagh and grow up in Milltown, right in front of the entrance to the golf club. Daddy was from Kells, County Meath. My mother was a Dubliner. But I was born at 32 Upper Beachwood Avenue. You never said Lower Beachwood Avenue," she said and then jokingly added in a posh accent, "It was very low class (to say Lower Beachwood Avenue). (It must be) Upper Beachwood Avenue. It was all that silly snobbery in Dublin about County South Dublin, North Dublin. God."

The social divide between the upper and lower Beachwood Avenue that she referred to is similar to the one that has always existed between north and south Dublin. When I mention that there was still a social divide running across north and south of the River Liffey in Dublin, she sounded surprised. "Really! You're kidding!" Maureen sighed and shook her head in bewilderment.

Maureen believed her fiery character, which she described as her "signature trademark" throughout her film career, was moulded by her two tough brothers.

"They saw to it that all the girls in the family were tough. And we were. The whole family: we were tough. We were all number one at no matter what we touched," she said. "We didn't brag about it. We were proud of it. We were so proud of the fact that we made our mother and father proud of us."

Even as a young teenager, the then Ms. FitzSimons stood out and virtually won every Fèis competition—a traditional Gaelic arts and culture festival—that she entered, which brought her to the attention of the Abbey Theatre as a potential future star.

"I was proud, but I wasn't egotistical about it," she recalled. "I was just thrilled that I was winning. So, I was hired by The Abbey. We used to get like ten shillings or a pound a week. But you were thrilled; you were proud of yourself."

As she was about to prepare for her first major role in a production at the National Theatre, a chance meeting with a popular American singer named Harry Richman in the Gresham Hotel led to her being offered a screen test by Elstree Studios in London. She was then signed up by a talent agency and offered a contract with the production company Mayflower Pictures, owned by the Anglo-Irish actor Charles Laughton and Erich Pommer—"the great movie producer," according to Maureen—who had discovered Marlene Dietrich.

"I'm not sure, but I think I was practically the only person that they signed and they signed me to a seven year contract. So, that was it," she said.

Her first starring role was as Maureen FitzSimons in a musical comedy, *My Irish Molly*. But her name was then changed after Laughton cast her as his leading lady in *Jamaica Inn* (1939), directed by Alfred Hitchcock, whose mother also happened to be an Irishwoman.

"It was Charles Laughton who changed my name," she insisted to me, making it sound as if she still wasn't too pleased about it all these years later. "He said, 'Oh, no, that surname would be horrible up on a marquee—Maureen FitzSimons. We're going to change it to O'Mara or O'Hara'. And I said, 'Oh, no. I'd like my own name'. And that was it—take it or leave it. But Laughton was a wonderful person to work with, believe me."

After the success of the Hitchcock film, Maureen was cast again alongside Laughton in *The Hunchback of Notre Dame*, which was to be filmed in America.

"I didn't move to America—I was taken to America by Charles Laughton and Erich Pommer," she said with great patois, making it sound like she'd been kidnapped.

Did she ever wonder where her career might have been if she hadn't met Charles Laughton?

"No, I think I'd be exactly where I am. Maybe a little further," she insisted with great gusto.

Astonishingly, only two hours before she boarded the RMS Queen Mary to America in June 1939, Maureen had secretly married George Brown, a production man on *Jamaica Inn*, after only a couple of dates.

As I wrote earlier, a stipulation for this interview was not discussing either of Maureen's first two failed marriages, because she was "embarrassed" to talk about those two big regrets in her life, I was told. I respected the stipulation during my two hour meeting with Maureen, but, in the past, she has spoken about how she felt pressured into the first marriage, which was conducted by a priest in Brown's sitting room. He had lied to the priest by insisting that the then 18-year-old Maureen was over 21. The marriage, which was never consummated, was annulled several years later.

On the boat journey to America, Maureen broke the news of the marriage to her shocked mother. She was subsequently urged by the film company not to tell anybody for fear of damaging stories surfacing in the press.

Soon after filming *The Hunchback of Notre Dam*, in an effort to prevent Mayflower from going bankrupt, Maureen's contract was bought out by RKO pictures, which she said "broke my heart", as she considered Laughton to be a father figure and wanted to continue working with him.

"They'd sell bits of you in those days. I don't know what they do today. But then they sold me first to RKO, then part of me to Twentieth Century Fox for *How Green Was My Valley*, one of the greatest movies ever made. Oh, it really was," she said.

"You'd be surprised at movies you thought were fabulous and they just made their way. And then something that you thought, 'Oh, good God did I really do that?' And it'd be a smash hit, you know? It's amazing what the public falls for."

Maureen went on to star in some of Hollywood's biggest movies, but insisted that she never allowed the fame to go to her head. "I had a fabulous mother and father and five brothers and sisters and they wouldn't ever permit you to get more important than you thought you were," she pointed out.

Yet despite such early successes, Maureen believed she wasn't being offered roles to match her raising star. She felt the studios' casting executives "resented" her because she refused to succumb to the so-called casting coach. "I wasn't a whore," she wrote in her memoir, *'Tis Herself*. (My signed copy takes a place of pride in my collection, along with the personalised autographed black and white photograph Maureen gave to me.)

In an effort to push her career in a different direction, Maureen made a conscious decision to change her on-screen image of someone who was merely part of the "pretty scenery" and sought out action-adventure roles.

"You had to fight, but not be rude or hurtful with anybody. You couldn't sit back and hope it's going to come and jump in your lap," she explained. "That's one thing, thank God, touch wood, I had wonderful leading men: Jimmy Stewart, John Payne, John Wayne, Errol Flynn, Brian Keith, and Anthony Quinn, who was very proud of the fact that he was born in Mexico, though he had an Irish name."

She also cemented her trademark reputation as a fiery redhead by insisting on doing all her own stunts. Maureen remembered how on her first action flick, *At Sword's Point* (1952), the director dismissed, out of hand, the idea of his leading lady doing her own fencing scenes.

"I heard these nasty remarks by the director, which I can't say I blamed him for because at that time women didn't do stunts. And the director was sneering, worse than sneering," Maureen recalled. "He was belittling the idea of a woman fencing. He was against it. The studio wanted it. I was trained by the fencing master from the Belgian army."

She continued, "And so the guys were saying to me, 'Get out there and do it'. I was ready to panic and run away. I had to step out of a coach and immediately start fencing because I was attacked immediately. And finally they said, 'Alright'. And I jumped out and, boy, I fenced their arses off! The director said, 'Cut! Cut! Print! Print!'

"You know, the whole place fell apart laughing, screaming, and applauding. They were so thrilled. Because it belittled . . . well, not belittled . . . it did what to the director? It made him look like a fool."

Proudly, like a peacock, she then also pointed out: "When I did *The Quiet Man*, I did all those things. I did so many pictures that involved fencing, fighting, punching, boxing, jumping off buildings, and everything. The only stuff I didn't do was on a horse, properly; I couldn't look professional on a horse."

Maureen remembered one particular stunt in *McLintock!* being so dangerous that she could have been killed if she didn't fall correctly. As she got up the ladder to the "second story to fall backwards" into a water trough, a stuntman coordinator suddenly warned her about the perils of the stunt about to be undertaken.

"And I said, 'Why the hell didn't you tell me that a couple of weeks ago when I agreed to do the bloody stunt?' she said. "I could have killed myself; if I had fallen long, I'd have hit my head off the top of the water trough and I could have broken my neck. . . . I'd have been dead'."

She paused to shake her head at the madness of it all. "If I fell short, I'd have broken my legs. But that was the one thing that frightened me because I thought, 'God, I may be dead in five minutes'."

It was a measure of the woman's gutsy determination that she still went through with the dangerous stunt. "I fell into the water trough and almost drowned and I had to get out and face Duke. Watch him, next time that you see that movie. Duke looked at me and he said, 'You didn't get your hair wet!' 'Oh, really!' That was his way of saying, 'Good girl'. It was his way of cutting the drama and making everybody laugh," she told me.

Even though she had a tough persona on screen, Maureen revealed that deep down she had a softer side, especially "if it has anything to do with kids and family".

Perhaps Maureen cherished the concept of family and love so much more than anything else because she was extremely unlucky in love until she met her third husband, Charlie Blair. As with her first marriage, Maureen almost immediately regretted her second marriage in 1941 to William Houston Price, who turned out, much to her chagrin, to be an alcoholic and womaniser. She first discovered his unfaithfulness less than two months after their wedding when a prostitute from a whore house called her up and asked her to pick up her husband, who had been missing for several days. Cruelly, she was told about one of his many infidelities the day after discovering she was pregnant! It also later emerged that her husband also had several homosexual relationships.

Maureen was initially reluctant to divorce him for fear that the inevitable negative publicity would shame her parents. She also wanted to believe that everything would change for the better after the introduction of a beautiful child into their lives; their daughter, Bronwyn, was born on 30 June 1944. Unfortunately, her husband continued on his downward spiral and she finally found the courage to file for divorce. On 29 December 1951—coincidentally the tenth anniversary of their wedding—Price "staggered out" of their home with a suitcase and never returned.

By the time the divorce was final in August 1952, Maureen was already falling in love with a Mexican businessman named Enrique Parra. He was married with children, but told Maureen that he was no longer in a loving relationship with his wife. Reluctant to get involved with a married man, Maureen hired a private investigator who verified that he was indeed in a loveless marriage and his wife had even taken a lover herself. However, even though she fell in love with Parra, Maureen feared that if their relationship was made public it could possibly ruin her Hollywood career, as had happened when Ingrid Bergman left her husband for the Italian filmmaker Roberto Rossellini.

The sex scandal that did eventually explode was not of Maureen's own making. In 1957, the magazine *Confidential* printed outrageous allegations about her having a "steamy interlude" with a Latin lover at the back of Hollywood's Grauman's Chinese Theatre during a screening of *Ben-Hur* (1959). Maureen successfully sued the magazine, after she was able to prove that she had been in Spain filming on the same night as the alleged incident in LA. The magazine went bust shortly afterwards.

"There was never any really privacy—you were always subject to the public's opinion of you," she confided in me. "And it had to be up to you to see that it never became a bad opinion: [that] it was always a good opinion, and that they appreciated you and liked you and liked the work you were doing. You had to stand up for yourself. It wasn't much different than being in school."

Did it hurt when the press printed negative stories about her?

"It did," she admitted. "It hurt if anybody was jealous of you or if anybody tried to talk against you, or criticise you. Oh, there was plenty of criticism. And jealousy. If you're severally criticised, it's tough to take and stand up under it."

By 1967, Maureen and Enrique Parra were drifting apart when fate stepped in and she was introduced by her brother, Charlie, himself an actor and Hollywood producer, to her third husband Charlie Blair, the man she describes as her true soul mate. They married on 12 March 1968 and were so inseparable that Maureen retired from her glittering film career to be beside the man she loved.

"I gave up acting because it was John Wayne who nagged me," she explained. "He was playing chess with Charlie Blair—the two of them were great pals—and I went out to see if they wanted anything to eat. And Duke said to me, 'Well, don't you think it's about time you quit?' And I said, 'Okay, I quit. I've done it right now'. And I did."

Maureen told me that she never once regretted turning her back on stardom, but she did return to acting in the 1990s and made several films, including the hilarious *Only The Lonely* (1991), alongside the late John Candy.

"He was a charmer," she said of the late Canadian actor, who died of a heart attack at the age of only 43 in 1994. "And he was coming here to play in my golf tournament and he had to go down south of California to do a certain thing and he died. So, he didn't [get to] come. But, boy, we were looking forward to him coming. Can you imagine if we had John Candy out on that golf course? God! He was a very, very nice person; a very strong Catholic. We used to meet after mass on Sunday, his wife and his kids and me and all of my relatives. We'd all meet outside of the church and we'd yakety yakety yak; we were all chatters, you know? And it was wonderful."

What's her favourite film that she was in?

"Oh God! When you make 63/64 movies, which memory from which movie [do you pick], you know, you think? God, you're now going to start me thinking. I loved the Hunchback, I loved *How Green Was My Valley*," she said. "I loved *Sentimental Journey* (1946), which was very, very, very sad. And it was number one in China."

Our conversation inevitably turned to *The Quiet Man*, which she made in her beloved homeland in 1951 with John Wayne.

"You'd be surprised at how many years it took to try to raise the money to make *The Quiet Man*," she told me. "It was a long, long, long time. Republic Studios [eventually] put up the money. We could never get the money anywhere. They'd laugh. They'd say, 'Poor Irish!' We made a movie just before we *made The Quiet Man,* [entitled] *Rio Grande* (1950). And when that was shown to the theatre men, [half-way through the screening] Ford said, 'Stop, stop, stop . . . cut'. And they said, 'Oh, we want to see it all'. And they created such a hullabaloo that they put the movie back on and let them see the whole movie. And it was then the head of this Republic Studios, when he heard all of that fuss going on, he agreed to finance the movie."

She added, "It was wonderful. The script, my brother sat with John Ford and he said, 'Tell me so and so. Tell me so and so. Describe so and so'. And we were thrilled."

Initially retiring from acting in 1971 after she made the western *Big Jake* (1971) with John Wayne, Maureen and her husband then founded a commuter airline, Antilles Air Boats, in the Caribbean.

"I never missed it [Hollywood], as I was so involved with the airline business," she insisted. "They even say that I was the only woman who was the head of an airline company. Oh, if you met Charlie Blair you'd say, 'What a wise decision you made'."

Maureen would later have a theory that her decorated war hero husband had never retired from working for the US government and was, in fact, using the airline as a "secret fleet" for the CIA to fly reconnaissance missions to monitor Cuba.

"He was a very brave man and part of the military, as you know," she said. "He was a general in the air force, but then he was in commercial navigation too. He was the senior pilot of Pan Am. He flew the first flight across the Atlantic to land in Ireland. He flew the first flight to land in Portugal. He flew the first flight over the Pole. That was militarily very important. The first flight in Africa. He did the first every where in the world."

Sadly, the man she described as her true soul mate died in a plane crash on 2 September 1978. He was making a routine flight from Saint Croix to Saint Thomas in a two-engine Grumman Goose when its port engine exploded, killing him instantly.

"I never questioned my faith," she said. "I believed in God and I still believe in God, but I did feel it was a terrible thing to happen to me. It was absolutely awful. And he was a wonderful man."

Did she still miss him every day?

Without missing a heartbeat, she answered, "Oh, God, yes."

But did time make it easier for you?

Maureen shook her head and her eyes filled up with tears. "No. No. No," her voice quavered as she answered me. "You wouldn't expect it to? I don't. He was my soul mate. Oh, boy, yes. Everybody that knew him here [in Glengarriff]; he's their soul mate too, you know?"

Maureen was given permission from the US President to be buried beside her husband at Arlington National Cemetery, described as the most important military graveyard in the States. But at her time of talking—only four years before her death—Maureen believed it would be a considerable while yet before she'd go to her final resting place.

"I plan to live to 102," she insisted. "Charlie Blair's mother lived to be 102. She was a fabulous woman. And, believe me, all of the enthusiasm and ambition of Charlie Blair, he got from his mother. She was a terrific woman. And she was from southern Donegal,' she said with her famous steely determination.

Sadly, this was one ambition that Maureen was unable to keep. She died at the age of 95-years-old in October 2015. She had been in remarkably good health at the time of her death. After beating cancer three times, including cancer of the womb, it was perhaps miraculous that this Hollywood icon was still going strong at the end.

As her close friend of over 30 years and personal assistant, Carolyn Murphy explained to me: "She is a mentor to many of us who have been victims of cancer and is very supportive when your are going through your treatments. Like all things, her feistiness comes out and she will say, 'Just get on with it and fight it. Keep a good attitude, and pray to God' in a tone that makes you sure that you will beat it—if you just listen to her. She is an advocate of not having fear when something hits you and her attitude is to do what you're told and move on."

I asked Maureen to what did she credit for her longevity?

"That's your gift from your parents. You inherit that. But then, of course, you can damage it," she said. "But if you appreciate what God's gift has given to you through your parents then you should do what you're destined to do. Of course, I guess I was always tough.

There's a couple of things that I don't do. I don't have whiskey or spirits, and I don't smoke."

She also credited going to bed early and eating "plenty of vegetables" and "some good meat" for her good health. "As a special treat, I have a rock bun with my cup of tea. Oh, they're gorgeous. You can't have anything better than that. Oh, God!" she said, laughing like a naughty school kid.

The negative aspect of living so long was that Maureen was constantly bidding farewell to friends and relatives who left this world before her. But Maureen took great comfort from the thoughts of an afterlife.

"But, at the same time, you always say to them, 'You know, when you get there [to heaven], help and tell them not to cast me aside! To let me come too!' And, you mean, heaven. But you do. You really do. I often think about how I am going to handle it. You know, when I get there," she said.

"And thank God I've never doubted. I never thought I was going to go down, I was always going to go up. But you do think about, 'What am I going to do? Who am I going to watch over? Who am I going to help? Who am I going to talk to God about?' You know, you really do. It's amazing."

Maureen said that when God did come calling for her, she'd "answer and go willingly".

What was heaven going to be like for Maureen O'Hara?

"Well, I hope all my wonderful relatives will be there. And I'll be able to watch a couple of soccer games," she said.

Did she have any big regrets in life?

"Oh! Maybe that I didn't fight harder for certain roles that I would've loved to have played. I don't know. To do a thousand things. I could never satisfy myself by doing a little bit of this, or a little bit of that. I'd like to have sang," she said.

How did she best want to be remembered?

"As an Irishwoman who made a success in the world; never let Ireland down. I'm very proud of being Irish. You've got to remember one thing that's so important—when you're Irish, you're Irish. And nobody is better than you or there is nowhere better than the country you came from," she said.

"Ireland is one of the great countries of the world and we have sent people out to every country in the world and they've done famous things and become famous people. I always wanted to do something important and big—be a great representative of Ireland."

When I told her that she could rest assured that she'd left behind such a legacy and will always be remembered as true ambassador for her country, Maureen modestly replied, "I hope so."

There's a saying that you should never meet your hero for fear of being disappointed, but it's a maxim that clearly didn't apply to Maureen O'Hara.

CHAPTER TWO:

Ireland's Favourite Adopted Son, Martin Sheen

It was an astonishingly candid admission for such a high profile Hollywood star to make. "I am proud of just a handful of films. I would say 90% of it was basically trash. I did it for the money, and most of the stuff I did was a great source of embarrassment to me," Martin Sheen confessed to me as we sat at the vast dining table in the aptly named Presidential Suite in The Westbury Hotel, Dublin.

After he opened the door to let me in to his room, Martin, who has played the President of America four times on screen, pointed to the suite's title on the door and good humouredly said: "Perhaps they should call it: The Former Acting President's Suite!"

Despite all the trash, Martin has appeared in many critically acclaimed movies, mostly notably *Badlands* (1973) and *Apocalypse Now* (1979). There's also been memorable turns in Martin Scorsese's *The Departed* (2006), Richard Attenborough's *Gandhi* (1982), Oliver Stone's *Wall Street* (1987)—in a role originally earmarked for Jack Lemmon—and Stephen Spielberg's *Catch Me If You Can* (2002).

Martin describes Francis Ford Coppola's war movie, *Apocalypse Now* as being "both a career-changing experience as well as a personal voyage" because it helped him to face his own "darkness and inhumanity".

After suffering the near-death experience of a heart attack on the set in the Philippines at the relatively young age of 36, Martin confronted his alcoholism and returned to his Catholic faith. "I had to come clean of that. I had to find myself," he explained. "That was a long and very painful journey, which culminated in my return to Catholicism."

Apocalypse Now took up 15 months of Martin's life and, after it finished, he spent the next four years focusing on inner contemplation and developing his relationship with religion and God, which he credits for keeping him sober. Eventually, Martin emerged re-invigorated from his new-found belief in religion, and was determined to have a positive influence on society, particularly with human rights issues.

When he's not making films or television shows, Martin can be found campaigning on a wide variety of social, political, and humanitarian issues. He set up a foundation to help the poor in Third World countries, and he frequently visits deprived areas to help "shine the press light" on horrible conditions. In fact, Martin has been arrested over 70 times for his involvement in many radical campaigns in America, including stances against nuclear weapons and the invasion of Iraq.

The *West Wing* star shocked the show-business world back in 2008 when he turned down roles and moved to Ireland—his mother's birthplace—to study. He regretted never undertaking a third-level education, and decided to live out his "romantic fantasy" of returning to his mother's homeland to study at the National University of Ireland, Galway.

It was during his time in Ireland that I first got to know him. I was fortunate enough to spend an entire weekend with Martin and his wife, Janet.

Apart from conducting this interview with the Ohio-born actor, whose father was from Spain, we went out to restaurants together; we went for walks and we even went to church together! In the Church, he patiently posed for countless selfies with fans. People were constantly approaching him on the street to shake his hand or ask for an autograph. At one stage, he wanted a packet of cigarettes but we both knew he wouldn't make it to a nearby store on a main high street without being surrounded by a swarm of fans. Instead, he had to hide down a laneway, away from the prying eyes, pretending to look at the display window in a jewellers, as I dashed off to pick up cigarettes for him. It made me feel sorry for him. I remember thinking, *This is too high of a price to pay for fame.*

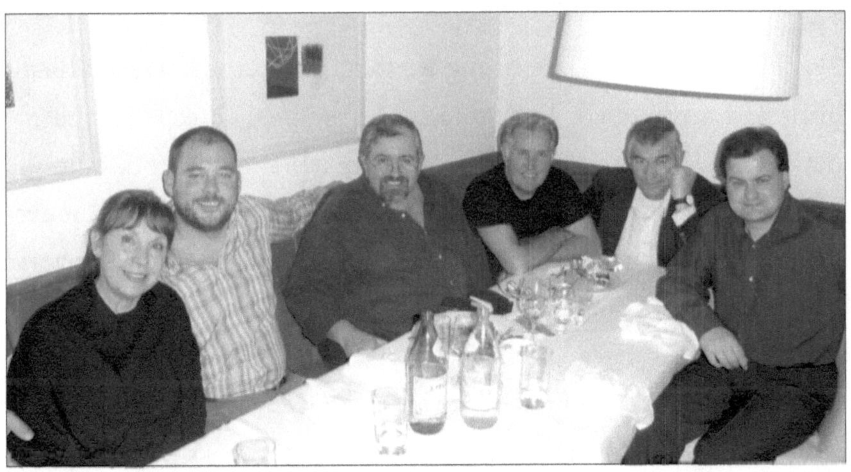

During the memorable weekend together, we discussed everything from movies, books and politics, to education and religion. He was one of the most open, honest and humble people I have ever had the opportunity to meet. As my friend (and actor) Jason Barry recently told me about Martin, "What a gem of a human being. Really interesting actor and person. I feel blessed to have shared the screen with him."

Jason added, "I remember when we were shooting *Monument Ave.* (1998) we only had him for a few days and we ran over. The director Ted Demme went to him cap in hand and asked for an extra day but explained they didn't have the money to pay him his usual fee. He didn't care. He loved the project. He wanted the role and the film to work so he turned up the next day for free."

Apart from being such a great guy, Martin was the perfect interviewee—unashamedly truthful and forthcoming. As I said about Maurren O'Hara, that old adage about never meeting your heroes was also certainly not true when it came to Martin Sheen.

O'TOOLE: Was it very difficult for you to drop out of school and focus on acting? I read that your father was very disappointed with your decision to try making it as an actor.

SHEEN: He was very angry and we fought about it. I was a difficult birth and nearly died, I am told, and they used forceps to pull me out into the world and they crushed my left shoulder. So, officially I could be qualified as handicapped because I have no lateral movement with my left arm. So, my dad looked at me from the old world perspective that I couldn't make a living doing manual labour, so that I would have to have an education. He singled me out of the nine boys and one girl to go to college and he put a few dollars aside each week and over the years it accumulated and that was the fund for me to go to the University of Dayton.

O'TOOLE: Is it true that you purposely failed your entrance exam?

SHEEN: I had to take an entrance exam but I didn't want to go. I couldn't make my dad understand that I didn't want to go—that I wanted to go to New York and start acting. He didn't want to hear of it. So, I was forced to take the exam and I threw it on purpose. I was 22 and this was not what I wanted to do. Out of a possible 100, I got a three, and I understand that it is still the record. And I probably wouldn't do any better if I tried my best! But that was it; he got the message and was furious about it. But I thought that maybe I should have went (sic) gone to a junior college, get some foundation, and then go to the university, but I said, 'No. I am going to New York'. And we fought about that. I borrowed some money from the local parish priest, who was very encouraging to me. He lent me a bit of money and off I went in January of 1959 to New York.

O'TOOLE: Did you eventually reconcile with you dad? Was he proud of your acting?

SHEEN: Once I got settled, and once I got committed to doing it, my dad blessed me. It didn't take long for him to realise that this guy was serious and he began to see me on television shows in the early '60s and realised that I had some measure of talent—that I could make a living doing this, then he supported me wholeheartedly. He was very proud, very much so.

O'TOOLE: Were you ever surprised by the level of success you achieved in acting?

SHEEN: Oh, no, no. I was never *not* an actor. I never had a memory of becoming an actor. I was always an actor. I just didn't know what it was when I was a child. All children have an innate kind of knowingness about themselves and they can't express it because they don't have the language and they don't have the experience, so they are left to their own devices to find themselves. It's universal mystery, I think, but children know themselves in ways that we can't know them. And I knew myself in that way and I didn't know what it was that I was feeling until I started going to the movies—I guess I was six or seven—and I gradually began to realise that I was one of them! I can do that. And I knew it instinctively; there was never any question or doubt—ever. And it was only a matter of time when I could go out into the world as a young adult and do it. It was just the next step, a natural progression. As far of the success of it, I knew that even when I was starting out that it was the only way that I would be happy in my life. If I did not do this thing I would never come to know myself and I would never be happy. So, I knew.

O'TOOLE: But did you not fear the possibility of failure?

SHEEN: I knew also that there was a chance that I wouldn't make a living, nevertheless that weighed against the life of the spirit, which was at stake, if you don't follow your heart. There is a lot more at stake than success or money—it's your spirit that will die and you will make other people unhappy. So, I committed to it right away.

I remember years later we were talking to a guy—I can't recall what the occasion was—but he was saying, 'When you were talking about all the hard time we had as young people over in New York, struggling and living in some very uncomfortable place, did you ever think about getting a job or going to school, or learning a trade?' And we kind of looked at each other and said, 'Gee, we never thought of that!' It never occurred to me! Or any of the lads I came up with. That would be like betrayal. You were an artist. You were an actor. You were valuable. Even if no one else saw it, it didn't matter, as long as you felt it was invaluable. Honest, it's important.

O'TOOLE: During those early years, before your big break, you were friends with Al Pachino.

SHEEN: Al Pacino and I came up together in the streets of New York. He's from New York, of course. We would recognise each others' dreams. We would say to one another, 'You're good'. Encourage one another. And it meant a great deal because we had good taste.

I remember Janet [Martin's wife] saying—she saw him acting in some little play off Broadway somewhere—'That guy is going to be a major star'. And we looked at her and said, 'Really? That's little Al!' She said, 'Oh, you watch'. And he was. He was the first one to breakthrough and no one ever—in the group that I came up with—equalled his success. He was that big a talent. We all knew it but we couldn't equate talent to success. Do you know what I am saying?

O'TOOLE: Yes . . .

SHEEN: We knew Al, for example, was brilliant but we never focused on, or were able to project his success. It was like that was out of our realm. There was no way that we could imagine that he was going to become the star he became. What was amazing to us was the talent he was. So, over the years, I would struggle from one job to another and I never made my living at it until the late '60s, where I could count on it. So that was 10 years I was doing it before I didn't have to do anything else. I knew that I could work at this thing—movies, television, plays, whatever.

O'TOOLE: You auditioned for the lead role in *The Godfather*.

SHEEN: I did. That's on record. It is in a documentary—I have never seen it, but I heard about it. I was doing a television show, a movie of the week in California, and they called me to come to New York and do a screen test for Michael. I was wrong for it, but you never pass up an opportunity. And I couldn't get away because I was committed to this film and suddenly there was an earthquake and the building we were filming in came down overnight; it was damaged, we couldn't film, they had to find another building. So, I had a couple of days off and I went to New York and I did a screen test. I had very long hair and I couldn't cut it because I had to match what I was doing in the film when we would re-shoot, when we would get back to filming. So, I had this enormously long mane and I had this army uniform on. I did a scene in the army with Kate.

O'TOOLE: Do you feel Al Pacino was the best choice for the part?

SHEEN: I remember saying to Coppola—that was not the first time I had met him. I had met him on another film before that, so he knew me—'If you don't use Al Pacino in this part, it would be like benching Joe DiMaggio in his prime'. Everyone knew that Al was going to get it. Everyone knew he was the only guy to play it. And Francis agreed. He said, 'Yes, he is the only guy I want, but they are making me do this'. The studio was forcing him to audition all these guys. I think they wanted Laurence Olivier to play it! And Marlon had to do a screen test!

O'TOOLE: You talk about Al Pacino being amongst your circle of acting friends when starting out in New York. Was Robert De Niro also a friend?

SHEEN: Not at the time. I came to know him as a fellow actor much later. I never worked with him and I would love to work with him. I think he is one of the best actors of my generation—or all generations. He's magnificent, a genius. I came to admire him, particularly when I saw him in *Raging Bull* (1980). I saw it in Paris long after he had won the awards when the film was celebrated. I wrote him a fan letter! I had never met him. Then, a few years later, I was in New York and he was doing a play and I had a friend at that theatre who got me tickets. I asked if I could go backstage and meet him and I did. I said I'd written him a fan letter and he said, 'Yeah, I got it. Thank you'. (*Laughs.*) He's very shy.

O'TOOLE: *The Subject was Roses* was your first big break.

SHEEN: Yes, I would say so. That would have been in 1964. It was the second Broadway show I ever did, but it was the first success I ever had. Both Jack Albertson and I were nominated for Tony's for the best supporting actor and he won. He played the father and I played the son. We reprieved our roles in the movie and he won the Oscar.

O'TOOLE: Do you feel the film captured the same atmosphere as the play?

SHEEN: No, in fact. Patricia Neal made her comeback in *The Subject Was Roses.* That would have been in 1968, I think, it was released in '69. We were not able to capture the same thing we had on the stage. In fact, I think Jack got the closest to it. But he had far more experience in film than I did. And, consequently, he won the Oscar, which was deserved. I watched the film every now and then over the years on TV and I just have a look and say, 'Oh my! I was not good at all'. But it was a good play.

O'TOOLE: You don't think you were good?

SHEEN: No, not particularly. I wasn't as good as I was on stage. On stage it was great fun and the movie was great work. There's a difference. I had a great time. I had a great deal of fun with the play, but when we got to the film it was a lot of anxiety. I wasn't comfortable in front of the camera. It took me many, many years to relax in front of the camera.

O'TOOLE: What is your favourite Martin Sheen movie?

SHEEN: Without question it is *Badlands*. When I got the part I had a different image of it, which couldn't have been further from the mark. Terence Malik, the director, moulded me into the character and opened up avenues. It was the little things. There wasn't much dialogue. It was visual, but it was behavioural. The character was very behavioural.

O'TOOLE: Would you have been inspired with that part by James Dean?

SHEEN: Oh, yeah. But not just with that part but my whole career. Everybody in my generation was affected by him—profoundly. Male and female, rich and poor, black or white, it didn't matter if you were interested in acting or not because he appeals to something in all of us, that great mystery of our common humanity. What he did for cinema was what Marlon and, I think, Montgomery Clift had done: they had transcended cinema acting. It had become behaviour. So, anyone after Dean was scrutinized based on that level of talent. He was a genius and he was able to transcend whatever character he was playing to his own personal behaviour. It looked like he was just being himself. He wasn't saying lines or following a script, he was just emoting what he was feeling at the time. He was the biggest influence on my career—by far. I didn't see him in a movie until after he died. I would have been about 15 before I saw *East of Eden* (1955) and I was never the same. There was no actor that had a bigger influence on me then James Dean—or on my whole generation. No one got close.

O'TOOLE: Francis Ford Coppola re-edited *Apocalypse Now* a few years ago. Which version do you prefer?

SHEEN: The first one.

O'TOOLE: Why?

SHEEN: Because it kept the energy and the focus on the journey and less on the plantation. I liked those scenes a lot and I remember filming them and being disappointed when I didn't see them in the original version. But when I watched the original version in its entirety and came to understand it as a journey inside—the journey this guy was on. And it was deeply personal—then I realised the genius of Coppola's vision. I was interested in all of the outside, the peripheral of the war and the character. He was more interested in what was going on inside the character and that's what he focused on, and I think the first version caught that.

O'TOOLE: Do you think the film realistically captures the horrors of Vietnam?

SHEEN: The film was not well received in the beginning. It was not nominated for anything. A few of the lads were nominated. I think it won one award for sound or editing, maybe cinematography, I'm not sure. But I remember thinking, when I first saw it, that it would not be realised for quite a while; that it was too big and it was too frightening. It scared people. It was only the Vietnam veterans themselves who started to go to it repeatedly and tell people: 'That's what it was like. It was insanity'. What you see in that picture is what it was for an American solider to experience in Vietnam. I came in as a replacement in that film. I replaced another guy [Harvey Keitel] and changed the whole structure. I was there for 15 months. I got a couple of weeks off every now and then.

O'TOOLE: You almost died from a heart attack during the making of *Apocalypse Now*. It was a film that changed your life.

SHEEN: That was both a career changing energy as well as a personal one because it made me face my own darkness and my own inhumanity. I had to come clean of that. I had to find myself—so that was a long and very painful journey, which culminated in my return to Catholicism.

O'TOOLE: Why was it this particular film—which is, ironically perhaps for you, based loosely on a novel called *Heart of Darkness*—that made you face your own darkness?

SHEEN: You see, I wasn't sure that I wasn't that character. It is not a very pleasant thing to deal with. I wasn't sure that that wasn't more of me and Willard. I had to define myself, so it took another four years of inner introspection. And I came back to Catholicism, but I came back out of love and out of freedom and joy rather than fear of condemnation, or going against my religion and so forth.

O'TOOLE: It is well documented that *Apocalypse Now* was a troubled film to shoot. Is it true that Marlon Brando was difficult to work with?

SHEEN: Oh, God—no! He was the easiest one of all [*laughs*]. We [Martin's family] adored him. He was a man after my own heart: great companion and humour. He was fun to be around. He went to great lengths to crack a good joke. He was very friendly towards everyone. The only thing he would not talk about was himself, or movies, or acting.

O'TOOLE: *Catch-22* by Joseph Heller is a wonderful book, but what went wrong with the film adaptation?

SHEEN: I think Michael [Director Mike Nichols] was a bit disappointed with it, that he wasn't able to capture the great depth of the book. It was not an easy film to do. We shot that down in Mexico primarily, and then we went to Rome for a little while and then LA, but it was a very difficult shoot. It was very big; there were a lot of aeroplanes and they are not easy to come by. We were in an isolated area. It was hard to get things. I thought he did a noble job really, but it was an impossible book to photograph. I think it was my third picture. I didn't have experience—I certainly didn't have any name; I played a tiny part, but he had some enormous stars in that film and he had to cater to them and it wasn't easy. He had his hands full.

O'TOOLE: You have only directed on feature film, *Stockade* [aka *Cadence* – 1990]. Why haven't you made any more?

SHEEN: It just takes so much out of you. To direct you have to be responsible for every part of the film. You have to prepare it. You have to get the script ready; you have to work with the writer; you have to be attentive to everything from casting to wardrobe to make-up to camera to lens to location to catering. Everything. If there is one guy who gets all the blame it is the director. He doesn't always get all the credit if it's a success. It's too big a job. I did it once.

O'TOOLE: Sounds like you didn't enjoy directing experience that much?

SHEEN: I really enjoyed the experience and I loved the players—all were friends. Laurence Fishburne was very generous to come and do it. Charlie, of course. My son Ramon was in it and a few other friends, most of them with experience and talent. It took a lot out of me for two-and-a-half years. We edited it in the backyard and in those days we didn't have electronic equipment, so we edited on the steam-backs, the old thing were you had to put a roll of film and a roll of sound and put them together and look at this on a little thing about this big [*makes a small square shape with his hands – JOT*] and it wasn't . . . I finished that film in '89 and we didn't release it until '91 and it was released at the height of the first Gulf war and no one saw it.

O'TOOLE: Was it very disappointing for you?

SHEEN: It was, yeah. I was happy with the film. I guess I might feel like an artist when you go into the museum and see your painting, you want to make adjustments here and there [*laughs*], change something or add to it, or take something out, or take the painting out altogether. I felt that way about it. I thought that it was a good and worthy and very honest effort. I didn't feel that it realised its potential.

O'TOOLE: Why not?

SHEEN: I didn't start playing that part, I started with a much smaller part, and then we changed protagonists and I had to step into it or otherwise we would have had to pull the plug. And F. Murray Abraham, another dear friend, came to play the part that I was originally playing, which was just a one-week part. I would have been able to focus, if I played that part, on the whole film. But when I had to jump in and replace the actor who plays the protagonist; I was in much more of the film and I was less attentive to all the other details. So, I think the film suffered as a result.

O'TOOLE: You played the American President four times. Which performance do you prefer?

SHEEN: The one I am thinking about is Kennedy, the mini-series. I didn't want to do it. I didn't think it should be done. I didn't think anyone should play it. He was too big a figure and there was no way you could capsules his life on film, even a short portion of his life. To take on that character—I mean, he was so much bigger than life; he was so heroic, beloved. And I didn't feel, not only I couldn't do it, but that it shouldn't be done. They kept coming back and back—it was a British company—and upping the offer and I said, 'No. It is not a question of money; I just don't want to do it. I can't do it'. And then my wife said,

'Well, maybe it is not a bad idea that you play him because you loved him. And by playing him, if you keep someone from playing him who did not love him, that would be a worthy effort. That would memorialise him in a much better light'. So that was the energy that I used.

O'TOOLE: Would you have liked *West Wing* to have continued?

SHEEN: In fact, they were talking to another network about a possible switch and go an eighth season and maybe longer. I was asked if I would appear from time to time as a former president and act as sort a Jimmy Carter type image or Bill Clinton type image. And I would go as a representative of the country just to represent the United States as a kind of elder statesman. I agreed to do that. In fact, the character would have had a chair at the University of Notre Dame and he would have launched a centre and build his library. That was sort of encapsulating my part if it did go to an eighth season. They were, in fact, talking to another network about making it.

O'TOOLE: What stopped it from happening?

SHEEN: When John Spencer died in December 2005, the wind left our sails and the boat stood still and we decided to abandon ship. He was such an integral a part of the focus and the energy and the image of the show that it was not possible for it to continue with any real credibility. We thought, 'We'll call it quits here'. John's death sealed the final season.

O'TOOLE: He was a good friend of yours?

SHEEN: He was a dear friend. He was like a brother towards me.

O'TOOLE: You don't mind sending yourself up! I'm thinking of that scene in *Hot Shots Part 2*?

SHEEN: 'I loved you in *Wall Street*!' That was Charlie's idea. I loved doing that (*laughs*). Humour comes out of the situation, not the character.

O'TOOLE: What was it like to finally get to work with Martin Scorsese on *The Departed*?

SHEEN: He is one of the masters. I met him once, years ago, and I liked him a lot . . . just meeting him socially. I am a huge fan of his work and I jumped at the opportunity to work with him. In fact, there was an Irish actor playing that part and he came to the States and was working, but he had some problems. He's known here. A popular player, but I couldn't tell you his name because I never met him. He had to come home. He had been shooting a couple of weeks, a couple of scenes.

They called me on a Sunday morning and said, 'We don't have time to send you the script, we'll send you a synopsis in a fax, but here's the story, you'll have to be out on the set in 72 hours; you'll have to take this fellow's billing and his money, and his contract'. It was a drop and a pick up. Do you know what that means?

O'TOOLE: No!

SHEEN: A 'Drop and A Pick Up' means they can work you for two weeks, drop you for a month, and pick you up and you have to be free.

O'TOOLE: So, you had to be very flexible with your schedule for this role?

SHEEN: Yes and it would take all the summer. Not all of the summer shooting because it was a small part. I would work a few days, then I'd go back to New York for a little while, then I'd go to Boston to work for a little while. I was still doing the *West Wing*. I had to shoot the final season and, so, it got a little dicey finishing *The Departed*. We shot this in the summer of 2005. This is when the majority—99 percent of it—was shot. They called me back this past summer just to do a few little insert shots. When they told me the parameters of the contract: that I had a drop and a pick up, that I had to take the same money, the same contract, everything the same, I said, 'What's the catch?' They said, 'Martin Scorsese's directing'. And I said, 'I'm in'. Without even reading the script!

O'TOOLE: Seriously, you didn't read the script before signing on?

SHEEN: Oh, I didn't read it. No. I just read the synopsis of it. It is based on a real story in Boston of this Whitey Bulger character. I couldn't pass up the chance to work with all those wonderful guys and Marty, who is real magnificent. I adore him. He was everything that I imagined he would be to work with. He was so kind and polite, bright and very, very funny. I mean, I laughed every day on the set. It was a laugh-fest. He was so funny and engaging. I was really, really disarmed and charmed by him. I loved working with him. He is a master. I wouldn't turn down the chance to work with him—I'd do an extra! I would. My son, Emilio, called me after he saw it. He said, 'It is the most violent and vulgar movie I have seen. I can't wait to see it again!' [*Laughs.*]

O'TOOLE: This was the second film you did with Leonardo DiCaprio. You did *Catch Me If You Can together*. Was it nice working with him again?

SHEEN: I love him too. He is a wonderful young man. He is very involved in the environment. He has an environment website. His mother founded it with him. You gotta check it out. He's concerned mostly with clean water. The world is fast becoming in need—particularly in the Third World—of clean water. It is the source of all life.

There is a crisis with clean water. He's an inspiration. He's a lovely young guy and he's brilliant. I saw him in—I guess it was his first film—*What's Eating Gilbert Grape* (1993)—and I thought they had really gotten a retarded child to play the part! He was so real.

O'TOOLE: You have been directed by your son in in two films, *Bobby* (2006) and *The War At Home* back in 1996. Do you like working with Emilio?

SHEEN: Oh, yeah. He is terrific. He's my hero. This particular film, *Bobby*, he has been working on the script since 1999. Getting it done was a very, very difficult time. Editing, scoring, selling the film has been a monumental, uphill struggle and he's taken a beating, but he's hung in there and he has a film that's very powerful. And I am proud and happy for him. I would love to work with him again.

O'TOOLE: Have you every regretted turning down a particular role?

SHEEN: Oh, there's tons of them. Oh God! *Blade Runner* (1982) was one I turned down. I never saw the complete picture, but I watched scenes from it.

O'TOOLE: Have you every regretted making any particular film?

SHEEN: Most of them!

O'TOOLE: Most of them? You are joking, right?

SHEEN: No, I'm serious. I did them for the money. I didn't want to do anything else and that was all I was offered. I am proud of just a handful of them. I would say 90% of it was basically trash. I did it for the money and most of it was television. I didn't do that many features and there were many features that I did that didn't get released in the cinema, they went straight to video. I have only done maybe a handful of feature films that I am proud of, that are good, that stood.

O'TOOLE: Which ones are you proud of?

SHEEN*:* *Badlands* and *Apocalypse Now* are the main two. I didn't carry most of them. I would say *Wall Street*, *The American President* (1995), *The War At Home*, *Gandhi*. Films that I did and that I am proud of—that made a difference in people's lives or, at least, made them aware of another possibility. That film you mentioned where I played a lunatic president: *The Dead Zone* (1983). Cronenberg is a wonderful director. And a few television shows. The Kennedy thing, I'm very proud of that. A few others, including playing Eddie Slovak, who was the only solider ever to be shot for desertion in the US Army since the Civil War, and that had an impact. *Da* (1988) was a very good film and *Judgement in Berlin* (1988) is not bad. Most of the stuff I did was a great source of embarrassment to me, frankly. And I think most actors feel that way.

O'TOOLE: I heard you have been arrested 70 times as a participant in various different protests and human rights campaigns?

SHEEN: No. I have only been arrested 65 times. I am almost up to my age [*laughs*].

O'TOOLE: What motivates you to participate in humanitarian work?

SHEEN: Well, the Gospel, primarily, motivates my human rights activities. The command of the Gospel to feed the hungry, to cloth the naked, house the homeless, to visit the imprisoned, to do justice, and to love, and to walk humbly. I think that's the only way you come to know yourself by serving others. There is so much growth that happens when you are involved in peace and social justice work because it takes you into areas that you would not normally go. And you touch people that you would not normally touch: the marginalized and the poor and the disenfranchised. You are dealing with people who suffer on a daily basis and who are left out . . . they have no voice, so you have to be a voice for the voiceless. But you grow in ways if you are willing to take the risk. It is risky, it is going to cost you something, you got to take it personally. If it's not personal, it is impersonal, and if it's impersonal, who cares?

CHAPTER THREE:

Conversations with Peter O'Toole's Daughter

Legendary hell- raiser Peter O'Toole once famously finished a play on a Saturday night and took his young understudy, a then relatively unknown Michael Caine, on a night on the town—only for them both to black out.

The last thing the young Cockney actor Michael Caine remembered was tucking into a plate of eggs and chips at a nearby restaurant. When they woke from their drunken slumber in a strange flat it was broad daylight and Caine enquired about the time, only for O'Toole to snap, "Never mind what time it is. What fucking day is it?!"

It was 5 p.m. on Monday—three hours until curtain. Caine was shocked to discover that they had spent two nights painting the town red—yet neither one of them could remember anything about it. Back at the theatre, the stage manager informed them that the restaurant's proprietor had banned them for life from his establishment. Caine was about to ask what they'd done when O'Toole whispered, "Never ask what you did. It's better not to know."

The stories of Peter O'Toole's hell- raising days are legion but few are crazier than what he did to celebrate the birth of his eldest daughter, Kate. His delight was unbounded and of course a few drinks were needed to wet the baby's head . . . but he ended up, as Katy told me, becoming so inebriated that he put a tattoo of a shamrock onto his newborn baby's bottom!

One can't even begin to imagine what the celebrated thespian—who announced his retirement from acting in 2012, before passing away at the age of 81 in December 2013—told his wife when she discovered the next morning that their new born baby not only had a tattoo but also the slogan 'Made in Ireland' etched onto her bottom. "If Social Services were around then!" quipped Kate in this rare in-depth interview about her famous father. As she later told me in 2018, Kate doesn't like to do interviews "about either of my parents" because "talking about other people really isn't my thing".

Recalling the tattoo incident, Kate told me: "My father was drunk out of his mind and delighted and thrilled. And with his doctor who was also drunk. They decided to have me branded on my ass with a thing that is supposed to be a shamrock and 'Made in Ireland'. That's the joke—'Made in Ireland' stamped on my ass."

Even though the tattoo inevitably became disfigured as she grew, Kate still sees the funny side of it. "When I was a baby, it was a shamrock. I think it was probably three cigarette butts, probably! As I say, Social Service!" she chuckled.

"When you hit puberty it was this dreadful thing on my ass. It is no longer nice. I thought, 'I'll go to the tattoo parlour and ask them to make it [back] into a shamrock because it's meant to be a shamrock and Made In Ireland is fine. I get the joke. So, I plucked up the courage—it took me months—and I finally go and they said, 'No, we can't do that. It doesn't work. Scare tissues'."

The disfigured tattoo is still there today—a clear reminder that Kate's upbringing was far from conventional, to put it mildly. Her father and Welsh mother Siân Phillips—who starred alongside her first husband in three films, including *Goodbye, Mr Chips* (1939)—first crossed paths and fallen in love when they appeared together in a stage play. "They were cast as brother and sister because they looked so similar," recalled Kate.

Kate looks remarkably like her father too. Looking at her blue eyes, it's hard not to think about the iconic image of Peter's piercing azure eyes gazing out from under the head cloth of his Kufiyya desert garb in *Lawrence of Arabia* (1962). "I don't think anyone on the planet has eyes quite like my father's, though!" she insisted. "I'm six of one, half a dozen of the other. It depends which way the wind is blowing."

But she felt temperamentally closer to her father. "We are peas in a pod. I was completely a daddy's girl," she told me.

Initially, her parents were steadfast against getting married after discovering the unplanned pregnancy with Kate. "They loved each other, but they didn't believe in marriage or see the point of a bit of paper," she said.

It was Marie Keane—a highly regarded Abbey Theatre actress, who worked at the RSC in England and was "Beckett's favourite actress"—who cajoled them into their wedding vows.

Kate recalled, "Marie said, 'You have to get married because one day that child might grow up and want to join the army or become a politician or something like that and he's going to need a birth certificate'. They didn't know if I was a boy or a girl.

"My father said, 'If he grows up to be that sort of an idiot then he doesn't deserve a birth certificate!' Marie said, 'Will you ever just get married—for feck's sake'."

So, reluctantly, they tied the knot in 1959—only a few months before Kate's arrival the following year. Sadly, the marriage would later end in a bitter divorce.

Kate was never baptised because of her parents' distain for religion, but Katherine Hepburn was her unofficial godmother. Urban myth has it that she was named Kate because of her father's close friendship with the Hollywood legend, with whom he later starred alongside in *The Lion in Winter* (1968).

"I don't know if it's true," Kate said. "I think the real reason I was called Kate is because my father was playing at the Royal Shakespeare Company when I was born in *The Taming of the Shrew*, which was one of his first big hits on the stage."

According to some exaggerated profiles—including one in an Irish national newspaper—Peter was so determined for Kate to be born in Ireland that he insisted to his wife that they move over here prior to the delivery. Kate giggled at such inaccuracies. "Oh, really! I was born in England. I have an Irish birth certificate. I was registered with the department of foreign births," she told me.

There has always been a shroud of mystery surrounding Peter O'Toole's own birthplace. Was he Irish-born or a so-called Plastic Paddy? That's been a question nobody has ever really been able to get to the bottom of. In his own memoir, O'Toole stated that he wasn't sure himself because—strangely—he has two birth certs: one giving Connemara as the origin of birth and the other as Leeds.

Nobody knows where he was born, Kate explained, because her grandfather was an illegal bookie who was always on the run. "I'm not from the working-class, I'm from the criminal class," Peter O'Toole once declared about his upbringing.

But didn't he once boast that he was born in Galway?

"No, he doesn't think Galway—he's never said that. Everybody else says that. Nobody knows," Kate said. "Look, his father—my grandfather—was on the wrong side of the law his whole life. We know nothing about him because he didn't want anybody to know anything about him. We don't know."

Did she ever ask her father about it?

"Yes. He doesn't know."

But one thing, as far as she is concerned, is crystal clear—Peter O'Toole's lineage was 100 percent Irish.

"The only thing for sure is that his grandfather's mother was an islander. She came from Omey Island," she explained. "Her family had land in Connemara near where we are—that's the connection. That I know is real."

Shortly after Kate's birth, Peter dashed off to film *Lawrence of Arabia*, the epic movie that would turn him into a bona fide Hollywood star. But it wasn't without its sacrifices—he didn't get to see Kate for the next two years while he was off in the Sahara and the Middle East. It wasn't until Kate's second birthday that he got to hold his daughter again when filming was wrapping up in Seville.

Despite being so young, the reunion had such an impact that Kate can still vividly recall the occasion. "It was the first time he'd seen me since I was a baby. I'd been living in Wales with Mamgu, which is Welsh for Grandma. She came with me to Seville," she recalled. "It was all very exciting, as you can imagine. He took me to a bullfight.

"After that I travelled quite a lot, almost every year of my life. I always had a nanny or governess with me; the first one was a Bedouin called Shufti, who came back from the desert with dad.

"As school progressed and exams became more serious, I had proper tutors to make up for missing weeks of classes when I went to Orinoco in Venezuela for months on end—that was for the film *Murphy's War* in 1970—instead of sitting behind my school desk."

When they were at their London abode, Kate and her younger sister Patricia both lived in a self-contained two-bedroom flat at the top of the six-storey Georgian house in the affluent Hampstead, with their nanny; while their maternal grandmother had her own flat on the first floor.

"It was very beautiful. Very posh," Kate recollected. "The main thing I remember as a child was it was like *Mary Poppins. Chim chimney.* We were definitely isolated on the top floor. It was like a Parisian flat with a little balcony and it looked over the skyline of London. The rest of the house was normal. But we weren't allowed into any of those rooms."

Is it true that she would have to make an appointment when wanting to visit her parents in her own home?

"Yes. That's right. That's the way I grew up. That was just it—the centre of the house was out of bounds. You couldn't go into any of the rooms without knocking first. We had an intercom system in the '60s. We called it the buzzer because it kept making a buzzing sound."

Any truth to the rumour that her parents had separated bedrooms?

"My parents had their own bedroom—they didn't sleep separately. They shared a bedroom."

Kate has vivid images from her childhood of witnessing the crime scene of the morning after of her father's wild soirées. Sneaking down stairs in the mornings, she'd regularly swing open the door of the gargantuan living room to set eyes on an assemblage of unconscious bodies—a who's who of London's high society—scattered on the floor in a drunken slumber and snoring in unison to the sound of a skipping record on a turntable.

She'd often have to tiptoe over a passed out Richard Burton to retrieve her school satchel. "I'd creep out before anybody woke up and started harassing me! As I say, social services!" Kate quipped.

"If you'd open the door there'd be just sort of dead adults—dead! The thing I remember most was it was like being in an aeroplane flying above the clouds because the whole room would be full of wonderful, blue stratus cloud cigarette smoke hanging in the room from the night before. This amazing, wispy, magical blue smoke wafting around."

As she got older, Kate would find her father's friends hitting on her, but she refused to divulge any names. "I'll tell you off the record," she sheepishly answered.

She does, however, admit that her first big crush was as a 14-years-old with their neighbour, the eccentric Peter Cook, who was then 36-years-old and flush with success from his comedic collaboration with Dudley Moore.

"He was absolutely bloody hilarious. I fancied him like mad. He was the first person I had a crush on. *On the record*—drool," she confessed.

What was it about him that attracted her?

"Physically, wit—everything. I flirted with him. *I did.* I was mad for him."

Unsurprisingly, he told her to, "Fuck off!" when her flirting became obvious.

The crush began when he would pop over to watch TV with her father. "It was so hilarious—he and my Dad used to sit and watch the football together and they'd turn the volume down and do the commentary. Eye-watering, hilarious," she said. "They used to watch *Come Dancing* together with the volume down and my dad would be saying things like, 'Cynthia tonight is wearing 5,000 yards of very sharp barbed wire'."

At the height of his fame, Peter had to beef up security because of fears that his two children could be kidnapped. They had to be escorted to school, which was only a stone's throw from the house. Was it a terrifying experience?

"Not for me because we were never told about it. We had an army of staff. But we had a few weird phone calls. I would pick up the phone sometimes and there would be a heavy breather on the other end saying, 'I want to kill your mother'."

She felt suffocated by the tight safety measures and would relish when her parents would visit their second home in Galway, where security was much more lax.

"That's why, to me, I'm completely opposite of most Irish people who grew up in place like Clifton in the '60s. To me Clifton in the '60s represented complete freedom because it was the only place I could be without the security guard," said Kate, who moved back into the area full-time after she had established herself in her own right as a talented actress.

"I know most people want to leave [Ireland] because they are choked by the Church and by all the limitations and all that, but for me it was the complete opposite of my rather stultifying, protected, body guarded life in London."

But the good times clearly outweigh such bad experiences for Kate, who travelled the world at her father's side. She was in Paris when her father made *What's New Pussy Cat* (1965) and *How to Steal A Million* (1966). "Romy Schneider on one side, Molotov Cocktails on the other—quite a combination," she joked.

She recalled playing cards with Sophia Loren "in her trailer between takes" on location in Rome for *Man of La Mancha* (1972). Another time in the Italian capital for the making of the critically mauled *Caligula*, she remembered John Gielgud, Helen Mirren, and her father "all in stitches at the lunacy of the entire production" of the film, which on release shocked audiences with graphic pornographic scenes that were controversially inserted in during the editing process.

The film was a disastrous experience for all involved, but it was an idyllic time in Rome for Kate, who remembered staying in a beautiful villa with "frescoes and catacombs and a magnificent pool lined with stones".

But cracks were by then beginning to appear in her parents' marriage. "My parents were on the brink of divorce then so perhaps not the happiest of times for them," she confessed. "I was too busy clambering around Roman ruins and falling in love with ancient history to pay much attention to domestic affairs."

Her mother eventually left O'Toole in 1975 for the actor Robert Sachs, who was 15-years her junior. Did it come as a shock when her parents' separated when she was 15-years-old and then divorced four years later in 1979?

"No. I had a feeling it was happening. I smelled it coming down the wire."

Was the split upsetting for her?

"No. People have their own lives to live," she replied, philosophically.

Kate's mother wrote in her memoir that she had endured "mental cruelty" during her tempestuous marriage to O'Toole. In Kate's own opinion, was it accurate?

"Who knows! You'd have to ask her. I'm sure she did feel that way if she said it. That's her opinion and perception. And perception is reality though, isn't it? We all have good days and bad days. Not everybody is a ray of sunshine all the time."

Did the book upset her?

"No, it's didn't upset me—not in the sense that you mean. She was a really good writer and the reason I didn't like her book was because it wasn't her best writing. I felt that she didn't want to write the book—her heart wasn't in it and I think that shows."

Perhaps somewhat surprisingly, after her parents separated, Kate's maternal grandmother—who used to live with them at their London abode before the divorce—stayed on with Peter to raise her two granddaughters.

"She never left, she stayed—my mother left. She wanted to look after me and my sister. She was the most wonderful woman in the world. Her attachment was to me and my sister," Kate told me.

Back in Connemara—in the "dream home" her parents designed themselves—Kate remembered her father having a string of girlfriends, many much younger than him.

"He doesn't have a partner [now]," she told me back in 2012, a year before his death. "He's had a succession of nice girlfriends. He dated Trudie Styler for a while. She lived with us in Connemara," she said of the woman who went on to marry English musician Sting.

Was it strange to see her father with younger women who were sometimes near her own age?

"If they're nice it's fantastic. It's got nothing to do with age, it's got everything to do with personality."

Courtesy of Mirror Images

The legendary director John Huston, who gave up his American citizenship and became an Irish citizen in 1964, was a nearby neighbour in Galway. When his wife Enrica Soma tragically died in a car crash, their youngest daughter Allegra stayed with the O'Toole family. It was subsequently revealed that Allegra was the offspring of an extramarital affair Enrica had with John Julius Cooper, the second Viscount of Norwich.

"Allegra is my best friend in the world since her mother died," Kate explained. "She was five and she came to live with us in the big fancy house in London while the Huston estate tried to figure out what to do with her. She also lived with us in Clifton. She also came on holidays with us because we used to go to France for two weeks every year, to Cannes before it became a nightmare."

Kate laughed at the absurdity of how busloads of tourists would descend on Clifton to take photographs of "the house where Peter O'Toole lived"—even though it was still only being built and was covered with scaffolding and there were mudslides everywhere surrounding the property.

"All the local businesses in Clifton used to say to the American tourists who had come off the coach tours in those days in the late 60s, 'Peter O'Toole has just built a house. You've got to go look at it'," she recalled. "So, we used to get actual coach loads of nuns, Americans, travellers, all kinds of people, just taking pictures of us at the house. It was mad, you know?"

Kate added, "It wasn't really a problem. It was hilarious because it was barely more than a construction site at that point. It was like, 'What are you looking at?' We just thought it was mad. Silly."

She remembered one funny episode when she mistakenly took Katherine Hepburn for a tramp when she called to the house unannounced.

"I was at the kitchen sink window looking down and there was this awful old hag wearing clothes suitable for the windy weather—a headscarf and a hat and an old jacket and a pair of sensible trousers but also with a skirt over the sensible trousers tucked into the boots," Kate said.

"And I just said to my mother, 'Oh, it's one of those travellers again to take a photograph'. And then she said, 'Oh, no, darling—it's Kate Hepburn!' And it was, just dressed for Connemara."

Amazingly, Kate said, she has only ever been upset once about something she read about her father. As a young child, she recoiled in horror when coming across a story claiming her father was on death's doors.

"I was in Connemara with my grandmother—both my parents were both away working—and I remember reading just a little paragraph saying that Peter O'Toole was dying of stomach cancer," she told me.

"I was completely devastated by it, because I believed at that age, as you do, that anything you see in print is true. I believed that that was case and it wasn't—it was some stupid ass story that got completely fucked up in the mix and had nothing to do with anything.

"And it was years before he did get sick. But that was my first experience of being really frightened because of his health. And that is the first time I've ever been hurt by a newspaper article. And because of that experience, fortunately, happily, it was the very last time because nothing has ever been like that since.

"So, frankly, if somebody writes that I look like a dog and I just climbed out of the back of the bus and I'm terrible in the play and I'm not worth tuppencewop, I couldn't care less. I couldn't care less about anything that I read in the newspapers since that very day."

A few years later in 1975, Peter was diagnosed with pancreatic cancer. "He nearly died. It was 50/50. I wasn't aware of it at the time. I knew he was ill but I wasn't told how ill. I didn't realise he might die," Kate said.

"But I did know that his life was completely changed when he came out of the hospital. My mother left. His agent had robbed him. Everything fell apart then. When he came out of hospital there was nobody there."

But Kate was there for him at the time. She was also by his side in 1978 when he almost died from a blood disorder.

O'Toole dramatically cutback on his drinking binges after being on death's door back in the late 70s. But he still likes an occasional tipple. "Especially when I'm around," she laughed.

She was also by his side last year when he was struck down with pneumonia and they feared the worst. She puts it down to a foolish decision to make a film in poor living conditions in Asia. "He was in Kazakhstan doing a dodgy film in very dodgy circumstances. He's much better now," she said, clearly relieved.

Was he worried?

"Yeah. Well, he's not getting any younger—79 going on 80. But he does look after himself."

During his twilight years, Kate visits her father regularly in London; while Peter liked to come back to Galway occasionally for visits, but they didn't talk regularly on the phone. "He doesn't do the phone. He doesn't know how to use a phone!" she laughed.

Despite the close bond that has always existed between the legendary Peter O'Toole and daughter, there was a time when they drifted apart, Kate revealed as we continued discussing vignettes about her extraordinary upbringing.

After we'd talked for a few hours, Kate—who good-humouredly refers to me as "Jason No-Relayshun" throughout our conversation because of our surname—opened up next to me about her parents' bitter divorce.

After her mother Siân Phillips had left her father for her younger lover, the family unit sadly disintegrated. Kate dropped out of school and went off to live in a squat with a boyfriend. What did her parents make of their 17-year-old daughter running off to live in squalor?

"I don't know—I never asked them! I was free to do my own thing. I mean, my mother was gone, so that was irrelevant what she thought anyway. My father was busy working. They weren't really paying attention to me then."

While living in the squat, she hung out with emerging bands like the Sex Pistols and waited tables in a trendy jazz club where Miles Davis was the resident musician.

In fact, her proclivity for having a good time seemed at times to almost rival her father's reputation as a hell raiser. She was sent home from a school skiing trip to Switzerland after being caught in a compromising position.

"I didn't behave myself," she sheepishly admitted. "I ended up in the toilets of the hotel underneath a big gang of Swiss army guys, all of whom I'd invited back and the geography teacher came in and she said, 'Oh, my God! What is going on here?' I said, 'It's called sex and drugs and rock and roll!' She said, 'Get out now'."

Kate paused to laugh. Quickly realising how she just made this anecdote sound as if she was the only female amongst the male companions, Kate immediately clarified the story by telling me: "Me and a few friends—I wasn't being gang raped by the Swiss army! No, it wasn't like that. But they had come in through the skylight. It was just girls on a school trip. I got expelled for that and neither of my parents passed any remarks. Why would they? For fuck's sake!"

Surely her parents were shocked by such behaviour?

"I don't think it shocked them. I think they were unshockable."

Kate had first shown signs of her rebellious streak when she ran away from home when still only a toddler. Recounting the story, she told me: "I was two, seriously. My mother remembers it. She was looking out the window and she saw me striding towards the Tube station with my bag stuffed with my dolls and teddy bears. And she sent the nanny out to get me. The nanny said, 'What are you doing?' I said, 'I'm leaving. I hate being told what to do'."

She certainly had a wild streak in her formative teenage years, but Kate was also sensible enough to stay away from hard drugs, which she put down to her "grounded Welsh part" on her mother's side.

"I don't like needles. But Grass is a good thing," she said.

It wasn't until she moved to America that she started taking cocaine. "You couldn't live in New York in the '80s and not do it [coke], darling," she laughed.

Did she become addicted to cocaine?

"Oh, no, I've never been dependant on anything or anyone. But it was more at the weekends," she said nonchalantly.

Her move to the US—and first foray into acting—was more by accident than design. Kate had dreamt of being a playwright but this plan changed after a traumatic break-up with her boyfriend with whom she shared the squat. To get over her broken heart, Kate jetted out to the US to visit her father, who was making a movie called *Svengali* with the Oscar-winning actress Jodie Foster back in 1983.

"I went to stay in a hotel with him for a couple of weeks. I was recovering. I was having a trauma. I was very fragile," she confessed.

It was Jodie Foster, who at the time was attending Yale University, while making films during school term breaks, who encouraged Kate to attend the prestigious university. "She said, 'There's a really good drama school, you should apply to get in'."

There was one inconvenient problem—Kate had never completed her secondary school education. She brazenly lied about having a BA from Trinity College on her application for an MA course in writing at Yale.

"That year there was a postal strike in Ireland," Kate recalled. "So, physically the admin woman at Yale couldn't ring Trinity or write to them. I'd passed through all the hoops and then it just came down to the technicality, 'Where's your BA?' I just said, 'I'm grand—I have my BA, of course I do. Yeah, yeah. You're just going to have to try to get hold of Trinity'. And they couldn't. The admin person said, 'We'll just fudge it for now and we'll sort it out later'."

Kate continued, "I couldn't do it now. It was amazing because not only did I get in but I got into the MA programme—having left school at 16! It was while I was at Yale that I got bitten by the acting bug."

Kate found Yale liberating because nobody there cared that she had famous parents. "America's different. America isn't as impressed by fame as people are here or in England," she explained.

Courtesy of Mirror Images

Kate had once contemplated attending the prestigious acting school RADA, where both her parents had excelled. "I physically couldn't go. I couldn't go into the building because at the bottom of it there was a bust of my father and, you know, boards everywhere saying things like the Siân Philips Memorial Trophy for best actor . . . it was like, 'I cannot go here. It'll fucking do my head in'. It was impossible; the whole place was full of ghosts.

"It would've been a nightmare. Every single day I would've walked in there I would've seen them. It's not what you need when you're trying to evolve. So, Yale was better because they didn't really have any consciousness of that, you know?"

Did she feel like she was living under the shadow of her father, or that people might think she was trading on the family name, when she finally broke into acting?

"No, because I was in America. It would've been if I had been living in England. Big time. I didn't get any jobs because of them [my parents] in America because America is very hard nosed. They didn't give a shit. All they care about is bang for their bucks."

Did her father give her any advice when she started acting?

"The only thing he said when I told him I was thinking of switching from writing to acting was, 'Can you starve?' I said, 'Oh, yeah. I can. Have done that living in the squat. Yeah, I can starve'. He said, 'Well then, you'll be okay'.

"He's always been good. He's always come to see me in everything I've ever done, really. He likes to keep an eye on me. He doesn't ever give me any advice. He's never taught me anything about acting. Never. He's just not like that."

Peter O'Toole once hopped on stage as a last minute replacement when an actor didn't turn up one night when Kate was starring in a Jim Sheridan's production of *The Hostage*, off Broadway in a tiny theatre in 1984.

"My dad came to see the show and the next night I must have mentioned to him that the black guy who plays the drag queen wasn't turning up and he said, 'Oh, are you short of a cast member? Well, I'll do it'," she recalled.

Sadly, father and daughter never shared any stage time that night.

And, despite talks about working together down through the years, they have never acted together since that one night in Brendan Behan's play.

Despite all the critical acclaim, Peter never won an Oscar—even though he was nominated something like eight times and was eventually given an honorary one. "I was sitting next to him when he didn't get it [for *Venus* (2006)]. He wasn't [upset] because he calls the Oscars—and this is completely on the record—the dog and pony show! It's High School prom for movie stars. It would've been nice to get that one," she admitted.

She revealed that he was pressured into accepting the honorary Oscar in 2003. "They forced one onto him. He said, 'No, I don't want it because it's not in competition'. He turned it down. They said, 'That's grand but we're giving it to you anyway because we call the shots. If you don't turn up you're going to look like shit. So, up to you'. Horrible," she said, shaking her head in disgust.

As she started out acting in New York, Kate was so desperate to stay there that she fell into a marriage of convenience". She needed a Green Card to work in the US and her then lover, also an actor, needed a UK working visa for a small role in Stanley Kubrick's *Full Metal Jacket* (1987) shot on location in London's docks, which were doubling for Saigon because the eccentric film director had a phobia about flying. Ironically, her new husband's big scenes in Kubrick's movie ended up on the cutting room floor.

"He wasn't the person I wanted to marry and I wasn't the person he wanted to marry. We were living together—it's not like he was a complete stranger and I paid a lawyer six grand," she said, laughing.

"I stayed married to him for quite a long time even after we'd broken up as boyfriend and girlfriend. I had moved back here for work. One day I got a phone call from his brother who's a lawyer who said, 'He's met somebody he wants to marry, so now it's time to draw up the divorce papers'. I said, 'Fine'. I hadn't spoken to him for years. It wasn't a big deal."

What did her parents make of the marriage?

"They didn't know! They know *now*. I wasn't in touch with them [at the time]; I was doing my own thing."

She never remarried, but almost came close on one occasion when she was in a long-term relationship that happened after she had moved back to Ireland. Did she have any regrets about not having children?

"No. I don't thing so. I have no patience whatsoever. I don't even like looking at babies! I like being on my own."

Has she ever had any high profile romances? After all, the gossip columns are full of stories about actors having flings on film sets.

"Not fit for print," she quipped.

Despite a fine body of work—including roles in John Huston's *The Dead* (1987), appearing in the Meryl Streep's movie *Dancing at Lughnasa* (1998), alongside Ewen McGregor in *Nora* (2000) and starring alongside U2's drummer Larry Mullen in his film debut, *Man on The Train* (2011)—one could hardly blame Kate for being irked by how the first information to come up on an internet search is that she was arrested for drunk driving in 2008. She received a three-year driving ban for being over the limit when driving home from the local hotel after a Christmas function to her home in a remote part of Clifton.

"I'm not proud of it, but neither am I covered in sackcloth and ashes. I am not the only person in the area who was doing the exact same thing that very night. I just ended up in the newspapers—that's the only difference," she explained.

"There is no public transport whatsoever out there. None. This isn't an excuse for what I did but it is very much the reason. That's an important point. Taxis are few, maybe four in total, and therefore impossible to get at Christmas, either they've been booked months in advance, or they're not working because they're at the big Christmas party with everyone else.

"I was wrong to do it—even if there were no other cars for miles around I still could have injured myself steering home like that. That's why I said [to the Garda], 'It's a fair cop'. I was over the limit and should not have been driving. End of story."

Typical of her optimistic nature, Kate tried to look at the positive side of the incident. "The ban was lifted two years ago," she said in 2012, "but I now prefer life without a car. I have learned my lesson. The punishment was 100 percent justified and I will never do it again.

"I am the poster child for how being punished for drunk driving can transform one's life for the better. I'm glad it happened. When I have the time I *choose* to walk six miles a day. Walking does very good things for one's mind and body. It's both energising and meditative at the same time. I thoroughly enjoy it and wouldn't dream of giving up the walks now. I'd never have discovered this if the ban hadn't happened."

Kate's father Peter announced his retirement in a press release in 2012. He wrote: "Dear All, It is time for me to chuck in the sponge. To retire from films and stage. The heart for it has gone out of me: it won't come back."

What did Kate make of his decision to retire?

"I can't improve upon his beautifully worded public statement which, as far as I'm aware, is unique. He's 80 and I believe he's earned a break—most people retire long before that age. I applaud him for setting his own agenda and doing it on his own terms," she told me at that time.

"As for myself, I feel a little too young to be contemplating the end of my career but ask me again when I'm 80 and I'll probably have some thought on the matter by then," she said, smiling, with a twinkle in her blue eyes that makes it hard not to make comparisons of her father—both physically and with her character, especially after listening to her extraordinary life story.

The adage about the apple not falling far from tree is certainly true when it comes to Kate O'Toole.

CHAPTER FOUR:

A Star Is Born, Saoirse Ronan

Saoirse Ronan was only eight-years-old when she suffered her first (and only) rejection. She auditioned for a role in *The Actors*, a crime-comedy starring Michael Caine and the Dublin-born thespian Michael Gambon, which was shot in Dublin and released in 2003.

"She really impressed the casting directors, but she was deemed too young and didn't get the part," her father, Paul told me during one of many conversations I had with him back when his daughter was first breaking into acting.

But the spirited young girl from County Carlow quickly bounced back and soon afterwards landed her first major role in the Irish-made TV drama series, *The Clinic*. While the mediocre film *The Actors* quickly vanished without a trace, Saoirse is having the proverbial last laugh, with a sensational movie career that is unrivalled by any other Irish actor at the moment. With already three Oscar nominations under her belt for her stand-out performances in *Lady Bird* (2017), *Brooklyn* (2015), and *Atonement* (2007), the now twenty-something has established herself as one of the most in-demand actress working in Hollywood these days.

I first came across Saoirse back in 2008 when I interviewed her shortly before the release of her breakthrough movie, *Atonement*. Our interview was actually the first time she appeared on the cover of a magazine. After that hour-long chat, for a few years I managed to keep in contact with the Ronan family—mostly through the odd call, email, or text—as I observed the continuing rise of Saoirse's star, which continues to ascend even today at a phenomenal speed.

I'm not going to claim to be a close friend of the family's, but they were very open and accommodating to me during those early years, helping me put together large features on Saoirse for the *Irish Mail on Sunday* and *Hot Press* magazine, which was actually her first ever cover story. There's been countless since.

After Saoirse returned home for a break during the filming of *The Lovely Bones* (2009), I had the pleasure of meeting her socially when she and her parents invited me to the Shelbourne Hotel in Dublin for afternoon tea. During our chats, I was struck not only by her poise, which she has in considerable abundance, but also by her genuine passion for acting and her determination to rise to the top of her profession.

Over tea and cake, she joked to me about how hardly anybody in Hollywood can say her name, which means freedom in the Irish language. "They have the biggest problem in the world pronouncing my name. You'd want to hear the stuff they come out with," Saoirse said, laughing.

But it seems that not as many people have as much trouble these days pronouncing Saoirse's name, considering that she's been talked about so much at the moment.

"Give them time," I reassured her. "When you're a big star, nobody's going to have any problem pronouncing your name in the future."

Saoirse got her first starring role in a big budget Hollywood movie at the age of just 13-years-old. It was a bolt out of the blue too. She was sitting, accompanied by her parents, waiting for a conference call with her new representative from CAA, arguably the biggest talent agency in the US. The Ronans assumed the phone call was to discuss the mundane task of fine-tuning the contractual details for Saoirse's latest co-starring role, alongside the legendary comedian Bill Murray, in the big budget sci-fi movie *City of Ember* (2008), which was being shot on location in Northern Ireland.

But the call turned out to be anything but routine. They heard the agent's voice boom out of the loudspeaker: "Are you sitting down for this?" There was a dramatic pause, before the agent revealed what was mind-blowing news: "They want you for *The Lovely Bones*!"

There was a pregnant pause. Had they heard that right? Did Saoirse's agent just say that she was actually being offered the lead role in the new Peter Jackson movie? It was one of the most sought-after parts in recent years, with literally over a thousand young actresses fighting it out for the opportunity to star in the eagerly anticipated adaptation, by the *Lord of the Rings* director, of Alice Sebold's hugely successful novel.

It took a while for the news to sink in. "It wasn't one of those kind of things where we were jumping up and down and screaming all over the place because it is a Peter Jackson movie," reminisced Saoirse.

"We were just sitting there trying to think of what they said. It's like the dream role. I don't think we ever jumped around—because we're still kind of amazed that we are even working with these people."

Jackson selected the young Irish teenager for the lead role after viewing an audition tape. Apparently, Jackson was so impressed with Saoirse's innate acting skills that he immediately called up the casting agent to reveal that he'd found "the perfect actress" for his next blockbuster. In fact, Jackson was so confident in her innate acting skills abilities that he didn't even bother meeting Saoirse until she flew over to the US to start filming.

"There is a fantastic casting agent called Jenny Jay," Saoirse explained, "and she had cast me for *Atonement*. She had seen me for a couple of more things as well, so I knew Jenny and she must have gotten into contact with my agent and I went on tape for *The Lovely Bones*—and we sent it off. They hadn't met me or anything when they gave me the part."

She continued, "I had to keep it top secret though—because obviously it is a Peter Jackson film and it is really high profile. I was on *City of Ember* up in Belfast and I knew about *The Lovely Bones* but I wasn't allowed to tell anyone for about two weeks or something and

I was just in agony—I just wanted to tell everyone, 'Oh, look—I'm in the new Peter Jackson movie!'

For those unfamiliar with *The Lovely Bones*, it is the story of a 14-year-old, brutally murdered rape victim, who narrates her story from heaven, as she looks down on her family as they try to cope with the tragedy. It was a taxing role for a 13-year-old to play, to say the very least.

"Once I read the script I just cried because it is so sad, but it is such a beautiful script. I've been thinking about the story. You see, it's a sad story but it's turned into something that is really beautiful," Saoirse explained.

"Susie has to learn to let go and that's kind of what the film is about—her letting go and her family learning to let go. And that's kind of what we all have to do when somebody passes away. So, yeah, sometimes I just go home and I get a bit sad and I've cried a few times, but you would though, wouldn't you?"

Immediately after wrapping up filming for *City of Ember* in Belfast in the summer of 2007, Saoirse jetted off to Philadelphia with her parents to start work on the voice-over narration of *The Lovely Bones*. In the end, Saoirse spent almost nine months of 2007 away from home.

"In 2006, it wasn't as difficult because I had breaks in between," she recalled. "I did *Atonement* and then I had a week in between that and *Death Defying Acts* (2007), so even that was OK because I got to come home and see my friends and everything. But in 2007, I finished *City of Ember* on the Friday and then I went over to America to do *The Lovely Bones* on the Saturday. *City of Ember* was up in Belfast and people were saying, 'You can go back to Carlow to see your friends'. But it's about five hours away, so we couldn't really because they were in school and I would be wrecked on the weekends. So, I didn't get to see them at all. I was really, really homesick when I got to America. When you are away, you realise how much you miss your home. I just missed the Irish food and the Irish people and everything, but it was great though."

In recent interviews, Saoirse revealed that she also missed her dog. But when she got home that Christmas, the dog, unfortunately, had absconded. "I'm missing her a lot more now," she said, sadly, at the time. "My nanny and granddad were minding her and she ran away and she's either in Dublin, somewhere in a nice house or I don't know—I don't want to even say it, but she's gone, I think."

During my first phone conversation with Saoirse, she was halfway through filming *The Lovely Bones* but was still sometimes finding it a surreal experience to be working on such a big-budget film. "I haven't really had any time to pinch myself. I haven't really had any time to sit down and go, 'Wow!'" she admitted.

"Sometimes when I'm on the set, I think about how I am with these people who made *The Lord of The Rings*. They won like, I don't know, 20 Oscars for it or something mad like that. It is amazing that these people are my friends now and not just the people who made *Lord of The Rings*. It is mad—but I am kind of used to it now. I can't believe how lucky I've been to work with all the actors and actresses I've worked with. It has been brilliant."

The past decade has been phenomenal for the young actress, who is now one of the hottest properties in Hollywood. By the time I'd met Saoirse that first time in 2008, she had already produced an impressive body of work; from the ages between 11 and 13 she already had six films under her belt and was nominated in the Best Supporting Actress category at the both Oscars and Golden Globes for her portrayal of Keira Knightley's younger sister in *Atonement*.

Unfortunately, Saoirse's dream of strolling up the red carpet on that particular occasion was scuppered when Hollywood screenwriters went on strike and it prompted the television network to cancel the show, after it was made clear that no Hollywood actor would cross the picket line.

Recalling the moment she learnt about the Oscar nomination, Saoirse told me: "I was trying not to think about it because I was doing *The Lovely Bones* in Pennsylvania and I was wrecked—I still am—as well because it was coming to the end of the shoot and I knew that the nominations were going to be announced the next day. I was trying to put it out of my head because if you get excited you could be disappointed, so I didn't really want to think about it. But then when it happened we were just jumping around. I think everyone on the set of *The Lovely Bones* knew before I did! And everyone in Ireland rang us—the time difference was just gone out the window. Oh, it was brilliant."

While she was very unfortunate not to win the Golden Globe or Oscar that year, there is no doubting that there will be other award possibilities for Saoirse in the not too distant future. She has already been nominated three times for an Oscar and she's still only in her early twenties. I'd bet the farm on her winning either one or both of these prestigious accolades before she reaches thirty.

Her affable father Paul Ronan is also an actor, who acted as a manager for Saoirse when she was starting out in the acting world; while these days Paul stars in an Irish TV soap, *Fair City*. He has starred alongside Brad Pitt in *The Devil's Own* (1997) and also had a leading role in the final series of BBC's *Ballykissangel*, which kick-started Colin Farrell's fledging career.

Even knowing the ropes as he does, Paul admitted that he was flabbergasted by his daughter's swift ascent to Hollywood stardom. "No matter how talented anyone is, it is a surprising rise by any standards," Paul reflected when the family finally got back home for a short break at Christmas 2007, before jetting back off to New Zealand in early 2008 so Saoirse could continue work on *The Lovely Bones*.

"She has surprised the hell out of all of us. I'm not surprised that she is an actor, but I am surprised with the speed because it rarely happens to any actor, of any age, of any sex, of any nationality. I wake up every morning with a smile on my face—happy for her. We are just walking on air. In fact, her whole family is walking on air. My brother Bobby has been battling leukaemia for two years—he's doing great now. The news that Saoirse was giving him from time to time was one of those things that was giving him a lift—so it's been great for him.

"Everybody is getting such a kick out of it. I'm happy that it has happened to such a good kid and happy that she is handling it so well. I wouldn't be happy if she was getting all this success and it was turning her head and was affecting her; then it would make me really very unhappy. I'd pull her out of the business as quickly as I could if I thought that was happening."

As the roles got bigger, Saoirse has refused to allow the obvious increased pressure get to her. "You can't really think like that because then you'll lose it—you'll go mad," she proffered.

"You have to take it as it comes and every role is different and every film is different. I'm just thinking about the character and what way we are going to do it, and stuff. It's really nuts what's happened over the past couple of years and especially now that *Atonement* is out, it is really big. You know, if you get really, really excited about it you'll probably like pass out or something. So, I have to be kind of calm—but still excited though."

She is 100 percent Irish, but Saoirse was actually born in the Bronx, New York in 1994. Her parents had immigrated to the States in the late '80s, because of the high level of unemployment back home in Dublin. Her mother Monica (neé Brennan) originally hails from the working-class north Dublin suburb of Cabra and had worked as a child actress herself, alongside the legendary Maureen Potter in the Gaiety, but hasn't acted since. Paul, who is originally from the tough neighbourhood of Ballymun, only a stone's throw from Dublin Airport, was working in a New York bar when he was persuaded to take up acting by Chris O'Neill, an actor from a once popular Irish TV show called *The Riordans.*

It was this thespian influence that had Saoirse acting—literally—while still in the pram. She got her first film role when she was about one year old in a film called *Exiled* (1999), in which her father played the leading part. Soon afterwards, her parents briefly discussed getting Saoirse seriously into the business. It didn't pan out. "We thought she was the cutest baby in the world, as you do when it's your kid," Paul recalled. "So, we thought, 'Ah, we'll put her in for an ad and we'll see how she gets on'.

"Years ago, in Manhattan, we'd brought her in for one of these auditions for, I think, a tyre or something. She was only a baby—not even a toddler—and I walked into the room and it was full of women and crying and screaming children—and they were all trying to get their kids to sit up straight. I saw the look on Saoirse's face when she saw this—a look of sheer terror—and me and Monica looked at each other and went, 'Nay, this is not for us. No way. We are out of here'. Straight away. We didn't even have to ask each other. We didn't want any kind of fear or anything negative for Saoirse."

The Ronans moved back to Ireland when Saoirse was about four-years-old.

Saoirse used to accompany her father onto the sets of films and TV shows he worked on. When she was only about two-years-old, the Hollywood heartthrob Brad Pitt used to pick Saoirse up and play with her between takes on the set of *The Devil's Own.* Unfortunately, Saoirse can't remember meeting Pitt. "I know I met him because dad worked with him on *The Devil's Own*. And Mam and Dad said he's a lovely, lovely guy, and that he was great with me," she said, laughing.

Saoirse told me that being around the film sets as a child proved to be ideal training. "It was great that I was able to go on set and see what it was like. So, I wasn't like completely clueless about how films were made," she said.

"But when you do it yourself you really realise what it is like. You have to think about what way you tackle your character and what way you deal with people on set. It was handy that I had been on a film set before and I suppose if I hadn't, you know, it would have been a lot more daunting. It did help in that way."

Her father remembers how she was constantly mimicking accents. "From a very young age, she had shown a remarkable imagination with accents and with inventing characters and just enjoying life—she was a very happy child," Paul recalled. "She was literally able to go into the corner with a bunch of toys and do plays with her dolls, and having them all doing different accents. I used to get such a kick out of just listening to her."

Saoirse agreed that playing with her dolls as a child helped her learn the different accents. "I used to have my Polly Pockets and it was kind of like a soap opera," she said. "They used to have affairs with different Polly Pockets and then they'd have babies with other Polly Pockets, but I had these two dolls that weren't Polly Pockets—you know *Arthur*? That TV programme? Arthur—he's a little animal fellow—and I used to watch that when I was younger. I used to play with Arthur and then I had Woody from *Toy Story*. So they all had boyfriends and they used to have like American accents, so that's kind of where the accents came from."

Her innate talent for accents has paid off. In the first decade of her acting Saoirse hadn't used her own accent in any of the movies she has made. She finally got to use an Irish accent in *Brooklyn*. "It's a bit weird because I haven't used my Irish accent on film in such a long time," she once told me before making *Brooklyn*. "The last time I did it I was nine or something. I think it would be nice. Actually, an actress said this to me: 'It's great doing your own accent because it's kind of one thing off your mind, that you don't have to think about'.

"You don't have to have a dialogue coach coming up to you and giving you notes on how to say a certain word, and you can just focus on the acting. I'm used to doing it now. I've got half of my brain for the accent and half of it for the acting! But it would be nice to not have to think about it."

Saoirse's second foray into the acting world was when, at the age of six, she starred alongside her father again. "It was a short film I put her in that was never released called *Keep Talking*," Paul recalled. "She was great in it. At the time, the girl directing it saw Saoirse hitting her marks, and moving on action, and being quiet when she was supposed to be. She had to do a scene where she pretended to climb over a big back garden wall and it was one of these pebble dashed walls. So, Saoirse would start the scene kind of hanging off this wall, try to keep her knees out, and then jump down—and she'd hit it every time," he says.

Saoirse enjoyed making *Keep Talking*, but she didn't consider acting as a possible full-time career. She explained: "That was for, like, a day and I was dressed up as a clown," she said. "It was a brilliant role, though. You hear people saying they wanted to act since they could talk and everything, but when I was younger I was thinking about school and playing with my friends and things like that. It was only really when I started to act in *The Clinic*—and I experienced it—that I knew I wanted to act. I did *The Clinic* when I was about eight and before that I had done school plays and things like that."

"Now," she continued, "Acting is not work, it is more of a passion. It is so much fun—especially when I do dramatic scenes when I have to cry and stuff, as you feel great at the end of the day. You feel like you do after accomplishing something. Acting is one of these things that I can't really describe—it's just like, why do you love your mum and dad? You know, you just do."

Even from the very start, Paul was reluctant to "ever push her in any way or even nudge her towards the business". The upsetting audition experience back in Manhattan always stuck in his mind. However, Paul eventually decided to get Saoirse some more acting experience after various people had commented on her obvious abilities. "I felt it was the right time," he recalled, "because she had such confidence with people and such a great imagination and exuberance. People used to look at her and go, 'My God! She's special' – just by the way she acted around people and carried herself. My agent Lisa-Ann Campbell said, 'Bring her in and I'll meet her whenever you are up in Dublin'. I brought her in one time—not to bring her in specifically—and Lisa Ann said, 'She is just adorable. She is amazing. We've got to put her out for stuff'."

The first role Saoirse auditioned for was a part in *The Comedians*, starring Dylan Moran and Michael Caine. Her Irish agent recalls how Saoirse "really impressed" the casting directors but, unfortunately, she was deemed too young for that particular role. "She didn't get that, but Lisa-Ann called up with an audition for *The Clinic* for her. She went in for the audition—and bang, got it," Paul said.

Saoirse recalled: "I just went to Dublin for an audition for *The Clinic*. I met the director and I read through some stuff and I actually read for a different part. It was weird because I thought I was playing one part and then I ended up playing a different part."

Saoirse earned rave reviews for her work in *The Clinic* and was cast the following year in another RTÉ drama, *Proof*. During the first week of shooting, the director Thaddeus O'Sullivan took Paul aside and declared, "Saoirse is going to be a major star."

Paul, who had worked with Thaddeus on *Ordinary Decent Criminal* (2000), figured that his director friend was being kind. Paul told me, "I really thought that he was just being nice to me because he knew me and he was a friend. I said, 'Yeah, thanks, Thaddy'. But he said, 'No, really—she is a star'. He said, 'Look at this', and he showed me some of the daily rushes and he said, 'Look at the way she does this scene. She would have been playing the lead role in my last film. She is a star. You just watch'."

The director's prediction was correct. "Basically she hasn't not gotten anything she's gone for since then," Paul said, proudly. "She has done six movies in two years and has turned down about four as well. There are scripts coming her way now, where people are not even talking about auditions and stuff, but they are talking about, 'Will you do the film?'"

It was while making *Proof* that Saoirse met representatives from Hubbard's Casting, who invited her over to London—at her own expense—to audition for the new Michelle Pfeiffer movie, *I Could Never Be Your Woman*, which was released 2008.

Normally poised in auditions, Saoirse was extremely anxious when reading for that particular role. "I got really nervous because I'd never done anything like that before, but it got easier and easier," she said. "I do still kind of get nervous sometimes. I get nervous about meeting the director a little bit because I'd be nervous about whether he's a nice guy or girl and whether they think about the character the same way I do. You know, I think everyone gets nervous, really—but not petrified."

Her next major role was as Keira Knightley's little sister in *Atonement*. Her performance in the film, for which she got rave reviews, made Hollywood sit up and take notice. When I interviewed

Jonathan Rhys Meyers in November 2008, he spoke glowingly to me about her performance. "I'm delighted for Saoirse Ronan. She is one of a few very beautiful, very smart actresses emerging from Ireland at the moment. She is superb in *Atonement*. It is a beautiful movie. Saoirse Ronan—I was really like, 'Wow! She is beyond fucking good'. I have never made a performance like that," he said.

However, it was almost a part that Saoirse didn't take. At the same time, a major Hollywood studio offered her a colossal three-movie deal that would have financially set her up for life. But Saoirse's parents could immediately spot the downside: she would be virtually tied exclusively to that particular studio until those three films were completed, which would mean she'd probably be in her late teens before completing the contract. Besides, Saoirse felt that the role in *Atonement* was a better choice, as she knew it would fully demonstrate her acting abilities. I re-watched the movie and was struck, once again, by how truly talented Saoirse was—and still is. Despite starring alongside some really experienced actors at their peak in *Atonement*, the novice Saoirse stole the picture.

Recalling how she fought for that role, Saoirse said: "I went on tape, like *The Lovely Bones*, and I sent it off and then they wanted to bring me over to meet Joe [Wright, director of the film] and I read with the girl who is playing Lola. I got called back and was trying on wigs and things like that. And Joe and I got on really well.

"Then my agent, Lisa, rang and she said, 'Listen, it's down to you and another girl'. And there was this other film that I'd been offered and she said, 'Do you want to go for that or do you want to go for *Atonement*?' And she told me that *Atonement* was going to be an amazing film. So, Joe and Jenny wanted me—so they had to fight for me a little bit and they did.

"I don't like to play characters who have been done before, if you know what I mean. There are some young actors and actresses—I'm not saying they're all like this, but there are some—who kind of play the same roles over again. So, I kind of like to have a bit of a variety. And the likes of Briony Tallis (*Atonement*) and Susie Salmon (*The Lovely Bones*), they've never kind of been done before, so people will remember them."

Paul added: "We have turned down some really big ones for smaller ones. Rather than snapping at money, Saoirse has guided us through what roles she loves. She knows when she likes a role herself. She reads through the script and we'll talk about role selection. I'd read the scripts of course—and the agent would—and we'd talk among us to see what is the most suitable. It is a collaborative effort."

Working on *Atonement*, Saoirse says she learned a lot from Keira Knightley and, in particular, the veteran actress and political activist, Vanessa Redgrave. "Vanessa is amazing. I didn't get to do any scenes with Vanessa because we were playing the same character. But we got to do rehearsals and everything and that was just fantastic. Besides her being such a talented actress, she also does a lot of charity work, as does Susan Sarandon. So, I like that they do that—that they put money to good use, you know?"

Even as a young teenager, Saoirse was already thinking hard about her future.

"You see, that's the kind of thing that I think I learnt from them (other actors)—how to use your career to your advantage. Is that how you say it? You should look up to them instead of these people who are going out at all hours and they are on drugs and everything," she said.

"I'd like to be known as an actress who does films that make you think about life and how things are in the world. I want to do a lot of charity work because I think if more actors and actresses do charity work then maybe, you know, the public will realise that there are problems in the world and we need to get them sorted out. I'd like to be like Susan Sarandon and Vanessa [Redgrave] because they are fantastic actresses."

Paul admitted that their lifestyle has dramatically transformed since Saoirse's acting career took off. "Monica went over and accompanied Saoirse when she did *Atonement*. So it did disrupt our lives because it separated us and we are never really separated," he said.

Paul also admitted that he is wary of the fame side of the acting game. "It is worrying," he said. "Any parent would feel the same. All you want is for them to be happy and have a good, full, normal life and to turn into a good person—that's all you want for them.

"When we were in Venice, I saw that same scared look that she had when we walked into that baby audition. I kind of got a glimpse of that when she stepped onto the red carpet at a pre-premiere photo shoot of her and Keira. They were standing to the side, but as soon as she walks on they're screaming at her. I kind of saw a little bit of fear on her face when she saw that, and it is daunting, when you go on and next of all there is like a sea of flashing lights and voices behind those lights shouting at you—it has got to be weird for a 12, 13-year-old kid.

"Stardom and fame and all that stuff can be a help or a hindrance in life—I'm just hoping that it will be a help to her. As it goes along, I think we are doing OK at the moment—but you don't know how it's going to turn out."

Despite all the glamour associated with being a rising Hollywood star, Saoirse was still very much a typical, down-to-earth teenager who loved sports (she is rugby mad and a Manchester United fan), listening to music (she is a big Snow Patrol fan), playing with her Nintendo Wii, and, more importantly, shopping with her friends. "The most important thing for me is to see my friends and go shopping and just do normal things that I haven't gotten to do while I was away," she told me.

Saoirse came across as so articulate and balanced in her approach that it was almost impossible to believe that she had just started secondary school at the time—though, she had to do most of her study "on the road". I asked if her friends look at her differently now that she is being recognised a real star—at least one in-the-making?

"My real friends don't and they are the only people that really matter," she said. "I mean, there's been a few people who—and it's understandable, really—a few kids who don't want to really talk to me or anything [*laughs*]. I don't know whether that's because I'm in movies now or they just don't like me—I don't know! But some of the boys and stuff have been a bit odd, but it's really . . . I think I have a few admirers in my new school!

"No, I'm only joking! I've got four best friends and they treat me the same, so they are really the only people who matter. They are thrilled [for me]. Before any of the films came out they were delighted for me but they didn't realise how cool it was and now that *Atonement* is out and is getting so much press and everything they've got like posters and . . . they are delighted. They are so excited."

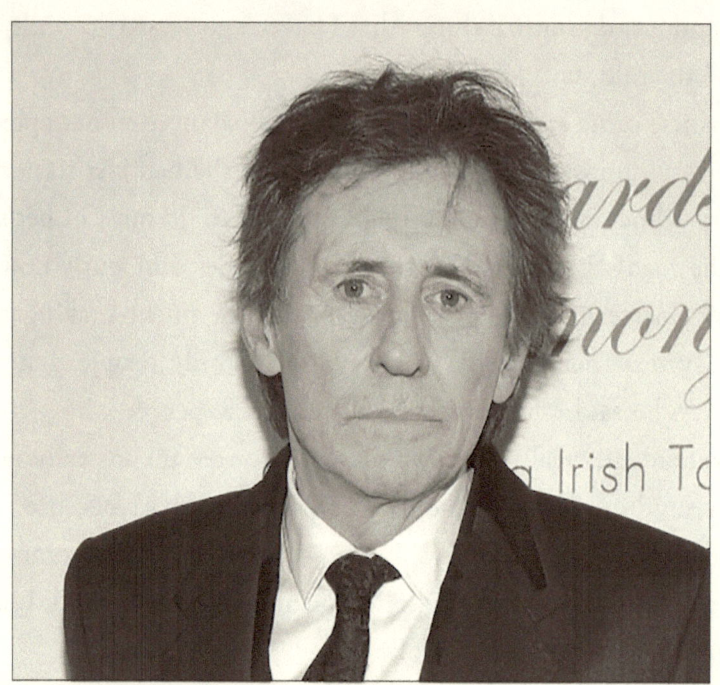

IFTA
AWARDS
FILM & DRAMA
RTÉ
SPOTLIGHT
The home of casting
ifb
IRISH FILM BOARD

CHAPTER FIVE:

Confessions of A Movie Star, Gabriel Byrne

Gabriel Byrne is one of Ireland's most successful and prolific actors to have made it in Hollywood. In an acting career that stretches all the way back to the late '70s, the Dubliner has well over 100 credits to his name, according to the online movie bible IMDb.

Byrne worked as a teacher prior to opting, at the relatively late-ish age of 28, to try his hand at acting. He had major roles in two of Irish TV station RTÉ's most successful television shows, *The Riordans* and *Bracken*, before emigrating to London in 1982. But Byrne insists he didn't go merely cross over the water merely for acting gigs. "It wasn't like a career step. I had always wanted to travel and to live in London, so I went," recalls Byrne.

The next eight years were a fruitful period as he notched up credits with some of the period's most influential, European-based, directors, including Ken Russell, Ken Loach, Michael Mann, Nick Broomfield, and Costa-Gavras.

At 40, in 1990, Byrne decided to break into Hollywood. It was a huge struggle as he jostled for roles. But his determination paid off and he went on to star in several Hollywood blockbusters, including

The Man In The Iron Mask (1998), *The Usual Suspects* (1995), *End Of Days* (1999), and *Stigmata* (1999), which received mostly negative reviews despite being a huge box office hit.

Apart from these commercial successes, Byrne has also collaborated with some of cinemas' most influential independent directors in recent years, including the Coen Brothers (*Miller's Crossing,* 1990), Wim Wenders (*The End Of Violence,* 1997), David Cronenberg (*Spider,* 2002) and Jim Jarmusch (*Dead Man,* 1995).

O'TOOLE: What motivates you when selecting your movie projects?

BYRNE: It is usually the director. Then I would try to be involved in stories that I would have a personal opinion about politically, or otherwise.

For example *Wah-Wah* (2005): Richard E Grant asked me if I would depict his father's life on screen and that was such an amazing compliment to me—that a man who was telling his father's story on screen would ask me to do it.

With *Jindabyne* (2006): the director said to me, 'I am not going to make this film without you. And if you do it, it will be a spiritual experience for you'. He came to New York to tell me that. And I said, 'I want to do it'.

Emotional Arithmetic (2007): the idea of two people being reunited as lovers, who had been through a horrendous experience in their childhood was something I found fascinating. Susan Sarandon was somebody I always wanted to work with. So there's always a reason, and it's always usually about the director, but mostly about what the story is trying to say. I have to say that a lot of the times I've worked in pictures, some of those stories haven't been told as well as I felt they could have been. In other words, the film didn't work, but that's the risk you take.

O'TOOLE: You have written, produced or starred in many Irish productions. Is it a case of wanting to push forward the film industry in Ireland?

BYRNE: There was a time when I felt idealistic about the idea of trying to get an Irish film industry off the ground. I made quite a few pictures here and I produced one or two. I had a bad experience with the last one (*In The Name Of The Father*, 1993). I had a very disillusioning experience working with somebody (*He was hinting at the director Jim Sheridan—JOT*), who I regarded as a friend, and that kind of put me off producing for a while.

So no, there is not any idealistic vision. If the script is good and I really like it, I will come back and do it. I worked on *Frankie Starlight* (1995) here with Noel Pearson and Matt Dillon; and I did *Into The West* (1992); and I did . . . what else did I do here? I haven't worked in Ireland for many, many years. I would love to do more here but, unfortunately, our film business is struggling, and there are not that many opportunities for me really.

O'TOOLE: How important is it that films are made by Irish people?

BYRNE: I think it is very important that we get to tell our own stories. How we are perceived, to a great extent, by each other, as human beings, is through film. There are still people who believe that Ireland is *The Quiet Man* (1952), *Ryan's Daughter* (1970), and *Far And Away* (1992). That's the Ireland of cinematic mythology, I suppose.

John Ford was a major mythologist. He mythologized the West; he also helped to mythologize Ireland in a way that has a certain amount of truth to it. But in terms of the depiction of a real and true picture of Ireland it is very much a chemically coloured version of Innisfree.

What's happening in Ireland now—a country that is going through such huge changes socially, economically politically—isn't being reflected in film. There are people, of course, who are really trying hard to make films about Ireland but they are facing a huge uphill struggle, not just in terms of getting finance, but in terms of distribution outside Ireland.

O'TOOLE: Are there stories to be told here?

BYRNE: Tons of them. In order for an Irish film industry to get off the ground it has to be able to make films that tell the story of who we are. But they have to be universal so that they can be watched outside of this country.

O'TOOLE: Ireland is known as a country of storytellers, but yet the majority of films showing in this country are American. Isn't this a form of cultural imperialism?

BYRNE: You have hit the nail on the head. It is a big question. If you go to America and, you go to an omniplex, the chances of you seeing an Irish film, an Israeli film, an Icelandic film, or an African film, are almost zero. In 1983, I think, 11 percent of the cinema-going population in America went to see subtitled films; it is now down to 0.1 percent.

O'TOOLE: Do you think we are becoming more Americanised?

BYRNE: I think that is not just true of Ireland, it is true of everywhere. Fifteen years ago if you had put a kid from Tel Aviv, Carlow, and Los Angeles into the same room they wouldn't have much to talk about. Now their reference points are so similar—not just with the one directional cultural American influence, in terms of technology. But it's as important for America to receive outside artistic input, as it is for us to take back the means of production for ourselves.

O'TOOLE: How can this be achieved?

BYRNE: That is a bigger question. Mainstream culture in North America has zero interest in Irish films. Zero. They have never seen a film from Ireland. They are not interested in seeing an Irish film. But if you go out to Santry or Tallaght, they can tell you what Adam Sandler's last film was. Independent film is struggling in Ireland, and independent film is struggling in America because [*pauses*] . . . it's kind of like the way of the newsagent guy on the corner who sold groceries is bought up by the big supermarket. That's kind of what has happened on a cultural level. The small man, and his individuality, is being rooted out and something bigger and more homogenous is taking his place. When I was growing up you could go see a film by Bergman, Fellini, as well as the more maverick of American mainstream films like Coppola and Scorsese.

O'TOOLE: Do you think there is too much violence in film today?

BYRNE: No. I don't think there is. I think people have always had a need to express violence fictionally and, if you go back to the Irish, Scandinavian, and Greek myths and sagas, they were all about violence. The inherent nature of men is to inspire towards goodness but [pauses] technology has changed, the world politically has changed, but the gene of violence has not changed. Mel Gibson said once, 'I watched westerns where people were hitting each other with chairs and shooting each other and it didn't make me want to go out shooting and kill people or hit them with chairs'. No, I think violence is a reflection of who we are—and films are always a reflection of who we are as a society, whether the film is good, bad, or indifferent.

O'TOOLE: What would be your favourite Gabriel Byrne film?

BYRNE: That is a very difficult question to answer because each film is tied up emotionally with my life at the time. I had such a wonderful time doing *The Man In The Iron Mask* with Leonardo DiCaprio, John Malkovich, Gerard Depardieu, and Jeremy Irons in Paris for four months, working with those incredible actors. The *Usual Suspects*: we laughed from the beginning to end on that picture; we shot it in 25 days. Bryan Singer was 24 and Christopher McQuarrie, who wrote it, was 26. Just being around that kind of energy was great. I have a huge fondness for *Into The West*. I have a great fondness for a film I did called *Polish Wedding* (1998), which I did with Claire Danes. I played a Polish baker. I have very happy memories of that. *Frankie Starlight*, *Miller's Crossing*. I think *Jindabyne* is an exceptional film.

O'TOOLE: *Jindabyne* was made in Australia.

BYRNE: *Jindabyne* is actually the name of the place where the film is set. It is based on 'So Much Water So Close To Home', a short story by Raymond Carver.

O'TOOLE: That was already made as part of *Short Cuts* (1993). Did you have any reservations about going back to a similar story?

BYRNE: In *Short Cuts* Robert Altman took, I think, maybe eight or ten of the stories and he combined them into one narrative that takes place over a day or two in LA. So I didn't feel we were repeating *Short Cuts*. The story is about a man and his two friends who discover a dead body and they decide not to report it until their fishing trip is over. The story is really about morality. We tend to think, in absolute terms, 'This is right; this is wrong'. But the film examines the complexity of it. From the men's point of view, what they do is morally justified but when they come back to their families their action is interpreted in a completely different way by people who weren't there.

O'TOOLE: Carver's story is profoundly emotional.

BYRNE: Well, it's a tremendously emotional film dealing with many themes: marriage; the way men respond to grief; the way women respond to grief; how communities are fractured by something as horrific as a murder. It is also about the nature of guilt and innocence and how, for example, the guilty can often go free, and it is the innocent who often suffer the most in the end. The central relationship of the film is between myself and Laura Linney, whose marriage is in trouble, and the effect of finding that body on our marriage.

O'TOOLE: You also did *P.S.* (2004) with Laura Linney.

BYRNE: I worked with Laura on a film called *A Simple Twist of Fate* (1994) with Steve Martin: we played an unhappy couple in that. And in *P.S.*, she asked me if I would play her husband. I never saw the film but I think I'm gay in it; I'm not sure [*laughs*]! She's an old friend, so we kind of knew what to expect from each other, but we had never played such emotionally complex roles together. Ray Laurence [the director] works in a very peculiar way. He does one take of everything. So we just took the bull by the horns and went for it.

O'TOOLE: I loved hearing your Irish accent in *Miller's Crossing* . . .

BYRNE: I had never heard anybody in a Hollywood film speak with a Dublin accent and, I said, 'You know, I want to be the first one'. I will probably be contradicted on this, but in a major Hollywood film, to have the main character be not from anywhere, not refer to it, that's just who he is, and to play it with a Dublin accent. But I thought, 'You know what? I want people to hear the Dublin accent and to hear an authentic Irish accent on the screen'.

O'TOOLE: Were you surprised by how big a hit *The Usual Suspects* turned out to be?

BYRNE: I was. Somebody told me that the film had made, at the last count, something like $165 million and we made it for $5 million. Somebody in MGM called me up and said, 'We are doing a new collectors' edition and we would like you to record an interview'. And I said, 'For what? There is a collectors' edition. Can you just explain to me what a super collectors' edition is?' And he said, 'Well, we want to re-package it and we want to add in . . .' I said, 'You know what you are doing? You're basically selling the same product over and over again'. I don't agree with it. It's like Manchester United selling a different strip every season to kids who can't afford it. A film is a film. I, personally, am not going to do an interview for somebody to rip off the public again.

O'TOOLE: I remember reading that you were confused by who Keyser Soze was?

BYRNE: I was having a joke. Bryan Singer had actually done such a good job that Keyser Soze could have been anybody up until the last moment of the film. In the very first sequence, the guy who shoots me in the head—with the hat and the gun—is me. It was supposed to be Kevin Spacey but the reason Singer put that in there was as a homage to *Miller's Crossing* when John Turturro says to me, 'Look into your heart', and I say, 'What heart?' and I shoot him. It's hard to tell but it actually was me.

O'TOOLE: You have only one director's credit to your name (*The Lark in the Clear Air*) and three screenplays. Are you tempted to direct more?

BYRNE: Directing a picture takes a good two years of your life. As I get older, I have less interest in spending two years making a film. I'm more interested in theatre, family, travel, reading, and being involved in other things.

O'TOOLE: Before acting you worked as a teacher—and also apparently as a bullfighter?

BYRNE: That's a thing that got into the papers. It's not true [*laughs*]. Skip that one.

O'TOOLE: Did you feel you would become such a successful actor?

BYRNE: No. I was a teacher up until I was 28 and, to me, the biggest kick I ever had was getting into the Project Theatre.

O'TOOLE: Which actors influenced you?

BYRNE: I know this sounds crazy, but I was hugely influenced by all the actors at The Abbey, people like John Kavanagh, Des Cave. I saw those guys when they were really exciting young actors at The Abbey. On television, one of the best naturals I ever worked with was John Cowley, who played Tom Riordan. He was the best worker of props I met in my life. He never did a scene where he wasn't doing something. He'd be repairing engines, cracking open eggs, and doing the crossword. He was a real method actor without even knowing it.

O'TOOLE: Which film actors did you most admire?

BYRNE: In film, the actors that I admired were O'Toole, Harris, Burton, Olivier, Richardson. I actually ended up—my very first job outside Ireland—playing a small part in a very successful mini-series called *Wagner* and I worked with Richard Burton, Laurence Olivier, Ralph Richardson, John Gielgud, Cyril Cusack, and Vanessa

Redgrave. I got to have dinner with Burton, Olivier, Richardson, Gielgud, and Cusack, all at the same table, and I didn't speak for the entire dinner. They were all heroes of mine. I admired Oliver Reed very much and I got to work with him as well. I worked with Richard Harris, Albert Finney . . . somebody showed me a list of all the actors and actresses I have worked with and I thought, 'Oh my God! This is astounding'.

O'TOOLE: After your initial success on Irish television, you went to London.

BYRNE: I had done a series, *Bracken*, that became kind of famous overnight. In 1982, I went to London and worked with Ken Russell, who was one of those crazy maverick directors, who was always doing really wild, mad films. He asked me to play Lord Byron in a film. Well, of course, it was thrilling to work with him. Then I did a play at the Royal Court with Ken Loach, which I think is the only play he directed in theatre. Then, I worked with Costa-Gavras, which helped me move into European cinema—he had directed two hugely successful films, *Missing* (1982) and *Z* (1969). Great, great films: he was probably the last great political director.

When I went to America I was completely unknown there, except for a British film called *Defence Of The Realm* (1986), which was a kind of a cult film in America. I didn't know it was a cult film until I went over there. But a lot of directors had seen it. Going back on it now, it was a film that was made in 1985 in England, and it was a film about the relationship between government censorship and the press. I thought it was a really brave film for its time; it pulled no punches and they actually killed off the journalist in the end. A man tried to tell the truth about the various worlds of the press and the government and the American influence on both.

That picture was seen by the Coen brothers and they asked me if I would come along and audition for a picture that they were doing, which I think at the time, every major actor that I knew of—Gary Oldman to Richard Gere—wanted to do. That picture was *Miller's Crossing* and that became my kind of entry card into American pictures. Subsequently with that, I again went the independent route and I worked with Wim Wenders, Jim Jarmusch, Bryan Singer. There were so many of them I can't remember! I went into a period when I went to live in Los Angels and I lived in Hollywood and I made Hollywood pictures. I made four Hollywood pictures, one after the other. I did *Smilla's Sense Of Snow* (1997), *Stigmata*, *End of Days* with Arnold Schwarzenegger and *Man in the Iron Mask*. That was my Hollywood period when I picked big Hollywood projects. I lived in Hollywood and I thought, 'I might as well make some really big budgeted Hollywood pictures', which I did. I had a great time doing them. Then I moved back to New York for family reasons, and then I went back into the independent world again. I did a picture with David Cronenberg called *Spider*.

I have continued to work now in New York independently, in independent films. For the same kind of reasons that I always had, I never set out to have a career in films and I never set out thinking, 'I will do this because it will advance my career'. I have always worked on the assumption that directors fascinate me because they are able to tell a story and if I think I would like to be part of telling that story, well then I will go do the picture with them. I have been very lucky, as you said, in the choice of directors that I have worked with. But, as I get older, I think the idea of travelling is not so interesting to me to work anymore, so I tend to stick around New York.

O'TOOLE: You went to Hollywood at a relatively late age for a 'new actor'.

BYRNE: I was 40 when I made my first American picture, which is ancient! I made the same journey, more or less, as Liam Neeson. We went to London together, and we ended up in LA together. I remember talking to him one day about how isolated we felt. 'Who are we? We are not American. We are not Irish anymore, really'. I did a picture with De Niro and Harvey Keitel a few years ago and they had voice coaches for the first time in their careers to teach them how to drop their American accents and De Niro said to me afterwards, 'Wow! I never thought that actually working on removing your accent was such a part of work when you are not an American actor', because they get to be American in everything that they do. I felt kind of isolated in Hollywood, I have to say, a little bit. I think it is much calmer now. I think Dublin actors, say, 'Dublin Airport straight to LAX'. And I don't think they have the same kind of fear, or trepidation, that Liam and I had going out at that time. Pierce Brosnan was also out there at that time, but he was working away on *Remington Steele*. To be an Irish actor at that time in LA was a very unusual thing.

O'TOOLE: You just mentioned Robert De Niro and Harvey Keitel. In 2004, you made a film, *The Bridge of San Luis Rey*, with them and Kathy Bates. What was that experience like?

BYRNE: When I did that picture with De Niro and Keitel, they had voice coaches for the first time in their careers to teach them how to drop their American accents and De Niro said to me afterwards, 'Wow! I never thought that actually working on removing your accent was such a part of work when you are not an American actor'.

Because they get to be American all the time. Working with De Niro was [*pauses*] . . . something happened to me that I never thought would happen to me. I was doing a scene with De Niro and I had what I think was the equivalent of a major attack of film fright or stage fright, which is a very terrifying place to be in. Again, I stress it had nothing to do with De Niro, but I had a very scary, personal, and emotional experience while I was making that film and it affected me in a deep way. And it affected the days which I worked with De Niro. I don't think, to the detriment of the film. I mean, I don't think people would have known what I had gone through.

O'TOOLE: Starting out, did you ever feel you would become such a successful actor?

BYRNE: I never did. I was a teacher up until I was 28. And, to me, the biggest kick I ever had was getting into the Project Theatre. When I look back at those days and I think of the people who were there at the time: Neill Jordan, Ciaran Hinds, Liam Neeson, Stephen Rae, Colm Meeney, Johnny Murphy, Kevin Rocket, Nigel Ralph, and U2 were practising down the road and busking up in Stephens Green, and Temple Bar was just a series of warehouses and unused kind of buildings. To be part of that ensemble was so exciting. It really was one of the happiest times of my life. I never lost my love for ensemble acting, which is why I love to go back to the theatre.

O'TOOLE: You come across to me as the type of person who is uncomfortable with fame.

BYRNE: It has given me a tremendous amount of gifts that I never would have had I not made pictures. I have gotten to travel to places that I never would have imagined; I have got to meet people that are just amazing; I have gotten to live in different worlds. That has been the most exciting part of it. I remember sitting on a plane and a movie of mine came on and I thought, 'If I get up now and go to the bathroom, you know, I'm going to have one of those moments'. And the guy beside me—it was on a screen that everybody was watching—was watching it and he fell asleep after ten minutes. You are constantly brought down to reality, especially when you come home to somewhere like Dublin—and I always felt a tremendous warmth for people in Dublin—and elsewhere. One of the great things about being in a film is that you can go anywhere and people have seen the film, so you are kind of on the inside almost immediately. But there are down sides to it.

O'TOOLE: Which are?

BYRNE: I am not somebody who likes to be in the limelight. I am uncomfortable with a lot of the attention. I tend to stay away from red carpets and things like that. I was presenting at the Golden Globes a few years ago. I was presenting best picture. But I got out of the car and I saw all the photographers and I just thought, 'I can't do this!' So I got the guy to drive me down a bit and I walked up behind the photographers and it was so easy. Without any fuss, I just walked right into the thing.

O'TOOLE: And then there's the critics . . .

BYRNE: And, of course, when you are an actor you have to face up to criticism. You've got to face up to praise and criticism. I don't consider myself to be famous, I consider myself to be well known to a certain extent, which is a lot of joy. I've worked with more famous people and I have seen it in action. I have seen people running for their lives because they are being pursued by mobs. I worked with Leonardo just before *Titanic* came out, and he had done *Romeo and*

Juliet. It was like being with one of the Beatles. There was a crowd running down the street and mayhem. I saw Richard Gere coming out of a place one night and photographers literary falling over bonnets of cars trying to get photographs. The look of fear in his eyes as he tried to make his way to his car; that kind of fame is scary. And then I know people who are completely addicted to it—they are absolutely addicted to the notion of fame that they can't get enough of it, and they'll go to an opening of an envelope. I don't want to do that either. I have no complaints about it really; my life is beyond my expectation. I never had any expectations. I wanted to get into the RTÉ rep when I was a young actor and I summoned up the courage and I cycled down as far as Donnybrook and I lost my nerve and I turned around and I went back home because I just hadn't the nerve to go in and do the audition. It wasn't even an audition actually, it was just to ask them about how you got in. I do feel a bit uneasy but I have to say that most of the time most people, 98 percent, are absolutely wonderful. They will say nice things to you.

O'TOOLE: Has there been any roles you regretted not doing?

BYRNE: I was going to do *Wuthering Heights* at one stage with my girlfriend of the time, Julia Ormond, and it fell through at the last minute. I would have really liked to have a go at that because I loved the book so much and I had seen the film many times. We were trying to come at it from a slightly different angle. I am sorry that I didn't do that picture when I had the opportunity. There is one other picture that I turned down that I hope you will forgive me for not mentioning because the actor who played it went on to win an Academy Award. I made a choice not do it and, you know, it is a funny thing about regrets, there are other things in my life that I have regretted, but I have never really regretted either doing a film or not doing a film.

O'TOOLE: I was going to ask you that—have you ever thought, "Well, maybe I shouldn't have done that one!'?

BYRNE: I think every single actor has thought that. That's one of the risks you take as an actor. You are just an actor in a film, you are not the editor, you are not the director, so you go along and you do it—and you do it for the reasons that you believe in. There are films that I have done that I regret how they turned out, but I have never regretted doing anything because something has always come from the experience, whether it was working with the people involved or learning something.

Every single actor, if there was a poster of his life and the subtitle would probably read 'In everybody's life there's a . . .' and the name of the film that maybe he shouldn't have done. I don't really feel that.

In a way, like most things in life, I learned a long time ago because I invested too much in the result. It was one of the mistakes that I made when I was younger I invested too much in the result and now I have learned to let go of the result and just do it, and just enjoy the experience of doing it and not to think, 'Oh, will this be a success? Will it not be a success?' Of course, you want it to be a success, but if it isn't, it isn't. If it is, that's wonderful. But, as an actor, to a great extent it is out of your control.

O'TOOLE: Having worked with Arnold Schwarzenegger, what do you make of his political career?

BYRNE: He is a very, very canny politician. If you look at the history of Arnold Schwarzenegger—a man with an unpronounceable name, who lifted weights, who came from Austria, who couldn't even speak English properly—and he became the highest paid movie star in the world. I don't think anybody's got more money per picture than he's got. He's a die-hard Republican, and he married a Democrat, and the line between entertainment and politics being so thin, he actually got elected, as Governor of California, on his screen persona to a great extent.

O'TOOLE: What is he like as a person?

BYRNE: Personable, funny, charming, likeable. That's not to say that I think he is a brilliant politician. I think he is a brilliant manipulator, mover, and shaker. He realised something a lot of Republicans didn't: that unless he changed his tune he wouldn't get re-elected. And he was one of the few who jumped off the bandwagon, abandoned the Republican mainstream political message and went with what he felt were the changes people were starting to demand in California. That was a very astute move.

O'TOOLE: What's your future plans?

BYRNE: I'm going into politics! If Arnie can do it, I can do it! [*laughs*] I'm going to take a lot more time out for photography, which I'm really interested in. I had an exhibition in New York for Unicef, and it was extremely well received. I'm going to go back on stage again this year, on Broadway. I would love to do Dublin and then Broadway. I'm going to do a couple of pictures next year and the year after.

O'TOOLE: How did you respond to the nomination for a Tony as best actor?

BYRNE: It's a funny thing, I get more pleasure out of been nominated for a Tony or wining the Outer Critic Circle Award then almost anything else because it's theatre—and theatre is where I began. Theatre shows you what you can and can't do. It tests your every reserve in terms of stamina, commitment, to reproduce highly emotional stuff eight times a week in front of a Broadway audience. There were times when I wanted to throw the towel in; I thought, 'I just can't go on tonight'. But you have to go on. You have to do it because the people who came tonight don't care about what you did last night.

O'TOOLE: What type of music do you like?

BYRNE: I listen to everything. I love traditional Irish music, classical, jazz. I have some secret vices, I have to say: I am a Julio Iglesias and Abba fan! But I do have to say, in my defence, I have an eclectic, across the board, appreciation of music. Now you know everything about me [*laughs*].

CHAPTER SIX:

The self-confessed eccentric, Patrick Bergin

He has starred alongside the likes of Julia Roberts and Harrison Ford in some of the biggest Hollywood blockbusters of the '90s, but these days Patrick Bergin is probably better known to younger viewers for making some quirky pop videos, or perhaps from more recent appearances on some British and Irish TV soaps.

He had a hit single a few years ago called 'Paddy's Revenge', which was an Internet phenomenon. It was dubbed "Riverdance On Crack" by the tabloids because of its unusual sound of an Irish jig mixed with dance music.

But despite its success, some music critics slated it and labelled Bergin as being literally "mad" for appearing in the hilarious pop video as a pastiche leprechaun performing a jig alongside scantly clad female dancers.

"Some people say I'm mad! I'm aware that people say that and I quite like it. Maybe I look odd? I don't know," he admitted when we met at The Forge studio where he was recording a song with Irish folksinger Eleanor Shanley.

"I have a bit of a mad streak occasionally. I may have a slightly different way of looking at things than the norm, so to speak. I just have different angles on things. I mean, I'm wearing wellies today, for example. There you go; it's as simple as that. No deeper than that. Wandering about in wellies!"

He added, "But I don't know what the problem was with 'Paddy's Revenge'. They were just jealous that I was with five brilliant looking women and I was having a ball! It was, 'How dare ya!' I mean, you can't fool people with this stuff. It was the biggest hit in Europe. Ireland used to be a land of saints and scholars, now it's musicians and actors. Same thing. The actors are the saints and the musicians are the scholars."

Regardless of such controversies and even the questioning of his sanity, there's no disputing that Bergin has genuine musical talent.

"I own a studio. I have a huge body of work, which I'm hoping to bring out now. I'm going to have an album out. I have two or three, to be honest, on the go. A couple of my songs have been used in movies. I think I'm going on the road next year. I think I'm going to do it before I need a walking stick," he joked.

It was actually his music that helped to put Bergin on the path to international stardom. After leaving school, Bergin told his father, "Look, Dad, If it's all going to be as fucking complicated as this, I'm out of here. Fuck it." Patrick moved to London and started up his own theatre group.

"It was the end of the '60s. It was Carnaby Street and the Rolling Stones. I saw the Stones in Hyde Park in 1969. So, what the fuck had Dublin got to offer when you could go to see the Rolling Stones in Hyde Park?" he recalled.

Almost every known actor, including Gabriel Byrne and Mel Gibson were considered for the lead part alongside Fiona Shaw in *Mountains of the Moon* (1990)—but serendipity landed the then completely unknown Bergin with the coveted role.

"Interestingly enough, I essential got that out of my music as well. I used to play in a bar up in Islington and a lot of media people were there. And, to cut a long story short, when *Mountains of the Moon* was being cast and I somehow got to see the casting agent and she said, 'You're the guy who plays in the pub! Oh, we love you!' Which was great. I believed—and still do today—what's coming your way is meant for you. I live in faith."

She then phoned Patrick's agent and said, "Let's make him a star!"

Recounting the story, Patrick shook his head. "I managed to nick it, as a result of that. It was an amazing platform and an amazing life-changing experience," he told me.

"A lot of young actors say to me, 'Should I go to LA?' I say, 'Yeah, by all means, go, but remember that Hollywood is essentially a private party. And you can go and try and gatecrash. Good luck to you if you can get in. But it's essentially invitation only. So, you make a bit of a reputation for yourself wherever you're based, as a result of that you'll get invited to the party'. And I was invited to the party."

And what a party it transpired to be for Bergin. When he headed to Hollywood for the premier of *Mountains of the Moon*, he found himself inundated with offers and managed to beat off many marquee names for the starring role opposite Julia Roberts in *Sleeping with The Enemy* (1991).

"The funniest moment was when I actually got the job. I went to a meeting to discuss it and I was extremely nervous. At the end, they said, 'Thank you, Patrick, we'll be in touch'. And I stood up and turned around and opened the door and walked into the broom closet. It was my reaction to that moment that the director, Joe Ruben, said, 'That's the moment you got the movie'."

The movie's theme deals with domestic violence. "A number of women came to me and said that they had found the courage to leave their spouses because of that film. It had given them the insight. It's a very serious film in that sense. We did our research about domestic violence," Patrick said.

With *Sleeping with the Enemy* number one at the box office, Bergin's reputation as the next big thing was cemented and he was offered the title role in *Robin Hood* (1991), with the beautiful Uma Thurman playing Maid Marian. Sadly, the film's thunder was stolen by the much inferior Kevin Costner version, which was released the same year.

"Uma Thurman was wonderful to work with. She was married to Gary Oldman at the time and I said, 'Let's run away together'. And she said, 'It couldn't possibly be worth it! Gary would follow us and find us and kill us!'" he laughs.

He must have got a lot of women throwing themselves at him during this period?

"Ah, Jaysus! All the time, yeah."

How did he handle that?

"I'm not telling you. There's too much detail there now!" he laughed again. "Ah, I would have to say that's exaggerated to say they were throwing themselves at me, but it's not a bad position to be in."

But, in truth, Bergin was never led into temptation by his new-found fame as his heart had already been stolen back in the early '80s by Paula Frazier, a British woman of Afro-Caribbean descent. They married at a lavish reception in Trinidad and Tobago in '92.

"I loved her before I even knew her name. Essentially, we met at a wedding, but I'd known her before that," he told me at the time. They have since broken up.

Bergin has certainly come a long way from his working class up-bringing in Drimnagh, South Dublin. He now divides his time between homes in LA and England, as well as his magnificent Kinnitty Castle Hotel in Offaly.

"I have a castle, I have a church, I have acres of land, I have shops. The castle is a very significant castle. Beautiful. At its earliest, they say it's 14th or 15th century. But it's unlikely to be that old; it's much more likely to be 1600s. It's wonderful down there. It's just absolutely gorgeous."

"In the same year that he got married, Bergin starred as an IRA man alongside Harrison Ford and Richard Harris in *Patriot Games* (1992). He admits to having many reservations about the film and reveals that he did receive some grief and criticism back in Ireland at the time for making it.

"It stereotyped the Irish very badly and its politics was abhorrent. I spoke with friends of mine and the general consensus was that it had given the Irish a bad slant, but my character came out okay.

"I fought my own corner. I said when I was offered the part, 'No, I can't do it'. And they came back and raised the money and I said, 'No, I can't do it'. They came back about three or four times and the money was raised. One obviously has to make certain decisions. I know 'no' is a very powerful word. For very often when you say 'no' to a project your money doubles."

"Eventually, the head of Paramount phoned me and said, "What's the problem? We've gone as far as we can with the money. Is it creative or money?' I said, 'It's creative. There's two speeches in this script that I couldn't possibly say. I think it's wrong. It denigrates'. He said, 'Send us what you'd say and we'll see if we can approve of it'. So, I did and they said, 'We can approve that'.

'And it would have been churlish and very arrogant at that stage to have turned it down. I can live with my role in the movie because I played it true to what I thought it would be. But the film itself . . .' his voice trailed off as he shakes his head, obviously still disappointed by it all.

He went on to star in some other great films in the '90s, such *as Eye of the Beholder* (1999) with Ewan McGregor and *Map of the Human Heart* (1992) with John Cusack. But instead of fulfilling his potential of becoming one of Hollywood's biggest stars, his career inexplicably went in the direction of B movies and TV shows, with titles such as *Back2Hell* and *Devil's Prey* (2001). With 84 credits of mostly B movies to his name, including six new ones in the pipeline, Bergin is rarely out of work.

"They were B movies. My first love is B movies. Always was B movies. I don't mean that in any arrogant way either," he explained. "I did whatever came my way. I just did what came my way. Things like *Map of the Human Heart*, which is a fabulous movie. It's like with most things, you get lucky."

At the time of our first conversation, Patrick was excited about two big films he had coming out at the time year, *A Kiss and a Promise* (2012)and *Dance of the Steel Bars* (2013), which was filmed in an actual Filipino prison.

"I was in that prison for a couple of weeks, shooting this movie. It's based on an inspirational true story about prisoners learning to dance to Michael Jackson's *Thriller*," he said. "I think it's one of the most important pieces of work I ever did."

But does he regret not making it in the business as a so-called A-list star?

"No, not in the slightest. Put it this way, I'm sorry some of those movies didn't make more money and then maybe there would have been a wider choice for me. Essentially, I enter things in good faith and I go for story, character, and location. I did whatever came my way. Things like *Map of the Human Heart*, which is a fabulous movie. It's like with most things, you get lucky. I believed—and still do today—what's coming your way is meant for you. I live in faith."

What about fame?

"I'd hate to be really famous, put it that way. Real fame is Tom Cruise type of fame. Or degrees below that, (like) when you have to have a minder and when paparazzi are parked outside your house. That kind of fame never happened to me. And thank God! Oh, I've been chased around occasionally by paparazzi and that's a pain in the hole, as you can imagine.

"For a certain period of it, I had a publicist. And if you have a publicist then you get a lot of attention; if you don't want attention, don't have a publicist. So, I don't have a publicist. That's a simple rule of thumb. Paparazzi told me that; they said, 'If you have a publicist, we'll come after you; if you haven't, we'll leave you alone'. So, I thought, 'Leave me alone'. And I sacked the publicist who was costing me ten grand a month. I think it was actually five!"

I was struck by his modesty; there was no ego on display during our in-depth interview.

"I'm not trying to be modest. I'm not like Bill Clinton who knows the power of humility," he said, pausing to laugh. "I thought that was the dodgiest thing I ever heard, somebody saying, 'I know the power of humility'."

Bergin and his older brother Emmet, who played Dick Moran in the Irish TV soap *Glenroe*, were inspired to get involved in acting by their father who founded a theatre group in Carlow.

Most readers would probably be unaware that Bergin's father Paddy was actually a Senator and a member of the Labour Party. Surprisingly, Bergin tells me how in the past he himself considered running for elected office.

He explained, "He wasn't steeped in theatre, he was using it for a purpose; he used it in a way of education. When my father was a campaign manager in and around Carlow, he was a county councillor down there also, he recruited, for want of a better word, his fellow workers. But without being anyway derogatory, some of them could barely walk or talk at the same time; they were country people. In order to give them confidence to learn how to speak, etc., with confidence, he and a number of others formed a group called The Carlow Little Theatre, which is still in operation. They presented him with an award a few years back, which I received on his behalf."

Bergin has a huge interest in Irish politics, with his ideological left wing leanings inevitably being shaped by his father.

"I'm certainly interested in politics. Whether one would have the necessary skills is another question. But I don't think anybody would vote for me! Would you vote for me? I think I'll run for Drimnagh. Or run away from Drimnagh!" he joked, laughing.

"I think there's ways to be political without having to be in Leinster House. I mean, hopefully through one's music. There's a couple of songs on the new album that tackle some of the subjects we're talking about right now, the banks and all that stuff. You can have quite an influence in that medium."

Bergin was also heavily influenced by watching his father on the picket lines.

"My father was very concerned about farmers and labourers and at that stage farm labourers were treated liked servants, it was like something out of the last century. My father wanted to raise their standard of living, so he organized a strike essentially. He closed all the factories in Ireland. He was threatened with excommunication and all sorts of business, but he insisted on presenting the case himself and went to Leinster House and won the case," he recalled,

"He got [the workers] wages and half time for all the time they were out on strike. But he himself was not given his job back and he eventually got his job back in Portarlington building the power station over there. Shortly after that, he became campaign organiser for the Labour Party and moved up to Dublin. I'd just been born and had spent two or three years up in Carlow before the family moved down. I was born in Holles Street [Maternity Hospital], but I was raised in my first three years in Carlow. We were living under the Labour Party offices in Earlsfort Terrace."

Bergin reveals that the recession that hit Ireland, which occurred almost a decade ago now, has him thinking even more these days about his deceased father.

"Recently, a couple of times I'd think of him and wonder what he'd be thinking, especially when he was steeped in politics. Dad said he used to talk to his father shortly after he died and would ask him advice. But he said after a couple of years his father stopped answering. Occasionally, I mean, very occasionally I would think of my father in that kind of way.

"It's a dreadful experience to lose your parents. Maybe to some extent, I don't know, my mother's passing was maybe a bit more [painful] . . . I don't know how to measure that. Certainly, being the last one to go, in that sense. In a very real physical way, you're connected to the earth through your mother, you know? The umbilical cord. For a short while after that passing you can get very reflective about exactly where you are in the universe."

Both his parents died from smoking related illnesses. He told me: "My father had a roundabout way of telling you things. So, one day he came to me and said, 'Do you know what emphysema is?' Basically, he was trying to tell me that he's dying. He said, 'I looked it up in the dictionary and it was defined as shortness of breath. When you think about it, isn't that what everybody dies of in the end?' He died of emphysema. My dad was 78, so it wasn't bad.

"And my mother was 89. My mum was wonderful. On her last day, she was searching for a fag in the bed before I realised that she was on her way out. She got to the hospital. They stabilised her.

"My sister said, 'Mum, I'm going back up to the house to get you your overnight stuff. And is there anything else you'd like?' Mum said, 'I'll have twenty Rothmans'. And just as my sister was leaving through the door, my mother leaned forward—this was the last words out of her mouth—and she said, 'I'll settle for ten'. That was her humour as well as anything else."

Bergin tells me how his parents met at possibly the most unusual and definitely most unromantic of places—at an IRA meeting!

"It was way back in the late '30s in Carlow. There was a notice in the local paper for a bicycle club meeting and it was a front for a Republican group, which my father was part of at the time.

"Mum turned up wanting to join the club and whoever was the organiser of the group said, 'Ah, Paddy can you take Nora home!' So, Paddy took Nora home and that was the beginning of their relationship."

A few months after this interview appeared, I was strolling around Dublin's inner city, waiting for a train to the midlands. As I turned a corner into an undesirable part of town, Patrick Bergin stumbled out of a bar. It was still not midday, but he was in good spirits, to put it nicely. I called out his name and he crossed the road to shake my hand. I asked if he liked our interview. There was a moment's silence as he digested my question. He then told me that he didn't like the article whatsoever, but added that it wasn't my fault. "The article was too honest," he reflected. There were, he added, too many home truths in it. I told him I was sorry to hear he didn't like, but again told me I wasn't to blame. I admired his honesty.

As he walked away, I noticed that he was still wearing his wellies!

CHAPTER SEVEN:

An Honorary Irishman, John Boorman

It's been over half a century since the renowned film maker John Boorman first jetted over to LA—on the back of his hugely successful debut flick about The Dave Clarke Five band—to make his first Hollywood picture, *Point Blank* (1967).

A hard boiled thriller, shot in 1967, it cemented Boorman's reputation as a brilliant new talent. On the set of the first film to be made at Alcatraz after the prison had closed, Boorman formed a life-long friendship with the film's star, Lee Marvin. Indeed, there was such a strong bond between the two men that Boorman named one of his seven children after the Hollywood star; and he made a documentary about Marvin in 1998, which he subtitled "A Personal Portrait".

The two men made *Hell in the Pacific* (1968) together, but it was Boorman's 1972 film, *Deliverance*, that made him a household name—even today, movie buffs still talk about the film's infamously brutal buggering scene, which leaves very little to the imagination.

Shortly before making *Deliverance*, for which he was nominated for Best Director and Best Film Oscars, the English-born Boorman relocated permanently to County Wicklow, Ireland. For almost half a century, he has made some of the finest movies ever to come out of Ireland, including the Cannes award-winning *The General* (1998) and *Excalibur* (1981). Then there was *Hope and Glory* (1987), which was nominated for five Oscars.

But there's also been some flops too; most notably *Exorcist II: The Heretic* (1977), which is often described as one of the worst movies ever made.

Boorman has written several non-fiction books. At the grand old age of 84, Boorman dipped his toes into the world of fiction with his first novel, *Crime of Passion*. He had clearly taken to heart the advice to write about what you know best: his highly entertaining novel is the story of a film director and producer who decide to put together a movie that is both sexy and violent enough to deliver them a worldwide smash hit.

O'TOOLE: Were you a big film fan growing up?

BOORMAN: At the age of 15, I was seeing everything that was on at the local cinema and I became very much a fan. I had to join the army for two years at the age of 18. A few months before I went into the army, the National Film Theatre opened on the South Bank in London and they showed all the great silent movies like *Intolerance* and Abel Gance's *Napoleon*. So, I haunted the place. I was steeped in the silent cinema. And then when I came out of the army, I got a job as a trainee assistant film editor. My career developed organically. I didn't set out to become a film director. I was interested in film—and one thing led to another.

O'TOOLE: Was your first feature, *Catch Us If You Can* (A.K.A. *Having a Wild Weekend*) with The Dave Clark Five in 1965, influenced by The Beatles' movie *A Hard Day's Night*?

BOORMAN: Yes. It came about because The Beatles' films were a great success. I had carte blanche to do whatever I wanted. The odd thing was, when it opened in America, Pauline Kael—who was a very influential figure in film criticism—praised it much more than it deserved! As a result, I started to get offers from the States. So, everything about my career has been a sort of a series of accidents.

O'TOOLE: The Lee Marvin vehicle *Point Blank*, which is regarded as one of the best film noir movies ever made, came next.

BOORMAN: Because of Pauline Kael's influence, this American producer came to London and gave me this script. He said, 'What do you think of it?' I said, 'It's terrible!' He said, 'I agree with you'. I said, 'The character is interesting'. So, we met several times and I described how I could see it developing and it touched something in Lee.

O'TOOLE: What do you mean?

BOORMAN: Lee was wounded in the Pacific War. But he was also wounded psychologically. He'd been rather brutalised. He was, in a sense, trying to redefine his humanity. And he could see a parallel to his own experience in this story about a man who is shot and left for dead and somehow comes back to life. I think this is what gives the film its power.

O'TOOLE: I re-watched it last night and it feels like a European art house film.

BOORMAN: I was very much influenced by Renoir. And I was very influenced by Harold Pinter in the dialogue.

O'TOOLE: You had carte blanche on *Point Blank* too, which is highly unusual for a novice in Hollywood.

BOORMAN: When I went out there, Lee Marvin knew better than I did how difficult it was going to be to make the film that I envisaged. So, he called a meeting with the head of the studio and the producers and he reminded them that he had script and cast approval. And they agreed that he had it in his contract. And he said, 'I defer those approvals to John'. And then he walked out of the room—and these guys were staring at me angrily! Here is this young English director who had total control over the film [*laughs*]. Lee was so supportive of me throughout.

O'TOOLE: Were you nervous doing such a big Hollywood production?

BOORMAN: There was one moment. We were in Alcatraz. We'd flown down from LA on the previous night and I was exhausted from the whole thing and I lost it for a moment: I couldn't think what to do. And Lee came over to me and he said, 'Are you in trouble?' I said, 'I'm trying to break down this scene'. He then started to act drunk! He started to shout, sing, and fall over. And the production manager came up to me and said, 'Do you see the state Lee's in? You can't shoot with him like this'. So, immediately the pressure was off me. All I needed was 10 minutes without the pressure to figure it out—and he gave me that.

O'TOOLE: Have you ever thrown a tantrum or screamed and shouted on set?

BOORMAN: No. I'm quite severe. I prepare very carefully and I give careful instructions to everyone on what they have to do. And if they don't do it, I have righteous anger!

O'TOOLE: How did you manage to persuade MGM not to take a scissors to *Point Blank*?

BOORMAN: There was a very good editor at MGM called Margaret Booth. She cut *Gone With The Wind*. She was a greatly feared woman because she re-cut all their pictures. So, I had to show the film to her and she made one or two suggestions, which were good, and I made the changes. And then I had to show it to the executives and they got up at the end and started mumbling about reshoots. And Margaret Booth said, 'You cut a frame of this film over my dead body!' So, that's how it came about. I was very fortunate.

O'TOOLE: The film you're most fondly remembered for is probably *Deliverance*.

BOORMAN: Warner's said they would do it if I get two major stars. Jack Nicholson was on the up at the time and I got him. And he said, 'Who's going to play the other part? What about Marlon Brando?' I went to Marlon and I spent the day with him. It was just before he made *The Godfather*. He agreed to do it. I said to Marlon, 'Ok, who's your agent?' He said, 'I don't have an agent anymore. I'm not in the business!' He said he hadn't worked for years. And he was considered box office poison. I said, 'How much do you want for doing this picture?' He said, 'I'll tell you what I'll do: pay me the same that you paid Jack Nicholson'.

O'TOOLE: So, why weren't Jack Nicholson and Marlon Brando in *Deliverance*?

BOORMAN: I went to Jack's agent and I said, 'What do you want for Jack to do the picture?' He said half a million dollars! Now, I knew that he had never been paid more than $50,000 for a picture! I said, 'That's outrageous. He hasn't done a big picture'. He said, 'Well, that's what we want. He's going to be a great star'.

I went to the studio and I said, 'You wanted me to get two stars. Here they are: Jack Nicholson and Marlon Brando'. And they said, 'Jack is up-and-coming and we'd like to do a picture with him. But Marlon Brando! Who cares about Marlon Brando? He's finished!'

So, I said, I think they'd match up very well'. He said, 'What does Brando want?' I said, 'I agreed to pay him the same as Jack'. And that killed it because Ted Ashley, who was running the studio, said, 'If I paid Marlon Brando half a million dollars I'd be laughed out of town'. So they said to me, 'Make it with unknowns, for a very low price'.

O'TOOLE: How much did you pay Burt Reynolds and Jon Voight?

BOORMAN: Very little. Burt got $50,000 and Jon got $75,000. Ned Beatty and Ronny Cox had both never made a film or been on a TV show. I made the film very cheaply. They kept beating me up about the budget and I cut everything back. I didn't even have an art director on the film. And then they still needed me to cut the budget. I had the money for a composer and an orchestra, so I cut them and I got two musicians to make the score—and that's how I got down to a budget of $1.7 million. Of course, the picture went through the roof and they made millions out of it.

O'TOOLE: You're not credited for it, but did you do a lot of work on the script?

BOORMAN: It was James Dickey's novel. He did a draft of a script before I came into the picture and then we worked together on a new draft. And then we fell out over the direction of the script and I took it on myself and wrote the final draft. But since it was based on his novel and they were his characters, he got the credit. The Writers' Guild was intent on protecting writers from producers—they gave him the credit. But that was OK because it was very much his story, his characters—and he deserved it. When the film was finished, Dickey was thrilled with it and told everyone, 'It's better than the novel'. But in later life, he disowned the film and sent his script to every studio, trying to get them to remake it.

O'TOOLE: I understand you had a very difficult relationship with the author.

BOORMAN: It was quite difficult. I mean, right at the beginning when we were rehearsing with the actors up in South Carolina and

Dickey was hanging around and was always getting drunk. He would only address the actors by the characters they were playing and it spooked them. We would be rehearsing all day and he would be sitting at the bar drinking all day, so by the time we had finished he was not in good condition.

I had cast him to play the sheriff. I said, 'You'll have to go. Let us get on with the film and you come back and play the sheriff'. He said, 'If I go you can get yourself another boy to play the sheriff'. And then he said, 'If I'm leaving, I want to say goodbye to the boys'.

So, I took him down to the rehearsal room. And he was a very imposing figure. He said, 'It appears that my presence would be most efficacious by its absence'. And then he left. And then Burt Reynolds said to me, 'Does that mean he's going or he's staying?'

O'TOOLE: There's a story that you fought with Dickey on set—and came out of it badly.

BOORMAN: Absolutely not! He's supposed to have knocked my teeth out—but miraculously I still have them!

O'TOOLE: Do you think, as Burt Reynolds character says, that it's justifiable homicide to murder a rapist?

BOORMAN: They debate it: whether they should go to the police or not. And they decide to bury the man and say nothing—and that all comes back to haunt them. What do I think [*laughs*]? It doesn't really matter what I think. It's what the characters thought that matters.

O'TOOLE: So what was going through the characters' minds?

BOORMAN: You had Ronnie Cox as the moral compass of the group, and he was all for reporting it to the police; Jon Voight was hesitant, he didn't know which way to go; and Ned Beatty sided with

Burt because he didn't want this whole thing getting around—being buggered. Lewis [Burt Reynolds] desperately wanted the experience of killing a man. He felt that his view of masculinity was that he had to go through fire—you had to experience these things—and the ultimate was to kill a man. So, they all had their different views. Voight was the indecisive character: the one who never really committed to anything, didn't really stand up for anything. So, he becomes the one who eventually has to make the harsh decision. He's the one who's most changed by it. That's the heart of it.

O'TOOLE: If you were in such a horrifying position, do you think you would've been able to draw the bow and arrow?

BOORMAN: No, I couldn't have done that. I have a shotgun, and many years ago there was a rather drunken burglar trying to break into my house and I got the loaded shotgun and confronted him. And I thought, 'What am I going to do [*laughs*]? I don't want to kill him. How shall I wound him? And where would I shoot him? Maybe in the feet or the leg?' And I knew the guy! He was a local labourer. And I thought, 'I can't shoot him in the leg because that would incapacitate him. He wouldn't be able to work as a labourer!' I couldn't bring myself to shoot him or wound him. But the threat of the gun was sufficient and he went off.

O'TOOLE: Your house was broken into by Martin Cahill, A.K.A. "The General".

BOORMAN: I was away, but the police identified him as the thief. He stole this gold record for 'Duelling Banjos' [from *Deliverance*]. I'm sure he was horrified when he found it was just gold paint on vinyl! And so I put that scene in the film [*laughs*]. I got my own back on him!

O'TOOLE: If you had been there during the burglary, would you have been able to shoot him?

BOORMAN: I don't think so. No, I'm pretty sure I couldn't.

O'TOOLE: Your last big budget Hollywood movie was *Exorcist II: The Heretic.*

BOORMAN: I was actually offered the original and I turned it down!

O'TOOLE: Why would you turn down directing the greatest horror film ever made?

BOORMAN: Because to me, it was a film about the torture of a child. And, as a father of seven children, I found that absolutely impossible to contemplate. So, with *Exorcist II*, I made the mistake of making a film, which in a sense, was an answer to the original. It was a big mistake because what the audiences were entitled to expect was more of the same, since it was a sequel. I think the film has a great deal of quality, but it was aimed at the wrong audience.

O'TOOLE: How did you rate Richard Burton—the star of *The Heretic*—as an actor?

BOORMAN: Richard had this fantastic voice, but he was not physical: all his acting was from the neck upwards. He couldn't use his body! He was the antithesis of Lee Marvin, who could use his body like a ballet dancer—so you could make complex shots and movements. Burton was static and I had to work the scenes around that limitation.

O'TOOLE: Brian Hoyle's book on your work mentions that you were struck down with a mysterious illness and almost died while filming *The Heretic.*

BOORMAN: We imported desert sand into one of the stages for a scene. It contained spores that cause Valley Fever. It causes very high temperatures. I was hospitalised and shooting was stopped for four days.

O'TOOLE: Did you turn down any other blockbusters?

BOORMAN: Oh, I've turned down projects that have made a lot of money—*Rocky* (1976) being one! My friend Bob Chartoff, who recently died, produced a couple of my films and he sent me the script and asked me to do it. I wrote back and said I thought the script was ridiculous. I said, 'Not only am I not going to do it, but I strongly advise you not to!' He put my letter in a frame and had it up in his office [*laughs*]! I turned down *Alien* (1979), which also made a lot of money.

O'TOOLE: Why did you turn down *Alien?*

BOORMAN: It was set on a spaceship and I didn't know what I could do to make it interesting. And, of course, that [film] had the wonderful scene of the alien breaking out of John Hurt's stomach. John was my great friend. He died just a few days ago.

O'TOOLE: His death must have hit you hard.

BOORMAN: Yes. We did two short films together. We did *Two Nudes Bathing* (1995) and *I Dreamt I Woke Up* (1991).

O'TOOLE: Was he good to work with?

BOORMAN: He was great. Always drunk but always good! This film, *I Dreamt I Woke Up*—someone put that on Facebook. You could have a look at that. It's partly documentary and partly spiritual. He plays my alter ego and we actually have scenes in which we talk to each other.

O'TOOLE: Was it a conscious decision to move away from Hollywood after *The Exorcist* sequel?

BOORMAN: I was getting more and more disillusioned with the studio system and living in Hollywood. And when I made *Leo the Last* (1970) with Marcello Mastroianni in London, I left LA to do that. I did the post-production at Ardmore and fell in love with the landscape and the mountains—and bought this house that I still live in, 45 years later. That became my home and my base and that's where I brought-up my children. And so, I elected to work at arm's length from Hollywood. In fact, I made *Deliverance* entirely on location in South Carolina, after I'd left LA. So I never had to go anywhere near the studio, nor did they interfere in any way.

O'TOOLE: Is it true that Stanley Kubrick was an uncredited technical advisor on *Zardoz* (1974), which starred Sean Connery?

BOORMAN: No. And I never discussed it with him. But I was inspired by the magnificent *2001* (1968)—to imagine that I too could dare to make a metaphysical futuristic movie.

O'TOOLE: You were good friends with Stanley Kubrick.

BOORMAN I was. I greatly admired him. For several years, Stanley would call me once a month, or once a week, always looking for information about film making, about the technical aspects, always asking about how I did a certain shot, a certain sequence and things like that. And I remember, after about three or four years, I said, 'We should meet and have lunch'. And he said, 'Why? We have a perfectly good telephone relationship!' [*Laughs*] But we did meet and we did have lunch. He was an extraordinary man.

O'TOOLE: In the poster for *Zardoz*, Sean Connery seems to be wearing a nappy. How did you talk him into wearing that?

BOORMAN: I had no problem with the red thing, but he was a bit reluctant to go into the wedding dress. But fundamentally, he's an actor and plays parts. He was great. I love Sean.

O'TOOLE: What happened with your planned *Lord of the Rings* movie?

BOORMAN: Before *Deliverance*, I wanted to make my Arthurian story and I went to United Artists with it and they said, 'We own the film rights to *Lord of the Rings*. Why don't you think about that? You're interested in this kind of thing'. So, I did. And I spent several months on making a script. It was before CGI. And not only did I have to find a way of making the story in script form, but I also had to find a way of solving the special effects problems, particularly, for instance, the hobbits being half the size of men. I researched all sorts of traditional film techniques. By the time I'd written it, United Artists had run out money and couldn't afford it. And so I didn't make it.

O'TOOLE: Whom did you have in mind to cast in the *Lord of the Rings? (Note: There was a rumour he wanted to cast The Beatles.)*

BOORMAN: The idea I had for the hobbits was that I would cast nine-year-old boys who were roughly half the size of a man and put on facial hair and dub them with adult voices. So, that might have worked but it might have not (*laughs*)! So, anyway, it's just as well I didn't do it. If I did make it, I think probably Peter Jackson's trilogy would not have been made. Anyway, all the research I did, I was able to apply it to *Excalibur*.

O'TOOLE: How do you rate Peter Jackson's trilogy?

BOORMAN: It is one of the great accomplishments of cinema. And so, in a sense, it was fortuitous that I didn't make it because it wouldn't have been anywhere nearly as good as Peter Jackson's. Because I didn't have the facilities of CGI to do those astonishing effects.

O'TOOLE: Of your own films, which is your favourite?

BOORMAN: I'm fondest of *Hope and Glory* because it's a film about my own family. It's a film that was very successful, with lots of Oscar nominations and prizes around the world. And it's probably the only film I ever made that had universally good reviews—except for one! And it was the very first review, which was in *Variety*. *Variety* said, 'It's not art and it's not commercial!' [*Laughs.*] And, of course, you only ever remember the bad reviews. When *Point Blank* came out, the review in *Time Magazine* was: '*Point Blank* is a fog of a film!' One line! That was it. You always remember the bad ones.

O'TOOLE: Technically, which is your best film?

BOORMAN: I've spoken about *Excalibur* and doing all the special effects with the camera—so that was certainly one. *Excalibur* was made before CGI. There were no post-production effects. All the tricks were done in the camera. It was probably the last effects picture to have been done before CGI. But, I think, oddly enough, *The Heretic* was the most complex in terms of special effects and the whole complexity of shooting it.

O'TOOLE: Will we ever see a new director's cut of *Excalibur*—or any of your other films?

BOORMAN: My movies are my cuts for better or worst. No wish to revisit.

O'TOOLE: Which of your films do you like the least?

BOORMAN: I asked Billy Wilder how *Buddy Buddy* had worked out. He had just finished it. He said, 'John, our movies are like our children. When we have a kid we hope he will grow up to be Einstein, but sometimes they turn out to be congenital idiots!' I don't dislike any of mine, but the failure of *The Heretic* was painful.

O'TOOLE: Who are the best actors you've ever worked with?

BOORMAN: I've had the privilege of working with some of the best film actors: Lee Marvin, Marcello Mastroianni—and I'd put Brendan Gleeson alongside them. Brendan Gleeson is one of the best film actors around.

O'TOOLE: Do you have fond thoughts about *Where The Heart Is* (1990)? Your daughter Telsche—who passed away from ovarian cancer in 1997—wrote the script.

BOORMAN: That went through a few incarnations! It started off as a modern version of *King Lear* where Sean Connery was to play the head of this corporation, who decides to retire and give it over to his daughters. It was a way of talking about contemporary young people. And then he fell out of it.

O'TOOLE: It was your first big Hollywood film after *The Heretic*.

BOORMAN: I had a big problem with Disney because they kept wanting to change it. And the head of Disney [*laughs*]—after we'd been struggling back and forth—said to me, 'The problem with this film is it's still a Boorman film and not a Disney film!' [*Laughs.*]

O'TOOLE: I can't even begin to imagine the ordeal you went through losing your daughter.

BOORMAN: You never get over it. It was a terrible thing to lose a child.

O'TOOLE: What's your fondest memory of Telsche?

BOORMAN: We were playing tennis on our court. It was a windless autumn day when a little birch tree caught a private breeze. It shook, and its leaves dropped in a shower. We were the [only] two people in the world who witnessed this and we smiled at each other. It was a metaphor for all the things of life that we shared together.

O'TOOLE: Is it why you never left your base in Wicklow—that she grew up in this house?

BOORMAN: Yes, that's true.

O'TOOLE: You've lived in Ireland for almost 50 years now. Do you feel Irish in any way?

BOORMAN: No, I don't feel Irish and I don't feel English! But I always felt European. I have a love of Ireland and a love of England too. But I don't feel connected. In England, I was always very critical of Britain and its colonial past. And I've always felt that patriotism is a ghastly thing. I don't like it when its ugliness appears in England. And also in Ireland. I find people cheering for their football team rather vulgar.

O'TOOLE: Has Ireland changed much since you came?

BOORMAN: Very much so. I think that two things changed. Well, first of all going into the EU and the EU put all the money into building roads and the infrastructure, which opened up the country tremendously. And then, the other thing was the big property bubble, which everybody who had a house became a millionaire and everybody got very cocky. And when it all came crashing down, I think, Ireland—the new Ireland with a recognition of technology—began to grow up after 2008. It was painful, but I think what's happened since then—despite an ineffectual government—it's growing in a very good way. There's a maturity that's come into Ireland, which I find very good.

O'TOOLE: Has the country improved since you attacked it in your movie *The Tiger's Tail* (2006)?

BOORMAN: Perhaps it's lost some of its easy-going charm from when I first arrived. But it's now much more rooted and much more mature. It's growing into itself. Ireland was the first country in the world to pass a referendum on same sex marriage.

O'TOOLE: Would you have believed it possible 10 or 20 years ago?

BOORMAN: No [*laughs*]! Especially as the Church had instructed every Catholic to vote against it. I think most people in Ireland didn't give a toss about same sex marriage, one way or the other. But it was a very good way of cocking a snoot at the Church.

O'TOOLE: Back in the days of the Troubles, did you receive any death threats from the IRA because you're English?

BOORMAN: One night there was a knock on my door and it was the Official IRA guys! And they said, 'We would like to use your land for training purposes'. [*Laughs*] So, I said, 'Do I have a choice?' And they said, 'Yes. We'd only want to do it if you approved'. And I said, 'Well, I'd rather not'. And they moved on.

O'TOOLE: Was that your only contact with the IRA?

BOORMAN: The only other connection was making *Zardoz.* I needed a lot of guns and I wanted to import them from London and there was strict prohibition about importing weapons, even though these weapons wouldn't fire bullets [*laughs*]. It was a big problem. It almost toppled the production. And then one of the carpenters came up to me and said, 'The lads above can get you all the weapons you want!' [*Laughs.*]

O'TOOLE: How did you solve the problem?

BOORMAN: I went to the government. Justin Keating was the Minister at the time and I told him and he sorted it out and I got the weapons. Anyway, I could've got them from the IRA [*laughs*]! My dealings with the IRA were, on the whole, rather positive!

O'TOOLE: *The General* is a black and white film—but it was released in colour and even dubbed in parts for the US market.

BOORMAN: I wanted to do it in black and white and we couldn't find enough black and white stock to shoot it because nobody uses it anymore. So, I shot it in colour and then de-saturated it to black and white. I hate the idea of it having a life as a colour film: it was lit for black and white.

O'TOOLE: You were criticised for portraying Martin Cahill as a lovable rogue.

BOORMAN: [*Laughs*] I got a lot of criticism for glamorising a gangster—despite all the cruel and brutal acts he committed in the film. The thing was, I kept making him do more and more nasty things and whatever he did, it didn't seem to make any difference—people just loved him. But I think it was partly to do with Brendan. You see, Brendan is a very, very beautiful man and somehow his beauty, his goodness shone through the character, even though it was so nasty. Hitchcock said, 'Only a good person can play a good person and vice versa'. But Brendan gave a brilliant performance in that picture. It launched his career. He is a wonderful actor.

O'TOOLE: It was widely reported that you retired after making *Queen and Country* (2014), the sequel to *Hope and Glory*. Will you make another film?

BOORMAN: Some mornings, when I wake up stiff and everything aches, I think not! But then on good days I think, 'Maybe I will'. I've got a project and I've got most of the money for it and I'm just trying to make up my mind. I'll make it in Ireland. I've got three scripts that I would've liked to have made, but I certainly won't make them all—I might make one of them.

O'TOOLE: You've just written your first novel, *Crimes of Passion*. Why did you decide to turn your hand to fiction?

BOORMAN: I write every day and I've written several books and I did this series of Projections [books] with Walter Donohue. So, I had this idea for a novel about these guys making a film and the sort of background to what goes on in the making of a film and how a film develops and takes on its own life. It's just being translated into French. Some people like it [*laughs*].

O'TOOLE: How closely does the protagonist Daniel Shaw resemble you?

BOORMAN: I put myself into the book as a character in the Cannes Film Festival because I wanted to separate myself from Daniel Shaw [*laughs*]! There are aspects of me in Daniel Shaw, but he's very different from me and from the way I work. He's a compilation of two or three English directors I've known. He's much more manic and possessed than I am [*laughs*]!

O'TOOLE: Was it a big leap, into writing fiction?

BOORMAN: Scripts are fiction—so writing scripts is not too far away from novel writing. The only thing is: when I look back at the book, I probably didn't describe the character enough. You don't have to describe the characters in a movie script because they are going to be up there on the screen. In fact, it's better not to put in too many characteristics because it can often dissuade an actor from playing a part—if you say that he's fat or sweaty, it's very hard to cast that [*laughs*].

O'TOOLE: What's next?

BORMAN: I'm writing another memoir, bringing it up to date. I call it *Conclusions*. I think it's the last thing I'll write. You know, I'm 84—things come to an end. I've had a good innings.

O'TOOLE: Have you started to think a lot about your own mortality?

BOORMAN: You have to wind down and it's very important for you to contemplate death. And that's what I'm doing. I think about it a lot.

O'TOOLE: It must be very emotional.

BOORMAM: No, it's rational. I've seven children and I've got grandchildren. In a sense, I stay alive for them rather than for myself. But I'm ready to go anytime that they call [*laughs*].

O'TOOLE: You had three children later in life, during your second marriage, which ended in divorce about ten years ago.

BOORMAN: My three young ones are grown up now. They're 24, 21, and 18. I'm very, very devoted to those three because they still need help and guidance and I love them dearly. I've always loved children. I've always loved playing with them and helping them and doing things with them. And that's been one of the great joys of my life. And I was very fortunate to have a second litter, as it were!

O'TOOLE: Are you religious?

BOORMAN: No. I was brought up as a Christian, but I'm not a believer.

O'TOOLE: So, you don't believe in heaven or hell?

BOORMAN: No. I believe in oblivion.

O'TOOLE: What are your thoughts on euthanasia?

BOORMAN: I'm all in favour. I think suicide has had a very bad name. But I believe that everyone should be allowed to end their life when they see fit. And the notion of what we see today—of people living into their 90s and living just a half-life, of pain and aching bones and dementia—it's a dreadful thing. Society is being plunged into this abyss of decrepit age, supporting a vast part of society which is old and useless. We should all be given a pill at the age of 80—it would solve all the problems [*laughs*]! Which means I would've died four years ago!

O'TOOLE: Would you go to Dignitas in Switzerland to end your life?

BOORMAN: I would find some way, I think, yeah. I don't know about Switzerland—but there are ways and means!

O'TOOLE: Do you have any regrets?

BOORMAN: Yes, I have lots of regrets [*laughs*]! I've worked incredibly hard and I've fought and struggled to make films and it cost me a huge amount of effort. And I think I've often neglected people I love, and my relationships, because of devoting myself so much to the work. That's my regret.

O'TOOLE: You never won an Oscar, even though you've been nominated five times—does it bother you?

BOORMAN: Not in the least [*laughs*]. If you look at the history of the Oscars their record is not great in terms of the films that have lived. A lot of great films—like for instance *Citizen Kane* (1941)—didn't win an Oscar. *Zardoz* was a complete failure at the box office. But that film has grown in reputation year after year. And it was recently restored. It has more and more followers ever year. I get so much correspondence [*laughs*] from these addicts. Often when you look at a film you thought was brilliant at the time, you see it ten years later and think, 'What did I really see in that film?' And vice versa: films that escaped you at the time often turn out to have a longer life.

O'TOOLE: Looking back at your career, are you satisfied with what you achieved?

BOORMAN: My only professional regret is that I didn't make more films. You know, making a film takes so long. You write the script, then maybe it doesn't work and you write another one, and then you try to find the money and you cast it and then you design it and then you shoot it and then you edit and then you promote it. It takes about three years. Whereas in the old days, it was more of a factory job: directors like John Ford would make two a year—because they weren't involved in editing the film. In a way, I much prefer being involved in the whole process. But it does take so much time. I've made—what?—16 films or something, whereas I probably could've made twice that much.

CHAPTER EIGHT:

The Importance of Being Brenda Fricker

Oscar winning actress Brenda Fricker can still recall the occasion vividly. She felt there was no point in living anymore. Out of sheer desperation, she made a decision to take her own life. In the event, somebody called an ambulance. It was touch and go, but the surgeons managed to save her.

Brenda remembers exactly what went through her mind when she came to, in hospital. "On the serious attempts—I would call them close to the wire—I remember waking up and thinking, 'Failed!' And then I'd think, 'You'll have to wait and try it again'."

Anyone who has had the pleasure of spending time in the company of Brenda Fricker immediately comes to the conclusion that here is a woman who has a penchant for being brutally honest while wearing her heart on her sleeve.

She's also a down-to-earth character who used to keep her Oscar on top of her fridge for many years. She holds the distinct honour of being the first and only Irish actress to ever win an Oscar for her portrayal of Christy Brown's mother in *My Left Foot* (1989).

But the little gold statue now sits proudly on a "respectable little shelf" in the sitting room of her home in the Liberties, a tough working-class district in the centre of Dublin. Film buffs might recall the neighbourhood in the bizarre little Gene Wilder film, *Quackser Fortune has a Cousin in the Bronx* (1970).

However, the old adage about fame and fortune not being able to buy you happiness is certainly true when it comes to this self-described "reclusive" and multifaceted woman.

Born in Dublin in 1945, Brenda was the younger of two children. Her mother Bida was a school teacher; her father, Desmond, was a journalist with *The Irish Times* before working as a PR man. She originally wanted to follow in his footsteps as a writer, but switched to acting when she was offered a part in the 1960s urban TV soap, *Tolka Row.*

Brenda went on to have a very successful acting career. She is best known to TV viewers for starring in the hospital drama *Casualty.* More importantly, she made cinematic history when she became the first Irish woman to win an Oscar for her role in Jim Sheridan's powerful *My Left Foot.*

But the startling truth is that Brenda has been putting on a brave façade for most of her life. Back in 2012, she stunned TV3 viewers when she revealed, on a midday chat show, that she had been suffering from crippling depression for 50 years. Things were so bad, she added, that she attempted suicide a staggering 32 times

"That was a mistake for me to say that," she told me, "I might have done something very silly like cut myself, which would just be a cry for help. I don't think they were serious attempted suicides.

"They were just screams for help and you just got so tired of nobody hearing you that I just went and tried it for real. I would say out of all of those there might have been two or three serious attempted suicides."

Yet even one attempt is alarming, I ventured.

"It is a lot; I agree with you."

Thankfully, at the time of our first conversation back in 2012,

Brenda told me she no longer harboured such dark inclinations—after discovering an unorthodox "cure" for her depression, some ten years earlier.

"I don't suffer from depression anymore, thank God," she told me. "I did for 50 years and then I fond a wonderful cure—if you like that word—having tried every combination of medication and having spent a small fortune that could buy three houses on Leeson Street, you know, on psychiatrists.

"I found this guy in Abbey Street and he has a treatment he does with Mozart music. Yeah, it's quite amazing. It lasts for three months. It takes three months and you listen to Mozart for two hours every morning for a week and then you have a break of about a month and then you go back and you listen to Mozart again every morning for about a week or ten days for two hours. You lie down [during it] and go to sleep after that. And then you have three weeks off or something and you go back and you wake up cured."

She continued, "When you go in first they have a graft thing to see whether it would work on you or not and if they think it will then he is in another room controlling what music is being played. You don't have to listen to a Mozart concert. They pick. We know that Mozart—certain parts of his music helped children learn how to read playing in the background.

"So, it's like based on that and for adults with depression that they've learned that certain bits work if you just play them. You wouldn't notice a gap in the music when you're listening—you would think it was just a lovely piece on Mozart. They are picking in the next room what they're playing. Selective pieces of Mozart are played for you."

I could sense that there is a real aura of contentment and inner peace surrounding her these days.

"It is an extraordinary thing to go through; as I said, 50 years of your life battling with this Devil everyday and suddenly it's gone. It really is like in the old days that you would call it a miracle—and you see the world with clear eyes for the first time; you can walk down the street without being terrified; you can think clearly. It's very hard to describe. It's wonderful," she said.

"I was willing to try anything—when you're that depressed you'll try anything. I went in not expecting anything and at the end of three months I walked out and it was gone. I've sent about five people to them and they've all been cured. These were people standing on the bridge waiting to jump, you know? And they're all laughing now. It's quite extraordinary."

Why does she feel that traditional routes of counselling and medication couldn't help her? In her blunt honesty, she describes it all as nothing more than a money-making racket.

"I can honestly look back on it again with 20/20 vision and hindsight and everything else. I've lost a lot of faith in psychiatrists. I think that no doctor or psychiatrists is going to advertise a cure that works because they really want to make money out of you. I think they want you to go and see them once a week for the rest of your life, paying €200 or something. It's an awful lot of money," she said. "And you're put on all kinds of drugs. If you look up the Internet on some of these drugs they put you on—Jesus, Mary, and Joseph!—it would frighten the life out of you.

"In this cure, there is no medication; there is no conversation—you just listen to selected certain pieces of Mozart that you lie down and listen to and you get up after three months and you're better. It's hard to believe but true."

After finally finding inner peace, did Brenda feel lucky to be alive today?

"No, I don't feel lucky to be alive. I'm not that keen on life—I don't mean that in any depressed way at all. I'm not depressed in any way; but I'm not a high-energy person. I enjoy the very small things in life and I toddle from day to day and some days are great and some days are not so great. I don't want to live to be 100," she insisted.

The issue of assisted suicides is a contentious but topical issue at the moment following the stories of terminally ill Irish people in recent times going over to Switzerland where such means of ending one's life is legal. Brenda told me that she would go over there to check into such a clinic to follow such a route to end her own life if she becomes terminally ill.

"I think I would try to go to Switzerland. I believe even if you weren't sick, if you feel you've had enough of life, that you want to go, you should be able to go. But I don't think that will happen in my lifetime or yours," she declared.

"I approve of assisted death. I think we should all have the right to die whenever we want to die. What else do you own? Nothing. You don't own anything at all except your life."

I wondered what exactly compelled Brenda to find herself in such a low place in the first place. Granted, there has been an astonishing number of tragedies in her life—she endured "five or six" miscarriages; her husband tragically died in an accident; it then fell on her to nurse her father in his dying days; and she even told me she still mourns the death of her sister, whom she "worshipped" and touchingly described to me as her best friend.

However, Brenda said, "there's no question about it", referring to the fact that the root of her suicidal tendencies can be traced back to how she endured extreme acts of violence at the hands of her sadistic mother.

"I think I would have handled all of those deaths much better if I had a different childhood. Or if I had found this cure much earlier," she told me. "She punched me half to death. She kicked the shit out of me.

Some friends that I had said, 'You can't be talking like that about your mother'. I said, 'It's the truth'. And it's not as if I'm telling lies about her.

"I was walking down the street with blood coming out of my legs. They [the neighbours] knew she was beating the shit out of me but nowadays neighbours wouldn't let that happen. But in those days everybody just kept quiet.

"I'm really trying very hard to forgive her—and I'm getting there. You have to forgive. You have to understand that she didn't know what she was doing; I think she was sick. I'm trying to come to terms with that now because I have a very good councillor who I go and see.

"Looking back on it now with hindsight, I would say that she was deeply troubled mentally in the sense that she was bipolar as it's now called, or manic depression as it was called in those days.

"But there was no one around to help her—doctors didn't know anything about it; nobody heard of it. But that's the only explanation I can put on this. She had two sides to her. And one was adored by people. She was a teacher and during the school holidays all these kids would come up on their bikes to see her because they were mad about her."

Brenda paused for a moment before telling me, "And at her funeral—Jesus Christ, I couldn't believe—people were coming up to me and saying, 'Oh, your Ma was wonderful'. She obviously had a side to her that I didn't see because at home with me she was very cruel."

Brenda thought that her father was unaware of the violence subjected on both herself and her older sister. "Next to [my husband] Barry, he was the nicest man I knew, but I sometimes wonder now, Did he know? Did he just mentally cut it off? Did he believe all the lies she told him? I don't know," she said.

Initially, Brenda who did some radio voice work as a child, intended to follow her father into journalism by getting a job herself at the so-called paper of record.

She got into acting fulltime "by chance" after receiving a phone call one day from the radio director who remembered her as a child actress and enquired if she would like a part in Ireland's first ever TV soap, *Tolka Row*, which was just about to go on air.

"He said, 'You'd be dead right for this'. I was sitting in my office at *The Irish Times* trying to be a reporter," she recalled. "My boss was in the room with me on the other side of the desk and he lost his head and he said, 'What are you talking about? Go and try it—the job will be here for you if you don't like it. You're only young once'. So, I went and tried it and here I am."

Brenda instantly fell head over heels for her future husband, the TV director Barry Davies—a contemporary of Mick Jagger's at school—at the Gresham Hotel back in the mid-60s when she turned up to audition for a play.

"He was waiting for his decree absolute and we were very well behaved—we didn't go into bed together until he got that! I don't know. There was some kind of moral streak in both of us. It was unspoken. It was interesting. Ah, he was just my soul mate; we knew what the other one was thinking," she said.

Was he her first big love?

"He was the first and the last. I came close to getting married loads of times, but when I met him I knew I'd only been playing in the ha'penny league, you know?" she said.

During one previous interview, Brenda spoke about how she felt she wasn't a good wife. What did she mean exactly?

"That would be a little bit of my mother coming through who told me I would never be very good at anything. She took all my confidence away. I'd get days when I was depressed, which I don't get anymore. But I would get days when I would think I was an appalling wife and an appalling person, an appalling actor. So, I may well have said that on a day when I was depressed. I can tell you now I know I was a great fucking wife," she said adamantly.

During their marriage, Brenda suffered from "five or six" miscarriages and they were thinking about adopting before Barry died. Did not being able to conceive her own child add fuel to the fire of her depression?

"It didn't really. I never had huge maternal instincts probably because of my relationship with my mother. I didn't have any of those callings to be a mother. When I met Barry we certainly wanted to have children. He more than me, I have to say, but anything he wanted me to do I would've done it for him."

She ended up divorcing Barry in 1988 because of his alcoholism. "It was very difficult. It was like Richard Burton and Liz Taylor," she told me. "Barry was becoming an alcoholic and I had dealt with that with somebody else in my youth and I knew where it would lead. He wouldn't admit it and I thought that the only way I can deal with this is to walk away from it.

"And I absolutely adored the ground he walked on. After all those years, it was still very much love. So, I divorced him to frighten him and it worked and he admitted that he was an alcoholic. I mean, we were still walking down the road holding hands even after we were divorced."

Brenda paused to giggle at this recollection. But then the laughter soon dissipated when she then told me: "He was really trying; he was going to AA meetings. And we were talking about maybe getting married again and then he died. He fell down the stairs—probably with a few drinks on him, I'd imagine."

Brenda revealed that watching her husband succumb to alcoholism swore her off booze. "I did drinking a lot—[enough] for about 14 women in my day, but I don't drink anymore," she explained. "I kind of went off it when it started to get a hold on Barry because we were great drinking buddies and he was a great drunk, a good drunk, but he started turning into a nasty drunk and that made me very slowly [give it up].

"It took me a long time—but I might have a Bloody Mary now once a year and that's it."

How did she manage to pick herself back up after losing the love of her life?

"I don't think I ever have, to be honest with you. One of my least favourite words is closure. I hate when people go around saying, 'You need to get closure'. I think that's the biggest insult you can give anybody is to have closure and put them out of your mind forever. You learn to live with the fact that they are not there. It's not just Barry; it's all the people who died, you just have to learn to live without them, you know?"

How long were they together?

"Gosh—it must have been half my life, 30 years."

When did he pass away?

"You know something, Jason? I've blocked all that out and deleted it. I spent time with psychiatrists trying to remember. I can't remember when we got married; I can't remember when he died; I can't remember any deaths—any dates, my mother, my father. I just wiped it all out."

Trailing through the archives, it appears that her husband died shortly after she was offered a role in *Home Alone 2*, which was released in 1992.

How come she never ended up in another serious relationship?

"I have this theory that when marriages break up because of one person dying that men replace and women grieve. It seems to be when I look around me that it's very true. Men get remarried much more often than woman do. I certainly never. . ."

There was once talk of her getting married to the highly regarded actor Peter Caffrey, who died at the age of fifty-eight in 2008. (As an aside, he starred in one of my all-time favourite Irish movies, *I Went Down*, which was released in 1997.) But Brenda insisted that there was never really a serious relationship after her husband died.

"I've had one or two little flings, but I still feel loyal to Barry even though he's dead and even though I divorced him, we never become unmarried," she said. "I mean, you can get a piece of paper that says that you're divorced but you don't ever get unmarried. We still love each other. The love is still alive in my heart."

A few years ago, it flashed through Brenda's mind that she was about to face the same death as Barry when she herself fell down 69 cement steps and shattered her shoulder and fractured her wrist.

"I would say that that would only take a second and a half really falling down the stairs. But in that second-and-a-half I remember thinking, 'Am I going to die the same way as Barry? Am I going to fall down the stairs and die the way he did?' she said.

"God, I didn't work for nearly three years because they had to do the operation four fucking times because it wouldn't take. They put in a titanium shoulder. And it's just not taking, the pain is excruciating and they want me to go for a fifth one and I just said no."

She misses her favourite pastime since the accident—playing snooker and pool. She reportedly used to beat all the cast members without fail when on film sets. Since retiring, Brenda has led a quite life. The last time we spoke Brenda told me that she mostly spends her days walking her rescue dog in the Phoenix Park, surfing the Internet, "downloading songs onto my iPod", and reading books with large text. At the time, she was also rolling up her sleeves and helping builders working on renovation working on her home in the Liberties. After making *The Field* (1990), she purchased a cottage in the south inner city area and eventually bought the two adjoining cottages and knocked down the walls.

She lives a very sedated life these days. "My eyesight is beginning to go, so reading is [harder]. I have to buy those books with big prints. I like eating and walking. A very boring life," she maintained.

While her phone never once stopped with offers to work in Hollywood or in the UK, before retiring, Brenda was irked by how she was rarely offered parts in home-grown productions in Ireland .

"It's crazy. It just ridiculous. There's nothing more I'd like than to drive the car down the road to go to work and drive home again. But that's not the way it worked out," she said. "I didn't live here for a long time; I lived in England for nearly 25 or 30 years. I was coming back and forward doing work here and then when my husband died and my father died and my best friend died—it was all absolutely dreadful time in my life.

"And I've virtually been living in Dublin back and forth nursing people and trying to look after them. And then when my husband died I thought I might as well stay here. So, I stayed here. Since then they just stopped asking me."

Is it truc that Brenda lost most of her money in the financial meltdown?

"I read these things and I wonder, 'Where the fuck did they get them?' That's certainly not true—I did not have any investments that were lost, no. I got rid of my stock before the recession. I sold them off before the recession. I don't know why. Good luck."

During our conversations, it struck me how the affable and obliging Brenda I was talking with was far removed the "difficult" actress that is constantly depicted in the many profiles about her.

"I don't know where that reputation started," she said, adding that perhaps it comes from how she was always down to business on the set and focused on her "passion for the work" rather than just sitting around idly with colleagues "chatting over tea" while waiting for the cameras to roll.

But she has accepted it's accurate to describe her as reclusive.

"Yes, I am. It's getting worse as I get older. People think you're unhappy if you're reclusive—you're not," she said. "I suppose it comes from how I was often very nervous of meeting people and being in groups—mainly because of the things my mother said and did to me, all of which I believed; she was my mother and she said them to me.

"So, I thought I was not worthy of being alive basically, of being on the planet. I was always very hastened to meet new people. I have four or five very close friends and that's enough to cope with."

She confessed that she felt winning the Oscar put her under additional pressure of public scrutiny. "It changed my life because I was a completely unknown Irish woman making a living treading the boards and, suddenly, the whole world knows your name. It was quite frightening. I found that sudden fame to be like going through the eye of the storm. It is quite scary," she revealed.

"Back all those years ago, we didn't know what Oscars were. I vaguely knew that it was something that happened in America. I just knew vaguely about it, but nobody here had one. We got five nominations for *My Left Foot*—it just blew a bomb off."

It annoyed her when the English tabloids declared her as a British citizen. At the time, she commented, "When you're lying drunk at an airport you're Irish but when you win an Oscar you're British."

She told me, "That's true—I did say that. And I was drunk when I said it, but I wasn't lying at the airport, that's for sure," she laughs. "All the English papers were saying, 'British actress Brenda Fricker wins Oscar', and I thought, 'Fuck you! How dare you!'"

Is she religious?

"Oh Christ! Do I believe in God? Some days I might believe in God for about a minute and then I can go for a year without believing in him. I think I'm agnostic. I genuinely don't know. I don't believe in going up into the clouds into heaven. I think it's much more complex and scientific than that."

An email from Brenda popped into my inbox back in 2016. In it, she was warm and likeable, but, also capable of being brutally honest, Brenda revealed that she felt elated to have officially retired from acting. She confirmed that she had made her last appearance in a 2015 TV show.

She was always uncomfortable with fulfilling the annoying obligations that are part and parcel of being a movie star—whether it's promoting films on the red carpet at Cannes, going to events like the Oscars, or conducting the humdrum interviews that are always written into movie stars' contracts when they sign up to make a film. She never enjoyed being in the limelight.

"I find it very difficult to go to big nights coming up," she proffered. "I find them very nerve-racking and I avoid that as much as I can. I regard myself as just like putting a DVD into the back of my head and you act the part for the night. Put on the face and say what people expect you to say and smile for the camera and get out as fast as you can. I don't mean to be rude about the people who put these things on or anything; I think they're wonderful but I'm just not that type of person."

But for someone who professes to cherish her privacy, Brenda stripped off naked into her the proverbial birthday suit for a painting. It was a subject that could still make Brenda blush, as I discovered when I broached it. She burst into a fit of giggles as she recounted how she was cajoled into doing it.

"To this day, I can't believe I did it. He [the artist Daniel Mark Duffy] had been months asking me. I said, 'Absolutely not. Forget it'. But I really liked him; he was a nice man and we became close friends. One day I said to him, 'Ah, fuck it—take the photograph'. He said, 'Sit in the chair'. And with one click it was over," she said.

"I still think, 'Did I do that? Jesus Christ!' But I never looked at the painting. He said it's his best work and I said, 'Great, just keep it that way—facing the wall!' I don't want to see it."

Does she have any regrets?

"My career, I don't have any regrets. In my life? I'm not sure it was the best idea to move back to Ireland but I don't regret it," she mused. "But I'm not sure it was the best thing for me to do. I left a lot of very good friends in London and it's more lonely here than it would've been in London. I was hardly home when they all died."

Would she now consider baring all in the more traditionally acceptable format of a memoir?

"I've been asked to a couple of times. I think I'd rather keep quite about my life. No, I don't think so."

No doubt many colleagues from the acting sphere will be breathing a collective sigh of relief with the news that Brenda Fricker—who certainly has a penchant for speaking her mind—isn't planning a warts-and-all autobiography.

CHAPTER NINE:

Johnny B Goode, Jonathan Rhys Meyers

"Let the Spanish Inquisition begin!" joked Jonathan Rhys Meyers, as we sat down in an alcove of the basement bar in the Merrion Hotel.

As you can probably tell from his opening quip, the Dublin-born Hollywood star is uneasy around the media. And this was even before—18 hours to be precise—that embarrassing episode in Dublin Airport, which resulted in his arrest for allegedly being drunk and disorderly. It is probably the type of incident that happens more frequently than is publicised but, unfortunately, it only makes the headlines when you're famous. After his release from Whitehall Garda station, Meyers appeared to sum up the episode when he told reporters: "I said the wrong thing to the wrong person at the wrong time."

I was very surprised by the incident, particularly considering that it was only the night before his arrest that Meyers had adamantly told me how he was finished with drink—for good. During a two-hour interview, the then 30-year-old Golden Globe winner frankly discussed his recent stints in rehab. He appeared very earnest about staying away from booze. "If you don't go out and do stupid things then they can't write about you," he told me at one stage.

But two days after his arrest, Meyers appeared to do another very stupid thing in public. He was photographed walking through the streets of London, taking a swig from a can of cider, at 11am. The image could have left a bad taste in my mouth. I could have felt that he had lied to me about his vow to steer clear of alcohol. Looking at the photograph I could see a deeply troubled man. I felt he hadn't lied to me, but perhaps something dramatic had happened to him since our conversation. Meyers' erratic behaviour was explained the next day when his publicist announced the tragic news of his mother's demise. She was only 50-years-old.

But while he was then at the very lowest point in his life, I felt

Jonathan Rhys Meyers will bounce back. There have been some extraordinary successes for the Cork-raised movie star during the past decade. The standout must be his Golden Globe winning role as Elvis, but other highpoints include winning the prestigious Trophée Chopard award at the Cannes Film Festival for his part in Woody Allen's *Match Point* (2005). Another highpoint was starring alongside Tom Cruise in the latest instalment of the *Mission Impossible* franchise, and he garnered rave reviews for his portrayal as a young Henry VIII in *The Tudors*.

O'TOOLE: Career-wise, the last 24 months have been extremely good for you.

MEYERS: You never realise how great things are going for you because you are there on the ground level—you've been there from scratch. It just becomes work. What's my next job or move going to be? You can't really sit back and enjoy it. There seems to be a certain element of overnight success about it—but it isn't, it takes ten years to be overnight successful! We have to lay the groundwork first and then suddenly a couple of things you do get noticed.

O'TOOLE: Winning the Golden Globe for the *Elvis* miniseries must have been very satisfying?

MEYERS: It has done lovely things to help me along in my career, but I have never stopped to enjoy it. I was very nervous when I got it. I refuse to look at myself accepting the award because apparently I look like a deer in the headlights! I was shockingly, shockingly nervous. I forgot to thank my managers, my agents. It was just terrible—it was a disaster actually. *Elvis* was a bit of a strange experience for me. I took on the role thinking it would be a bit of a joke at the start and that probably nobody would see it. And then the further into shooting I got, the more I realised that people would see it.

O'TOOLE: As your profile grows, the media intrusion must be very difficult. Is it possible for you to have a normal lifestyle?

MEYERS: I've got loads of fucking normality in my life, really I do. I don't live as special as you think. I don't have the same paparazzi chasing me as somebody like Sienna Miller, God love her, or someone like Colin [Farrell]—every move he makes . . .

O'TOOLE : But you are getting up to that level now.

MEYERS: I'm more famous in America than I am here. It's kind of strange. But I'm very happy with that because if I wanted to be famous anywhere in the world, America is where I want to be famous.

O'TOOLE: Any time I open a paper these days there are paparazzi shots of you.

MEYERS: Well, they do, especially when you are in town doing *The Tudors* and stuff like that. There are not that many celebrities around and they've got to put things into the newspaper. I certainly don't court it.

When you become famous you've got to start living your life in a more controlled way. You've got to think the situation through more because you don't have the same sort of anonymity as other people. What you do can sometimes get written about in the newspapers.

So, therefore you've got to make sure that you don't do anything that could end up being gossipy. There is sort of like a very, very easy way to deal with the media—if you don't fuck up, they can't print any fuck ups! Of course, they can make a couple of things up—and they do make things up—but they've got to sell newspapers every day.

O'TOOLE: Does that not piss you off?

MEYES: No, because I know, personally, what's going on in my life.

You only realise how much bullshit there is when you work with somebody like Tom Cruise. I was seeing Tom every day for six months, but I was reading things about him that were completely untrue because I was there. Absolutely mad stuff. You can't even entertain it. It is the nature of the game. But my job is in the public domain, so therefore it is pretty much open season. It's a Catch-22. Listen, I asked for it, so I'm not going to moan about it.

O'TOOLE: But the media attention must be difficult for the women associated with you?

MEYERS: Yes, it is harder for friends who are girls because they have their own lives and their own friendships as well with other guys. And sometimes that can be difficult, it's like: 'There's a picture of you with Johnny Rhys Meyers in the newspaper saying you are going out together'. And it's like, 'Well, we're not. We were just shopping'. If I say hello to a girl, sometimes it ends up in the newspaper and you just don't see that her husband is standing there—conveniently out of the shot. In America now I have got my house rented out to a producer and his wife was having a shower one day—I have this really nice glass shower—and got a very nasty fright when somebody's telephoto lens came through the bushes to photograph her in the nip, thinking it was probably some liaison of mine.

O'TOOLE: The rumours on the Internet can also be vicious.

MEYERS: The other night I was in New York, after the premier of *August Rush* (2007), and somebody just turned on the computer and said, 'Would you like to see what they are saying about you?' And she put it up on the screen and I was, like, shocked and within about half-a-minute I asked her to turn it off. This is why I don't go on the Internet. There are many weird, weird people out there expressing their opinions on the computer. Do I give a fuck about some dude sitting in his room commenting about whatever to do with me? It's got nothing to do with me. It is somebody else's thing. So, I don't get involved.

O'TOOLE: Do you think your movie, *August Rush*, has some similarities with your own upbringing?

MEYERS: Not really, apart from my father, who was a musician, who wasn't there—that's pretty much where the comparison stops. I'm not a musical genius. I've never been to an orphanage . . .

O'TOOLE: I read you have been in an orphanage. Is that bullshit?

MEYERS: Yeah.

O'TOOLE So are there a lot of untruths out there about you?

MEYERS: There is. It kind of stemmed from this article years and years ago with this horrible, horrible woman. It was really strange. I don't quite understand this, but I gave my time to do a three-page interview in a magazine and then they are negative about you. It kind of really fucking annoys me. I'm nobody's fool.

So, it has made me very cautious when I'm doing interviews. I just put my guard up because anything I say can be twisted around. I did this *Details* article and even the editor wrote a note at the start of the magazine saying, 'Yeah, the guy who did the article with Johnny Rhys Meyers, his mind wasn't really on his job because he'd lost everything in a Dublin casino that night before gambling'. And he decided to take it out on me in the article. That's even written in the magazine. And it's kind of like, what a fucking cock sucker!

And that time I did an article for *The Sunday Times*, that woman had been ringing up family members, just pretending to be this nice old lady to sort of get behind the scenes information. I think that can be kind of snarky. So, now I don't suffer fools easily at all and if anybody asks me a question I don't want to answer, they get a very quick 'fuck off'. And if they don't like it they can leave.

O'TOOLE: All the background articles out there on you are very Dickinson. They make your childhood sound very bleak; it's as if you grew up in the '40s during the war.

MEYERS: Listen, that's also the fantasy as well. It's kind of like, 'Discovered in a pool hall', for *War Of The Buttons.* To a certain element, that's true, but that is pretty fantastical, you know what I mean? Or it's like this kind of Oliver Twist fantasy they have about me—to rise from a street urchin to being this movie hero fella. If that's what feeds their fantasies that's fair enough. But that's not the truth.

O'TOOLE: What is the truth?

MEYERS: The reality is less fantastical and much more dull and boring and drawn out. Normal working class. If we could find work we'd be working class. The criminal class. That's what we were—the criminal class [*laughs*].

O'TOOLE: I don't want to go down that road. I can just imagine the tabloid headlines.

MEYERS: I can imagine it [*putting on a satirical broadcasting accent*]: 'Rhys Meyers is part of the criminal class. Links to West Dublin gangs!' [*Laughs*] 'Where were you on the morning of August—whatever—when your man was shot on the strand?' I mean, for fucks sake, don't be ridiculous. No, regular working class Ireland in the 1980s. But when you say that to somebody in an interview in America—and I describe what Ireland was like in the 1980s—you might as well be talking about the 1940s because to them it's bleak.

O'TOOLE: But your upbringing wasn't poverty-stricken?

MEYERS: In a world of poor we were poor. There was certainly no one with any real money; there might have been someone who had an extra 50 to 100 quid in their pocket every week and it would have seemed like they were far richer but they probably weren't. Things were tight for everybody. But, you know, they kind of make up this fantasy—and let them make it up.

O'TOOLE: You left school early.

MEYERS: I certainly didn't like school. Myself and school never got on. I never really thought I would do very, very well in the academic world. I'm too individual as a person and I can't work within the factory. So, to spin a term, I couldn't be the Orwellian worker—it wouldn't satisfy me enough. I'm not very good at brownnosing. I'm not a very good toadeater. I think that when you are living in a business or academic world there is a certain amount of toadying that you have to be able to do. There is a certain amount of politics to get to where you need to go. It is not all about talent; it is about who you know as well as what you know. I don't think I would have done well at that. The only thing I was going to do well at, in hindsight, was something that was really sort of an individual talent.

O'TOOLE: Acting would have been like an escape route for you?

MEYES: Well, yeah. Acting is that fabulous career for people who really don't want to work very much. That's not from me. I can't claim that quote—that quote has been bandied around as long as actors have been bandied around. It is the ultimate sort of dosser job.

O'TOOLE: Is it true that you have a drink problem?

MEYERS: I can't drink at all. I don't drink. It is not that I drank a huge amount or drank for a very long time; I'm just one of these guys that it doesn't suit at all. For me, basically, I don't drink because I can't; I don't drink because I shouldn't—regardless, I can't, nor should I—but I don't drink because I don't want to.

O'TOOLE: I understand you attended rehab earlier this year?

MEYERS: I've been more than once. I think rehab is very, very good if somebody needs it. It is very good grist for the mill, but the reality of the situation is if you don't want to drink because you think you've got a drink problem, stop fucking drinking. It is that simple. You can go into all the programmes and you can read all the books, but the basic gist of it is: don't drink under any circumstances.

I remember seeing a videotape, while I was in a treatment centre, of this priest. He was an alcoholic who helped a lot of guys stop drinking. And that was his basic thing—if you don't want to drink, don't drink. From there on it is all fucking gravy. It is very simple to figure out. At this point in my life, I want other things that drink gets in the way of.

O'TOOLE: I'm getting the impression that you fear indulging in alcohol could thwart your career ambitions?

MEYERS: I want to focus on building a good career, but I just don't want to be that fucking arsehole sitting in the pub and someone turns around and says [*puts on a perfect Dublin working-class accent*], 'See him there at the end of the bar? He could have made a fucking fortune. He went over to Hollywood and fucking everything and he just fucking pissed it up against the wall. Fucking good luck to him!' I just like to be alert to the opportunity. I think that's really what luck is. Luck is sort of preparation meeting opportunity. When someone can really see a gift horse when it's up there fucking smacking its mouth.

O'TOOLE: Not drinking must be very difficult?

MEYERS: Of course it can be a little bit difficult. Life comes with its own sort of chariots of doom and gloom and chariots of happiness and joy. There's fucking times when you just want to go out with your mates on the lash. Of course you want to do that. But there's this other thing I want to be more. It's really that simple. It's not huge. It's not complex. I'm not on this incredible spiritual path. I don't claim to be on a quest or a journey, other than trying to live every moment and get the most out of every moment that I possibly can. This moment in my life does not include going out and getting drunk.

O'TOOLE: Was it difficult for you to go through the route of rehab?

MEYERS: Going into rehab is probably the easiest thing to do. It is coming out of fucking rehab that is hard. Going in there is difficult as well because who wants to spend that first night in fucking rehab? Nobody wants to do that. It's a very lonely place and I'm not going to bullshit you, I'm not going to say it is all joy, sweetness and light—it isn't. You really feel like you fucked up and you're useless.

In that sort of situation everybody cares about you; everybody is very in tune with their feelings. Nobody wants to offend anybody. It is very easy to stay sober in rehab, but it is much more difficult when you are out in the real world with people who really don't give a fuck. You get out into the real world and it's, 'Fuck you, buddy! And if you have a problem with it—fuck you again!'

O'TOOLE: Do you think being a famous actor gets you less sympathy and understanding about your problem?

MEYERS: Ahh, no! I mean, they expect it of you more. Yeah. They are kind of like, 'Oh, he's an actor'. It's like par for the course. 'He's

Irish'. There's actually a term in rehab and AA and stuff like that called 'CIA': Catholic, Irish, Alcoholic. There's a lot of that.

O'TOOLE: So the stereotype of us Irish being alcoholics is alive and well in LA?

MEYERS: It is not just alive and well in LA—it is alive and well all over the world because it is fact and the reality of the situation is that we do drink a hell of a lot more than most nations in the world. And you don't recognise it until you leave. We have that stigma attached to us. They are not shocked to see an Irish actor going into rehab, or Colin going out and getting drunk, or going into rehab himself. It is not unusual. And it is not unusual for actors. Everyone in LA has some sort of programme, regardless. Candy anonymous! It's that bad.

O'TOOLE: Is fame everything you'd imagined it would be?

MEYERS: No, it is nothing like I'd thought it would be because you don't really feel it. I just feel like an actor who is out there trying to do well. Someday, hopefully, I'll sit back and go, 'Wow! I have passed that threshold where my fame is more secure'. I think there are a couple of actors who are very lucky, they are at that stage were someone like Tom Cruise, Mathew McConaughey, and Brad Pitt can sit back and relax. They are what you would call modern classics, at this point. With any luck, hopefully in the next three, four, five years I'll give a couple of very, very good performances that will allow me that time to sort of settle and refocus. I think that if the wheels don't buckle, if I can keep my focus and if I can keep my fucking ears open and my ego to myself, I can learn a lot more and I can possibly do one or two really important things in the next ten years.

O'TOOLE: I was surprised to learn that you didn't have any formal training in acting. It doesn't show in your work. That's a compliment.

MEYERS: Thank you. When I get cast for a film now they are not only taking on somebody who has a percentage of talent, but with me they are now taking on someone with 12 years of experience in front of a camera and on a film set. It can make a huge difference to how a film is paced out and how a film goes when you've an actor who knows why a scene is being shot a certain way, knows how to hit his mark, knows how to work the camera, what the lighting is for and why it's there. It is totally different than working in theatre. Film is a technique.

O'TOOLE: Which of yours films are you most proud of?

MEYERS: I'm not sure about that because I can't really judge it. But I can tell you that there are a few that I'm not very proud of. I've just made a bunch of things that I'd rather not see on my CV—things like *Killer Tongue* (1996), *The Tribe* (1998). I didn't like my performance that much in *The Governess* (1998) because I'd done it so quickly after I'd completed *Velvet Goldmine* (1998) that I hadn't got out of that campy glam rock phase.

O'TOOLE: You obviously still have a hunger to become more successful?

MEYERS: Of course I'm hungry. Nobody gets into anything to go to the middle. Of course I want to go to the top of my game. I would like to start doing roles and becoming more prolific. I would like to enjoy getting better at what I do—I really would. The money and the fame thing is grand. I just want enough money where I'm comfortable and I don't have to think about it—that's the plan. If people want to pay me millions of dollars to do a film, that's good.

O'TOOLE: I understand that you are going into the gym in order to beef yourself up in order to get away from playing the androgynous type of roles.

MEYERS: Absolutely. It's everything you think it is. It's methodical. It's for a purpose. You physically have to develop yourself. I want to do leading men parts, so if that means I have to do a bit of extra time in the gym, to put a bit of weight on to become more physically imposing, then that's part of the job too.

O'TOOLE: You recently made this comment in an interview: 'There's something about the way I look that lends to the fact that I could be a little cruel. There's definitely a darkness in my physicality'.

MEYERS: I said this in an article and the fucking quote has been bandied all over fucking America. I think I got a little bit misunderstood. It was just this fucking asshole in this *Details* article. He was being snarky and he was like, 'Do you think the way you look has had a lot influence in how you get your films, you know, in being as famous as you are?' And I was like, 'Fucking doh!' I said, 'It's very fucking simple. You take someone like Brad Pitt, who is an incredible actor, but he's as famous as he is because of the way he looks'. It's a given.

Any actor who does not realise that the way they look determines the roles they play is a fucking idiot and shouldn't be involved in the business anyway. Then I read in an Irish newspaper: 'Johnny takes a swipe at Brad Pitt'. I don't swipe at anyone and I especially don't fucking take a swipe at Brad Pitt. Am I a mug?

O'TOOLE: But being a film star is more than just looking great, right?

MEYERS: The thing about film is you don't have to be the best looking guy in the world and you certainly don't have to be the best actor in the world, but you do have to be interesting and photogenic. Some people who aren't the most handsome men are very photogenic and very alive on camera—someone like Robert De Niro. In *Taxi Driver* (1976), you just can't take your eyes off him. Or in *The Godfather Part II* (1974).

It takes a very interesting person like Francis Ford Coppola to get Bobby as a young Marlon Brando. It is fucking genius casting. Looking at Bobby, he's like, 'You can't be Brando but you can be Vito Corleone'. I would like to work with somebody with that fucking depth. It was the most brilliant casting of fucking all time. I would like to work with someone with that level of insight into how a person should be cast.

O'TOOLE: His daughter is doing some amazing work these days.

MEYERS: I'd love to work with Sofia Coppola. I loved her film *Marie Antoinette* (2006). I thought it was one of the most beautiful things I'd seen in a very long time. I was never really into Kirsten Dunst. I always thought she was a very good actress, but physically I never thought she was gorgeous. I never thought she was beautiful. I never fancied her until I saw her as Marie Antoinette. I think I fancied her more because of her role, more than any other actress in any other role that I've ever seen. She caught my imagination—totally.

O'TOOLE: When you immerse yourself in a role do you ever find yourself becoming infatuated with your co-star?

MEYERS: There are little elements of them that you have to fancy, to a certain extent. That is part of the job. The nice thing is you are working with people who are extraordinary or beautiful for one reason or another. It is not hard to fall in love with Scarlet Johansson. She is very beautiful, charming, sexy, intelligent, wealthy, famous. She's got all of these 'zzzz' things going for her. It is very easy to fancy someone like Natalie Dormer, who is playing Anne Boleyn. She is very sexy, very vibrant, very intelligent. Or Radha Mitchell. Or Keri Russell. These are all very beautiful girls. So, it is very easy to pretend to be in love with them. I can pretend to be in love with most people, I think, for a short period of time.

O'TOOLE: But do you have affairs with your co-stars?

MEYERS: You don't take it home with you. I don't have affairs with actresses. It has been eight years since I had a fling with an actress; I was like 22. It is not a good idea. When you start having sex with them the chemistry slightly goes because you've had what you're not meant to have yet! Sometimes you can really pick that up, sometimes you can't. Sometimes the chemistry is just electric because they are having great, extraordinary abandoned sex with each other.

But more often than not the chemistry dies as soon as you start having sex with somebody. So, if you are going to have an affair with an actress you are working with, it is probably best to do it after the film. Even better to do it on the publicity tour [*laughs*] because you have to really like each other by the time the film comes to being distributed. You don't want two boring actors sitting there trying to complement each other or being snarky to each other—when really all it is, is an affair that went sour. So, you have to stay professional from that point of view

O'TOOLE: Now that you are famous you must get women throwing themselves at you?

MEYERS: I don't get that really. You know what; I'd like it if a woman would throw herself at me. I would love to see somebody literarily throw themselves at someone [*laughs*]. I don't see it as much, but I think people around me see it more than I see it myself. Girls are usually more discreet than throwing themselves at someone. I don't think they are as blatant as [*makes a girlie screaming sound*]; I think they are much more savvy [*starts winking and makes a clicking sound*].

O'TOOLE: You don't seem to have a problem doing gay love scenes. A lot of men would be uncomfortable with that.

MEYERS: Fuck 'em! I've never really had a problem with it because it is just part of the gig and I can sort of pretend to do it. I can't bring my own personal morality into what I feel about roles because it just wouldn't work. Otherwise, if I have a problem with that then when does it stop? I have had to do things that a lot of fucking men just wouldn't do.

I had to do a scene were I got raped up the arse by Malcolm McDowell in *I'll Sleep When I'm Dead* (2003). I've had to come out of the North Sea balls naked—nobody wants to come out of the sea balls naked, let me just tell you that, on camera. I know a lot of fucking actors who would have turned around and said absolutely no way. Their pride and their ego wouldn't let them do it.

When I was doing *The Tribe*, Jeremy Norton was really uncomfortable doing our three-way scene. Ewan [McGregor] didn't really like doing the kissing scene in *Velvet Goldmine*. In *Titus* (1999), I play Chiron, who, along with his brother Demetrius, rapes Lavinia, chops her hands off, and cuts her tongue out. Does that make me a rapist in real life? If it is a gay scene and I've got to be naked with a man, kissing a man—and if that what the role needs and requires—then that's what I'll do. Moralistically, as an actor, I have to be, to a certain extent, in limbo.

O'TOOLE: On a personal level do you feel in limbo?

MEYERS: I'm always in limbo. I'm always ready to go off and do a role wherever it is—that's the nature of my job. Some people may find that kind of shallow—and to an extent there is a shallowness because my depth I very much keep for myself. I wear my heart on my sleeve a lot because as an actor it is very much what you can bring to the surface. But also, I tend to not get attached to people and places and things because I might not be there all the time. So, there's a certain amount of limbo that you exist in.

O'TOOLE: What type of music do you like?

MEYERS: Everything. I've got an iPod with a bunch of stuff. At the moment, I find myself actually listening to a bit of '80s music. Bruce Springsteen. The first album I ever bought was *Born In The USA*. So, I'm revisiting Bruce. *Magic* is a very good album. I'm listening to Genesis. I found a really good compilation by them on the Internet, so I downloaded it. Some of it is just great catchy tunes, but then some of it is too '80s, some of it is too much like Hughey Lewis and The News—I don't want to go quite there! I've a lot of The Cure.

O'TOOLE: Do you have The OKs [his brothers' band] on your iPod?

MEYERS: I certainly have The OKs on my iPod. I have a really good demo of a song that my brother Alan wrote called 'Grace' and it's such a gorgeous song. My brother is just such an amazing songwriter but he hates every song that he writes 20 minutes after recording it. They are very fucking talented lads. I would like to see them do something. I'm not quite sure if I'd ever work with them. After *August Rush*, a lot of people in America have been asking me if I'm going to be releasing an album because I sing the songs on the soundtrack.

O'TOOLE: You also sang on the *Velvet Goldmine* soundtrack.

MEYERS: But on *Velvet Goldmine* I was 19-years-old and I hadn't really sung much, but they were sort of glam rocky songs, so some music magazines in England were sort of really harsh—but again, fuck 'em. For something like *August Rush* they were closer to my own voice, but they were also songs that were written for a film—and they were good songs and they suit the film—so, I would like to see what my voice would be like if I recorded a song that I found which I really desperately wanted to record. That would be a little bit more interesting. Maybe with my brothers in a few years time, but not on a professional level.

O'TOOLE: Did you sing in the *Elvis* miniseries?

MEYERS: I only sung for a couple of seconds in the studio scene. [*He then does a brilliant singing impersonation of Elvis for me—JOT*]. It was all Elvis' tracks. It was the first time that Elvis' masters were ever used because when John Carpenter made his film with Kurt Russell, they had to get somebody in to sing like Elvis. They didn't have the rights to his music.

O'TOOLE: What makes you tick as a person, it can't all just be about the work?

MEYERS: At the moment it kind of is. But I like the work; I like going to the gym; I like hanging out in London and Camden; I like watching TV. I like very simple things. Somebody asked me recently what was my favourite holiday destination and I said home! Home is my favourite holiday destination. A fucking cup of tea, sitting down in front of me TV, a nice football match, me cigarettes there—that's a holiday.

The thought of flying 11 hours to some fucking beach sort of drives me mad—I can't even think of it. Some exotic palm tree location? No! I want to go home. Music actually takes up a big part of my life—more than I thought it would. Listening to music, playing music.

I've got a dog called Bruce. It's really strange because I always thought these guys who have little dogs—and they love their dogs—were fucking saps. Well, I'm a total sap for this dog. A wasp stung him the other day and I couldn't be consoled. I was rushing into the hospital and everything—and it was kind of like, this is a fucking dog! The dog is kind of my baby replacement. I'm 30 and I feel like I should be a father in some way, but . . . let's have a dog. I don't want to have a kid, I want to have a dog! Much nicer!

O'TOOLE: So is parenthood something for the future?

MEYERS: I don't know. I'm just not quite sure. I love kids, but I'm just not quite sure if being a father is me. I'm just not quite sure that I'm that guy. If I get a phone call at the eleventh hour—to fall into the lead role of some super spectacular film somewhere because someone's dropped out, then I'm gone. It would be hard if it's your baby's birthday—your kid's taking his first steps—and you are up the top of a fucking mountain in East Africa making this big epic movie. And it is hard for the mother. Whatever about the fucking father running away doing his adventuring and being Mister Movie Star and cool and famous, it's hard for the mother to stay behind and sort of rear the child and have all that responsibility all the time. I'm not sure I can inflict that on someone.

O'TOOLE: Sure, when you are 50 or 60, as a big Hollywood actor, you can marry a 25-year-old and start a family then.

MEYERS: Now, you behave yourself!

O'TOOLE: Would you describe yourself as a religious person?

MEYERS: I definitely think there's a spiritual path. I'm more spiritual than I would admit or realise about myself, but I don't practice any type of spirituality. I'm certainly not a religious person, but I am respectful of other people's religions and their rights to have their opinions. I don't believe they should be fucking shooting each other with AK-47s to settle it out. I'm more of a realist.

CHAPTER TEN:

A Survivor's Tale, Peter Sheridan

Peter Sheridan was playing in the garden with his four-year-old grandson last year when he found himself flabbergasted and at a loss for words when asked, "Grandad, what did you do in the old days?"

It suddenly made the then 60-year-old feel like he was from the Stone Age, but it also inspired him to reflect on his past by writing a candid memoir—which was released in 2013—that was addressed directly to his grandson to comprehensively answer the question for him when he's old enough to understand.

Perhaps Peter, who has already written two best-selling memoirs dealing with his childhood and his father's complex love affair with another woman, subconsciously also wanted to outline all his achievements in theatre because his career has been overshadowed by the phenomenal success of his Oscar-winning older brother Jim, who directed *My Left Foot*, *The Field* and *In The Name of the Father*.

"It's weird—people you don't know go, 'You're the movie director's brother?' It's kind of like, 'Actually, we're equals', you know," he told me.

The two brothers originally started out together when they established The Project Arts Theatre. But while Jim used this as a stepping-stone to launch himself in Hollywood, Peter's own career trajectory has taken many dramatic twists and turns during the past 30-odd years.

Peter and Jim were first introduced to the stage as teenagers by their distraught father following the death of their younger brother Frankie from a brain haemorrhage.

"He didn't go to work for months after Frankie died. He always had a dream to be an amateur actor. He took that opportunity in the wake of Frankie's death and started a drama group," Peter explained.

Eventually, the two brothers took over the running of the amateur theatre group and toured the country with a production of *Waiting for Godot* in 1971. It brought them to the attention of Colm O'Brian who asked them if they were interested in using his Project Arts Centre to stage plays.

This ultimately led Peter and Jim to founding The Project Theatre Company in 1976, which quickly established them as the *L'enfants terribles* of the Dublin theatre scene with their many controversial shows. "It was absolutely insanity for five years," he said. "It never stopped."

It certainly sounds like it from listening to Peter reminisce about their times in charge. Perhaps the biggest controversy was when they caused outrage getting the Gay Sweatshop Theatre Group from London over to stage a play about homosexuality—over a decade before it was eventually decriminalised.

"The idea of gay men and gay women onstage caused an absolute furor. It's the only show I was ever involved in that got a standing ovation before the show started," he said. "It was such a feat to actually get the play on because we all had to get our way through these protestors who were outside with placards. We had protestors outside and inside the theatre.

"It caused an argument with Dublin Corporation because a lot of the councillors were very conservative and very Catholic. They put a proposal to suspend The Project's grant and that was carried. We finally got it reinstated but there was a whole campaign involved in doing that. I tell the story at some length in the book."

They also hit the headlines when Jim got into a fight with ex-Sex Pistol singer John Lydon (A.K.A. Johnny Rotten) when he pulled out of a planned concert at the last minute.

"Jim went over to London to confront him because he said he'd headline that gig and then he said he wasn't coming. There was a row in a house in London. The papers picked it up. It was headlines here back in Dublin," Peter recalled.

Who won the fight?

"I say Jimmy did actually."

They got U2 in as a last minute replacement and this lead to the future superstar band being offered to play at The Project every Saturday night for a six-month residency. But this too caused unforeseen problems when an anti-U2 gang of thugs stormed into the venue in an effort to disrupt their concert.

"One of them produced a knife and Mannix Flynn wrestled the knife off the guy and ran up the stairs and hid the knife," Peter said. "But somebody had phoned the police and the cops arrived saying, 'We heard there was a knife produced. We want the knife.'

"And we were all like, 'We didn't see any knife!' And Mannix looking at me looking at U2 looking at the cops! And the cops went off then and left us alone. That was a classic incident. I actually don't tell that in the book."

Peter remembered Phil Lynott on another occasion grappling Bono "in a headlock and wrestling him down onto the floor" in the Project's foyer back in 1982.

"My two boys were in the audience and they were so impressed that Phil Lynott and Bono were at a play that their dad had written. At the interval, we were messing around the foyer and Phil was saying to my son, 'What football team do you support?' I said to Bono, 'You're not interested in football, sure you're not?' Which he wasn't," Peter said.

"Phil then caught Bono in a headlock and started wrestling him down onto the floor, saying to him, 'Northside boys against the Southside!' My kids thought this was the best thing ever—two rock stars fighting over what football team they supported and where they came from."

The Sheridan brothers finally left The Project behind in 1980, with Jim then immigrating to New York to direct at off-Broadway theatres. But Peter shocked everyone by opting to take a year break from theatre to go off and run a market stall selling radio and stereo equipment in The Liberties.

"I learnt one thing in the markets, I'm not a salesman," he quipped.

For Peter working in the market was simply a means to an end to put food on the table for his family. Peter had met his wife Sheila when he was 16-years-old at a dance, but she rejected him because he was "too small" and also happened to be two years younger than her.

He recalled, "It was such a put down—I got mouldy drunk as a result of that. I got very drunk and felt sorry for myself."

But three years later Sheila, who was by then involved in the theatre group herself, was won over by Peter's charm. "I never thought she had any interest in me after that first encounter, but she asked me out to her house to help with an essay—but I didn't know it was actually a come on!" he said, laughing.

"It was a total whirlwind. Once we had that first kiss we were never out of each other's company; we lived in each other's world completely."

Within three months Sheila had fallen pregnant with their first of four children and Peter proposed. But her father was infuriated that his daughter was going to marry someone from the wrong side of the tracks.

"Her family didn't think that I was a good match," he confessed. "No. Her father was very against it."

The couple spent their first three-and-a-half-years living in a mobile home in the back garden of a council house in Crumlin, Dublin. "We'd absolutely no money. It was a huge struggle to try and make a few shillings in Ireland at that time," he said.

They eventually moved into a house when Peter found himself taking over The Project Theatre, but even then they were still watching every penny. "In The Project, me and Jim split a salary; it was £57 a week split between the two of us," he said. "That's so we survived. It was always like living by your wits."

After the self-imposed sabbatical from the stage to work in the market, Peter then formed an amateur theatre group in his old neighbourhood aimed at inspiring novices to get involved in acting. He directed them in a sell-out show at The Project, which prompted the future Oscar-winning director Danny Boyle of *Slumdog Millionaire* (2008) fame to invite the cast to stage the play at The Royal Court Theatre in London.

"It probably was, in my ways, the highlight of my theatre career at that time because it was so unusual to take a group of people with no background in theatre and do plays with them that became really successful," he said.

Peter next headed over to LA in 1987 for three months to direct Colm Meaney in a play he'd written about the contentious H-block hunger strikes of 1981 by IRA members.

"The show was the show that got Colm the gig on *Star Trek*," he explained. "They were saying to me, 'You're crazy to be living in Ireland. You should be here. You'd have a huge career here if you came over'. My plan was to direct that show, come back to Ireland and take that family out. That's where the book ends."

At the time of talking to him, Peter was planning to write a sequel to explain why his shot at a glittering Hollywood career failed to materialise.

It certainly didn't help matters that he was battling with demons in his personal life and was fast on his way to turning into a full-blown alcoholic. But the sojourn to LA turned into a nightmare for Peter when he found himself getting hooked on cocaine.

"I'm just at the coke problem when the book ends because my coke problem really kicked-in when I went to the States and directed *Diary of A Hunger Striker*," he said.

"I was living in downtown LA, which is a really dangerous place. I was drinking in bars that I shouldn't have been in, really dangerous places. I got on great because I could play pool. If you can play pool in America they love you. And I'm a pretty mean pool player. So, I could play and the Mexicans and Salvadorians loved me—the only white guy in the bar!

"I got very close to a guy, Cuban Mike, who was the main coke dealer in downtown LA. He took me under his wing, loved me—so I had a steady supply of coke for three months every night.

"I had occasionally dabbled, a line of coke here, a line of coke there before going to LA, but it wouldn't be anything. This was like a permanent supply where I didn't have to pay for it and it was a guy giving me as much coke as I wanted on any given occasion and I really got into it and I loved it. I got very partial to it. It's a great ego booster.

"And I came back from America knowing that I really had to do something about it. It was a very important juncture in my life because I realised that coke could become a huge problem very quickly so I cut it out. I came back to Dublin and I cut it out. The alcohol was still there, but I knew I had to do something about it."

Peter eventually faced up to his alcoholism two years later in 1989 when he was in Edinburgh doing a play and suffered a terrifying panic attack, which prompted him to attend AA meetings.

"The show opened and I went on a little bender. I was walking down the street and I had a panic attack at 11 o'clock in the morning. I was consumed with fear. I didn't know where I was. I didn't know what fucking city I was in. The streets were crowding in on top of me terrified. Petrified. It shook me to my core," he confessed.

"And it was the panic attacks really that got me in the end—not the falling down drunk or not being able to get out of bed in the morning. I decided to come home and really give it a chance to stop."

Peter's drinking came close to destroying his marriage. "There would've been issues in the marriage. A lot of rows around drink," he said. "Sheila used to write letters to me about my behaviour on drink and leave them on the table. I kept all the letters. They will feature very strongly in the next part of my memoir. Wonderful, brilliant, fantastic letters. They are the letters of someone really pleading with somebody to do something about their drinking."

Peter wrote candidly in his critically acclaimed memoir *Number 44*—a title derived from the number of the family home—about the tragic death of his younger brother and about how he himself was sexually abused by a lodger staying at the family home.

Did he believe that grappling with these traumatic events was at the root of his addictions?

"You can analyse yourself and think, 'Oh, that's the reason why'. But there are other people who would have those experiences and not end up as alcoholics. So, in a way it doesn't matter. It doesn't matter what the cause or what you think the cause had kick started something," he said. "The actually truth is I was using and abusing alcohol to cope with my everyday reality. All that matters is maintaining that sobriety."

Peter, who has been clean and sober for over a quarter of a century years, said he would never been tempted to hit the bottle again.

"But I'd have to walk away if somebody took coke out of their pocket. I wouldn't want to sit around and watch somebody snort coke up their nose," he admitted.

"But the funny thing is I have never been in that situation in 23 years. I've never been sitting at a table where somebody took out a wad of coke and started putting it on a mirror."

In the same year that Peter was wrestling with his drinking, his brother Jim directed *My Left Foot*, which was based on Christy Browne's autobiography *Down All The Days*. Was it frustrating that he wasn't working on the film?

"It was a bit because the story was one we had done on stage together. I wrote the adaptation of *Down All The Days in* 1981 and we put it on in the Oscar theatre. And I knew Christy better than Jim knew him. I was closer to Christy.

"So, there was this odd thing in my head of like, 'Oh my God! He's doing it. He's doing a movie about a guy I know better than he knows on a story that I've written for the stage——and now here he is'. There was a kind of uneasiness around at that time, but we did try to work together on stuff after that."

Why didn't they work together at the time?

"When *My Left Foot* happened I think a lot of people were saying to Jim it might be better for him if he made a break on his own. 'Get away from your brother. Use this as a vehicle to establish your own career as a movie director'.

"A lot of people were advising him to steer clear of a relationship with me on it because it might diminish his status within the project. And so he did. I don't think it was a rejection of me, but it was just an acceptance that that reality was the one that he bought into.

"And I suppose because it was a new experience for him. The Coen Brothers hadn't happened, so the director/auteur thing at that time was very much an individual thing. A director would be a director, whereas when the Coen Brothers and the Farrelly Brothers came along they showed that two people can actually do this job together. So, I think we missed the boat at the beginning when he did *My Left Foot*."

How did he feel on Oscar night?

"That's a bit strange alright. It is weird," he said. "Suddenly people are defining you as being somebody's younger brother who is much, much less successful. But I kind of don't see it that way. But that's the perception because movies and Oscar nominations matter so much that it catapulted him right up there in that world. I have no ungood feelings about that."

Peter's shot at a Hollywood career was then derailed when Sean Penn walked out on his film about Brendan Behan only days before the cameras were to roll back in 1996. What were the mysterious "personal reasons" for Penn's decision to quit so suddenly?

"I don't think he was ready in his head to play Brendan, but he couldn't bring himself to say, 'Look, I'm not ready'. So what it became was he said to me, 'If I go to Dublin to take on this role, Robin is going to move state with the kids and I'll never see them again, so I can't come'," Peter explained.

"I couldn't in my heart say, 'I still want you to come here'. How could I say to a guy 'My film is more important than your family?'"

It was a shock for Peter who had bonded with Penn over a four-year period as they worked on putting the film together.

"It's so difficult. You spend four years trying to put a movie together and if it doesn't happen, it's soul destroying," he said. "You think, 'I put all that energy into something and it has disappeared in front of my eyes'."

Peter ended up only ever directing one film based on Brendan Behan's experience of being incarcerated in a borstal as an IRA volunteer during World War II.

"The budget was based on Sean being in it. So, then when we got to do *Borstal Boy* (2000)—which is a much smaller version of that story—the budget shrank from being a $10 million picture to being a $1.5 million. I never got paid. I never got my director's fee," he pointed out.

At the time, Jim was talking about directing *Sheriff Street Stories*, a film based on their childhood, which still hasn't been made yet. Jim spoke about wanting to get Brendan Gleeson to play their father. But Peter admitted to having mixed feelings about the project.

"It's kind of awkward because his memory and his view of growing up is so different to mine. It's amazing that within the same family two people can have different experiences," he said.

"I was close to my dad and he would've been much closer to my mother emotionally. He fought with my dad, whereas I would've been more my dad's favourite. The film is kind of a conflict with the father that I don't quite get because it wasn't my experience of him. My experience of him was much warmer, much more paly.

"I find it hard to get inside Jim's story. It doesn't resonate for me in the same way that *44* resonated for me. It is my version of the story. And in order to make the film Jim bought the rights to *44* because he really didn't want me making a film."

But despite such differences of opinion, Peter insists they won't fall out.

"Jim and I don't quarrel in that way. He's dead sound," Peter concluded.

CHAPTER ELEVEN:

The Distinctive Character Actor, David Kelly

As the minuscule Dictaphone was placed down on the table, David Kelly said in his instantly recognisable thespian accent: "They are wonderful. They are so small. The wonderful thing about them is it stops men saying mine is bigger than yours! Now they are saying mine is smaller than yours!"

The 78-year-old veteran character actor, who was accurately described on his Wikipedia page as having "quirky looks", started performing in the Gaiety Theatre at the tender age of eight. After his screen debut in 1957, Kelly appeared constantly on television and in films. He played lots of small parts in big films and as many big parts in small films. He had blink-and-you'll-miss 'em roles in the likes of *The Italian Job* (1969) and *Quackser Fortune Has a Cousin in the Bronx*, but the movie parts have gotten bigger as he's headed towards retirement age.

When I pointed out to him that career-wise, the last 15 years of his career had been amazingly good, Kelly laughed.

"They've been great," he agreed, "because all the competition is dead—they're all gone!"

Joking aside, Kelly acknowledged that things could have turned out very differently. As he revealed during this very personal interview, he might—like many of Ireland's leading actors and writers—have drunk himself into an early grave. Instead, he knocked the booze on the head and focused on the work. From that moment on, things clicked for him. After his appearances in *Fawlty Towers* and *Strumpet City*, bigger offers started to roll in, particularly for TV shows and theatre. Kelly then had a co-starring role in Roman Polanski's *Pirates* (1986), followed by a solid performance in Jim Sheridan's *Into The West*. He belatedly hit the big time Stateside in 1998, when he played the lead role in *Waking Ned Devine*, which resulted in a Best Actor nomination from the Screen Actors Guild. It was a film that also turned him into an unusual sex symbol—thanks to his "Full Monty" scenes—for the OAP generation!

In his twilight years, he has appeared as Grandpa Joe in *Charlie And The Chocolate Factory* (2005), a rare outing as the villain alongside Timothy Hutton in *The Kovak Box* (2006), and with Robert De Niro and Michelle Pfeiffer in the blockbuster *Stardust* (2007). Since Kelly's enduring performance as Grandpa Joe, he has been discovered by a new, younger generation. This was evident when, moments after this interview finished, he was approached by an excited teenage girl as we strolled down Wicklow Street in Dublin.

"Next time you're in Hollywood, please tell Johnny Depp that I was asking for him!" she giggled.

Kelly turned to me. "You wouldn't believe how frequently that occurs to me these days," he smiled.

But despite the hundreds of television and movie roles, he's perhaps best known in the acting world for his work in the theatre, which culminated in an ESB Lifetime Achievement Award in 2004.

A true gentleman, Kelly later phoned me to thank me for taking the time to interview him. The pleasure was all mine.

O'TOOLE: Back in the '50 and '60s, you worked with many of the legends from the Irish acting and writing community. It must have been a very Bohemian culture in Dublin back then.

KELLY: Absolutely—and I'm delighted that you asked me that because I'm sick and tired of 12-year-olds telling us how terrible the '50s and '60s were, that it was this grey town. And if you didn't go to Mass, a priest would jump out of a bush and beat you to death. It's so tiresome because they weren't bloody well there and they don't know. Of course there was poverty, but nothing like the poverty that existed in London, Paris, and Berlin. It was a wonderful town and the people were a great deal nicer. Wonderful things were happening in the theatre and in the arts. Certain writers said, 'The whole place was grey'. It was grey inside the pubs where a lot of them stayed—about to write the great novel, which they never did. And if you go into the same pubs today, they're still pretty grey *[laughs]*.

O'TOOLE: Many of your acting contemporaries spent a lot of time in the two pubs—The Plough and The Flowing Tide—near The Abbey.

KELLY: You see, we're in a job like journalists, where basically we're free to drink. Back then, in the acting profession, you were free during the day and playing at night, but then you could take off afterwards. Or, if you were rehearsing, you were doing that during part of the day and were free at night. So, it was easy to drink. Also, it was considered kind of stylish for writers and actors to drink. 'Like, me and Hemingway—we drink heavily!' *[Laughs]*. I drank quite heavily, but I never drank with him. He never asked! There was a certain kind of kudos connected with the drinking. Thank God, that's gone—it's no longer considered that smart.

O'TOOLE: Did you ever have a problem with alcohol?

KELLY: I would never deny the fact that I'm an alcoholic. I don't drink and I haven't had a drink for 35 years, which is great. I've a lot of people to thank for that, and especially my good friend Ray McAnally because he had gone through it himself. When I woke up in the Home For The Bewildered, here was this snug, well-dressed gentleman sitting at the end of the bed. And I thought, 'Oh, God, not Ray! Go away. Leave me alone'. And he didn't. He stayed with me, putting up with the most appalling abuse from me—and the most appalling language mixed with the abuse *[laughs]*. But he never left me alone, he was with me every day. He was at the other end of the phone for me up until the day he died. A great and loyal friend.

O'TOOLE: How did your problem with drink start?

KELLY: I went to London in 1949, had a look at Big Ben and thought, 'How lovely', and got a pain in my belly as it struck—and I went down like a ton of bricks. It turned out to be an ulcer. When I was on stage I'd have to time the vomiting—from the pain—which eased the pain for an hour-and-a-half between takes. One worked under extraordinary difficulties. It wasn't a question of giving up drink, but I couldn't drink—I'd have a bottle of stout and if I had a second bottle of stout I'd keel over with pain. I got it when I was 20 and the doctor kept saying, 'Have the operation', which was a dodgy operation back then. I woke up one day and I was 40—and I had this illness half of my life—and the Abbey Theatre rang, asking me to play

Lazarus. I thought, 'Jaysus, I knew I looked bad—but they want me to play Lazarus!' So, I went in for the operation and I was out in three weeks—cured. Ulcer gone. I never looked back.

O'TOOLE: So, when you hit the booze, it was a case of making up for lost time?

KELLY: There was time to be made up. I poured out the vodka and there was no reaction at all—except happiness! And the next few years—though very forgetful—were very happy! I think I'm a reasonably civilised man, but I did drink like an animal for a period after that. I was an alcoholic. I am an alcoholic.

O'TOOLE: Do you regret that?

KELLY: Oh, Jesus yes. There are whole periods of the '60s I don't remember. It's the classic saying: if you remember the '60s, you weren't there! I recall being asked if I can remember where I was the day Kennedy was shot and I said I didn't know he was dead until 1972!

O'TOOLE: Can you recall your very last drink?

KELLY: I gave it up on March 28, 1972. It had never interfered with the work, except at the very end. I was playing Oliver Plunkett in The Gate and I was trying everything to get it together but I couldn't stop the shakes. It went badly. And, I thought, 'Something has to be done'. I can recall it vividly. It was a fairly large one. Two large vodkas and over to the pub to get a bottle, had a couple there, and came back and finished off the bottle. And then I kind of blacked out. That was the last one. It was a big one, as I say, but it really was the last one. So, I went into the Home For The Bewildered with the blessing of the family. I was determined that this was the last one. And I never missed it. People say, 'God, you must have great willpower'. I've no willpower at all. It had nothing to do with willpower.

O'TOOLE: Do you think you'd have ended up dead if you hadn't stopped drinking?

KELLY: I can tell you when I would have died. I would have been dead in about 1975 or 76. That would have given me another three or four years at that rate of drinking. I'd hardly have made that. At the outside I'd have been dead by 1976. And you wouldn't have had to put up with me *[laughs]*. . . .

O'TOOLE: How did your family respond?

KELLY: They were great because I was just welcomed back with open arms. I didn't lose my family—I didn't lose the kids. They hugged me and welcomed me back. I can remember looking and seeing these little eyes, strange, looking at this kind of monster and wondering,

'What's wrong with everybody? Because I'm in great humour'. They're bad memories. They've all not forgotten them, but they've certainly never held it against me. And later on, when they were growing up—and maybe coming in a bit late and I was saying, 'Where were you until this hour of the night?'—it was never thrown back at me. Never once. I love them dearly for that.

O'TOOLE: Were you afraid that your children might end up with a drink problem?

KELLY: I'm delighted that both my kids enjoy drink and they do it very sensibly. I was terrified that the alcoholism might be passed on—or, even worse, that they might turn out to be teetotallers. Neither of those things happened. So, I've been a terribly lucky man all round.

O'TOOLE: Jack Lemmon's alcoholic character in *The Days Of Wine And Roses* (1962) would hide the bottles. Did you?

KELLY: Oh, yes. I used to hide the bottles. The only thing I ever planted was a bush in the front garden, a big box bush. And when the winter came, the leaves disappeared off that, there was this wonderful—Disney couldn't have created it—Christmas scene of these glittering, sparkling jewels in the hedge. They were all empty vodka bottles, which we hadn't seen when the leaves were on the thing. It was one of the most beautiful scenes—memorable. But you'd hide the bottles under the bed and then the wife would make the bed and take out the bottle and just put it on the table. It would annoy me, so I'd hide it again. I would think, 'Maybe she'll lose her temper and throw it out, so I'd better have another one'. And then you'd forget where you've hidden them. We were finding bottles strapped under the table—that's a very good place, incidentally—and in the garage.

O'TOOLE: How did your wife handle it?

KELLY: Terribly well. She was generous enough to regard it, you know, as a disease. I obviously couldn't help it. It must have been—well, it was—extraordinarily difficult for her. I'm the one who hasn't got that many memories of the bad times. But, of course, they were sober—they remember. No, the subject was never thrown at me. It was just a welcome home and that was wonderful. So, there is hope. . . .

O'TOOLE: Did you manage to forgive yourself?

KELLY: I'm the only one who hasn't fully forgiven myself. It's alright to say, 'It was the drink—it wasn't you', but it was a bad scene. I used to think that maybe my career is gone, or whatever, because it's a small town. But it never happened and they invited me back to The Gate a year later. I came out of the hospital and I was pretty shaky. Hugh Leonard said, 'You better get well soon because you're doing a play called *The Virgins*, which I've written for you, for Thames Television. And you're cast!' And I said, 'What? In three weeks? I can't do it!' He said, 'Yes, you can, because you're booked. We fixed it with your agent'. I was terrified. Jaysus, if they just saw me—because I wasn't well! He said, 'Yes, you are—you skinny whore!' *[Laughs.]*

O'TOOLE: Were you depressed?

KELLY: No, I was just worried. The first year, I suppose, I used to get peripheral neurosis, I think you call it. This tingling sensation on the lip when passing a pub—as if you were walking along the edge of a cliff. They say the temptation is always subconsciously there: *Will I go mad suddenly and jump?* The worry that something will happen and I'll go in and have a drink—and that worry would make me break out in beads of sweat. I never did, but the fear was there that I'd do it and ruin everything. Ray's policy would be to never let any alcohol near his house. He'd say, keep it away. I mean, you only have to reach out your hand to get a bottle—you don't even have to go to a pub. I approached it differently. I don't advise other people to do this but, I thought, I've got to live with it—so my house is like a distillery. I pour an awful lot of booze because all my friends drink. I pour but I just don't take any myself. If I can't stay sober with a bottle of vodka in my hand I'm gone. You've got to live with it. Now, that is not recommended by AA and I'm not recommending it to anyone. In my house, I've got to do it that way.

O'TOOLE: You must have socialised with Brian O Nualláin (aka Myles na Gopaleen and Flann O'Brien), who was a legendary drinker?

KELLY: Oh, yeah. I think he was a great writer but he could be very grumpy. And I brought him to Mercer's Hospital because he'd fallen off the stool and wasn't in a good way. Then I dropped in to see him and he had gone! When I got back he was sitting up in the bar at Neary's. That's where we all sat. There's a famous story told about the wrong people. It was not Brendan Behan—it was Sean O'Sullivan, the painter, Myles na Gopaleen, and Jimmy O'Dea in the Holy Hour, standing outside Neary's with the tears rolling down their eyes, saying, 'There's no characters left in Dublin! Ah, Dublin's changed'. And there were the three of them. That's a true story, but it has done the rounds and has turned into Brendan Behan and somebody else. I can remember another funny incident: I had a great artist friend, Tom Murray, who was terribly upset because he couldn't get his medication. And O'Sullivan said, 'Why?' And Tom said because it's closed for lunch. And he said, 'We'll open it!' And he went over and kicked the door in.

O'TOOLE: Thankfully, drinking didn't stop you from going on to produce an amazing body of work.

KELLY: Ah, thanks. I've done my best.

O'TOOLE: You starred in one of my favourite Irish films, *Quackser Fortune Has A Cousin In The Bronx*, alongside Gene Wilder.

KELLY: That was fun. Gene was very pleasant, but I was disappointed with him because he bitched about *Willy Wonka And The Chocolate Factory* (2004). He said very nasty things about it. That, I thought, was unpardonable. And then to prove how unpardonable it was, he admitted that he hadn't seen it! I thought, 'Oh, Gene! Very vulgar. You are a bitch for that'. I thought that was nasty. We said very nice things about him during the *Willy Wonka* interviews. Incidentally, we didn't tell him that Roald Dahl went to his grave hating every second of *Willy Wonka* because, for a start, it was *Charlie And The Chocolate Factory*—but you couldn't say Charlie during the Vietnam War because it meant something else; so they had to change it to *Willy Wonka*—that annoyed Dahl because Charlie is the main character and Willie Wonka isn't a very nice man and the child saves him.

O'TOOLE: How did you get the part of Grandpa Joe in the Tim Burton version?

KELLY: My agent said, 'I think you're going to end up in *Charlie And The Chocolate* Factory'. And I said, 'That'll be the day'. Tim's people rang up and said, 'Is there any chance that you could get to London tomorrow?' And I said, 'Well, it so happens that I will be in London tomorrow'. I was going over for a custom fitting to Pinewood, and Tim's people said, 'Can you be in Pinewood?' And I said I would be there and they said, 'This is meant to happen'. Zanuck met me at the gate and said, 'Come on in and meet Tim'. I went in and he said, 'I won't hold you up, David. Just one question: This is going to take six months—and looking at that frame—is there a problem there?' I said no. I still wasn't quite sure if I was getting Grandpa Joe or the other grandpa. Tim said, 'That's the only question. I think we're in business. That's great', and he said to Zanuck, 'You know, David says fine, so get onto his agent'. Three minutes later I was over getting fitted for *Nanny McPhee*. It took three minutes. People asked were the auditions very hard? No auditions. I was just handed the thing on a plate.

O'TOOLE: It must be a long time since you've had to audition for a part?

KELLY: Oh, I never audition. I've lost parts over that, but auditions are stupid. I will read worse than anybody you've ever met. If you don't know my work—or you haven't seen it—you are not going to tell by my reading whether I can act. A big director in Hollywood asked me if I'd come up and audition. But my agent explained that I didn't audition. He said, 'That's alright. I respect that'. I went up in a taxi to the BBC and there he was—I won't mention his name to anybody—and he said, 'Will you read that for me?' I said, 'You know very well that I won't read'. He said, 'That's stupid . . . what kind of ego . . .' I said, 'I don't know your work! Would you like to show me a couple of your films?' He said, "You have a fucking nerve!' I said, 'That's exactly the way I feel'. But I didn't get the part [*laughs*].

O'TOOLE: Did you hit it off with Johnny Depp?

KELLY: We had a great time together. To show just what a magic guy Johnny is: he came over to me and said, 'You're from Dublin. You must know the work of Harry Clarke; do you?' Now, you don't expect that from a young Hollywood star. To know Harry Clarke, the great stained glass artist who died in the late '30s. I said, 'How do you know Harry Clarke?' He said, 'Oh, I have two of his cartoons at home. Two of the charcoal drawings for some Dublin church window'. We were also both jazz fans. He was a great personal friend of the clarinettist—what's his name? Not Benny Goodman, better than Benny, the greatest of them all. It will come to me—and he gave me some of his records that had been given to him. We used to swap records. In the lifetime achievement thing, Johnny made a lovely video, which was shown and sent to me, saying, 'You're my hero and always will be'. He said the most beautiful things about me and then it had Clive Owen, and a whole load of other wonderful people, saying nice things about me. It nearly reduced me to tears. It was terribly moving.

O'TOOLE: You're so hip now you've even appeared in a Playstation game.

KELLY: Yes and, of course, being a sex symbol in *Waking Ned!* [*Laughs*]. It was great fun being totally naked on a motorbike! I was worried about the motorbike because I'd never driven anything in my life. They said, 'It'll be dead easy. It'll only be about 35 miles an hour'. Thirty-five miles an hour is Steve McQueen as far as I'm concerned! In the scene, he has to be naked because he can't get into his clothes quick enough. He has his helmet and boots on, but he is stark naked, and says, 'Ah, to hell with it', and jumps up onto his bike and takes off. But they made a bit of—I don't know what you'd call it—an elastic pouch to cover one's embarrassment. But the cameraman said, 'I've bad news, you are so bloody skinny! Underneath the brakes I can see the indentation of the elastic. Would you mind getting rid of it?' And, at this stage, I knew I was going to meet my maker in a very short time [*laughs*]. I was frozen—and I was going to die anyway—so I didn't give a damn and I took it off. We did it nude. I think a lot of old ladies who were out for walks had several heart attacks!

O'TOOLE: That film was well received in America, resulting in you being nominated for some top awards there.

KELLY: I was nominated alongside Billy Bob Thornton, Ed Harris, and Robert Duvall for the Screen Actors Guild, which is arguably bigger than the Oscars in Hollywood. We were all sitting together and it was great to see the four nominations coming up. It went to Robert Duvall, who deserved it of course, and he's one of my favourite actors. But to be in that company is a huge honour. Duvall said, 'Nobody remembers who wins—but they do remember who's nominated'. At least 5,500 Hollywood actors voted for me, or I wouldn't have been in that position. I also won the Golden Satellite Award, in Hollywood, as the best performance by an actor in a musical or a comedy film.

O'TOOLE: Despite the accolades, you didn't stay and make movies in Hollywood. Why not?

KELLY: I was offered a seven-year contract after *Waking Ned.* It was a company that represented one of the big studios. I thought, 'What am I going to do in Hollywood in my 70s? At this age, am I going to uproot my home in Dublin and move to Hollywood, which is the ugliest place in the world, to do shit for seven years?' My son says, 'It's rather camp to be offered a Hollywood contract, but isn't it much camper to say no?!' [*Laughs.*]

O'TOOLE: But why didn't you try Hollywood earlier, back in the '60s or '70s?

KELLY: Oh, if somebody had offered me a role—God, yeah. I talked to Clive Owen when they discovered him. Clive was offered a two-year contract—and he was doing nice work with the National Theatre in England—and he said, 'I'll never forget it. I jumped at Hollywood. I sometimes used to cry, sitting outside in the car, to go in and do shit—when I could be back in London, with less money, but doing my job. Doing beautiful work'. And he said that was the worst period. So, I said I'd turned down seven-years and he said, 'Very wise'. You don't do that in your 70s, for God's sake!

O'TOOLE: Do you think the booze restricted your career?

KELLY: It wasn't that at all. You didn't get the chance to do films in Ireland. We had one of the most beautiful studios in the world in Ardmore, and English and American films would come in. If you were an actor in the Abbey you might get a few lines as a walk-on. But there was no Irish film industry. It's not that long since they started to make films here. At the time, we used to ask Ardmore, 'Could we have the studios? We've got the actors; we've got cameramen; we've got writers—we can make films. And we'd do it on shares'. They would say, 'Oh, no. You have to pay the rent'. And it sat there. Through my lifetime—50 years—that sat there. We used it—one of the major studios—to rehearse *Glenroe.* It was madness.

O'TOOLE: I won't mention any names—but there are some young Irish actors appearing in films that might look good but can't really act.

KELLY: No—because you can't do it without the groundwork. You can't do it without the absolute desire and passion to come across those wonderful moments that happen—not all that often—where you are actually transported and there's a kind of ecstasy, which doesn't last a run. It may not last for a whole performance. But there are those moments when you know why you are doing it. That is a kind of magic. Nowadays, the kids are not coming in because they are dying to act—they are coming in hoping to be rich and famous. They want to go to Hollywood and become Colin Farrell or Liam Neeson. It won't happen. The schools are churning them out. Everywhere you look there are acting students.

O'TOOLE: You worked with Roman Polanski on the *Pirates* film. Did you ever discuss his penchant for young girls and, in particular, the time he was arrested for having sex with a minor?

KELLY: I know all about the scandal. He told me the story about how he was going to go to Sing Sing prison forever—that was a set-up. I've seen the photographs of her—and she was only 14-and-a-half as it turns out—but, by God, she was a well-made 14-and-a-half (*I've since interviewed Samantha Geimer myself and learnt she was actually only 13 – JOT*). Her mammy had sent her over to Polanski to be photographed in the nude for the magazine. He was very upfront about the little weakness—and liking young girls. It is totally untrue to say that he fancied children. He was not a paedophile. He liked young girls. You are talking about 18 and that. He said to me once, 'I don't know what the fuss is! Don't you like younger women?' And I said, 'At my age, there isn't any other sort!'

O'TOOLE: Did Polanski ever confide in you about the murder of his actress wife, Sharon Tate?

KELLY: Yes. The man had a horrendous life—the murder of his wife and the unborn child. They [the Manson Family] ripped her open and the child was murdered as well. And, of course, he had such a bad name because of the film he made, *Rosemary's Baby* (1968). He just made that when Sharon Tate was murdered and the small minds thought, 'Oh, that gang! They are all into dope and black magic'. People were very nasty. He got a bill the next day for blood on the carpet. And he was under suspicion. He told me that he was pathological himself about it—you'd have a drink with him and he'd take away your glass to match the fingerprints to the thing. A terribly sad life. A great director. Terribly loyal to his actors. We got on well.

O'TOOLE: What's your favourite role?

KELLY: I always say my next one! I suppose it would have to be Samuel Beckett's *Krapp's Last Tape*. It's beautiful. I played that in 1959—probably the second or the third production of it anywhere. And I've been playing it all through the '90s—in Australia, three tours in America, and Spain. I've played it everywhere. Over 50 years, between theatre and film, you do so much that it's really very hard to say which is your favourite. But that was terribly important to me. One churns out a lot of rubbish over a lifetime but one hopes that, as well as the rubbish, there's some that's very good. The great thing about growing old is that your memory slips and, happily, you tend to forget the bad. (*A few days after the interview, David Kelly called me at home and asked me as a favour not to print a quote in which he compared his performance of Krapp with another famous actor. He didn't want to appear as if he was boasting, which was a measure of the gentleman – JOT.*)

O'TOOLE: You'll always be remembered for playing the hapless Irish builder O'Reilly in *Fawlty Towers*.

KELLY: That'll be on my gravestone! I get cheques from all over the place for that—usually for six pence or something like that. They repeat it so much that you do get a little kind of pension. I'm very big in Malawi! I only had nine minutes playing time in it. They are great scenes—terribly funny. It grows in people's minds—they think you were in all of them. As Manuel pointed out to me, 'We broke our asses doing it and they all say, 'Oh, I love the one with O'Reilly, the builder'. And I've counted the bloody thing—you're nine minutes in it'. It's actually one of John Cleese's favourites. The first six were far better than the other six. He didn't want to do the second series, but the BBC wanted another six episodes because it was huge. They are wonderful, but the first six really are gems. Do you know what type of audience we had for that episode? They'd gone down to Thomas Cook and they'd got three coach loads of tourists from Iceland. As John said, they were sitting there thawing out and smelling of fish blubber! And they frankly wanted to be somewhere else [*laughs*].

O'TOOLE: You worked with Laurence Olivier, just before his death, in *The Jigsaw Man* (1983).

KELLY: I had one scene that took the whole day to film with Laurence Olivier—just the two of us. He was wonderful to play to. He was very sick. He was dying. When you do the reverse shots you want a stand-in actor, but for somebody of Oliver's standards I stood in while he did his lines, but on the reverse they said, 'Larry, you needn't stay. David doesn't mind if somebody stands there as an eye line'. But he said, 'No, no. I wouldn't do that to an actor'. And I said, 'Please, I don't mind,' because he was promised rest. But he wouldn't go. He stayed there and he was like falling down tired, but he fed me the lines and then he'd say, 'Is that OK? Is that position OK?' Beautiful, beautiful man.

O'TOOLE: Do you have any disappointments or regrets about your career?

KELLY: No, because—I think it's especially something alcoholism teaches you—regrets are a waste of bloody time. Regrets? I've had a few but, then again, too few to mention. Forget it. You are wasting your time and God's time. Just don't do it again [*laughs*].

O'TOOLE: Are you going to continue acting?

KELLY: I'd never retire. I think retiring is a very vulgar word. You know, the people in ordinary jobs who work all their lives doing a job they hate, make a lot of money and have a second house and a fourth car, and retire at 60 and go on a cruise, have a heart attack and die! That's a terrible life. I'd never retire—I just do far less now

CHAPTER TWELVE:

Beyond the Breaking Glass, Hazel O'Conner

Hazel O'Connor burst onto the big screen almost 40 years ago with her astonishing performance as a drugged up singer in the smash hit film *Breaking Glass* (1980). It won her glowing plaudits from Cannes' notoriously fickle film critics when it premiered at the prestigious festival back in 1980.

The film portrayed the life of a young punk singer whose meteoric rise to fame led to her personal disintegration. But, as the actress and singer revealed to me, it was very much a case of art imitating life—as she used her own experiences of being a drug addict to help flesh out her brilliant portrayal of a character heading towards a nervous breakdown.

"I've had a very raucous life," she said simply. "I had a boyfriend who was into cocaine and for about a year it could have gone very badly for me. I started to take coke with him and then I needed to take coke and he needed to take coke and there was no relationship anymore—it was just about cocaine and I didn't like it."

Though she was only 25-years-old when she made the film, Hazel had already experienced poverty and rape and enough of her own addiction to drugs to draw on for her brilliant portrayal of a character heading towards a complete breakdown.

"I wised up one day. Luckily, I started to have horrible nose bleeding things and they really frightened me. I'm a bit of a baby about things like that, so I don't drink because I hate throwing up; I hate ill-health. And I looked at my ribs and I thought, 'I could play a tune on these ribs! I'm skinnier than I've ever been and I'm not happy and this guy and I aren't happy and this is not a nice thing'."

For the sake of her own health and sanity, she went to Germany and joined a three-piece all-girl group and found the willpower to stop taking cocaine. She focused all her renowned energy on becoming a star.

"I got away from the scene and I cleaned up and I never took it again because I know what a fool's errand it is. I can't bear people who are known for taking cocaine because that's so boring."

Still, even though she and her boyfriend had parted, she would let him stay with her because she cared so much for his daughter.

"She grew up to be a beautiful girl, not addicted to any substances, and she lived in LA. When I lived there, she took me out to the best lunch ever and she said, 'You were the only one of the grown-ups that used to look after us kids'.

"I didn't remember. I think I used to take them to the seaside because I like the seaside. But their mothers and fathers didn't because they were always a bit kind of squatty and druggy and I was a bit younger than the rest of the people.

"When I came back from the singing—my first singing experience—I was clean. I didn't want to be part of this relationship and so I said, 'That's it, we're over', which was sad because of the little girl. But she's remained my surrogate niece or whatever and she's a great woman now with her own kids."

It's all the more surprising that Hazel ended up addicted to cocaine because, as a teenager, she had sworn to herself that she would never take heroin after witnessing a friend overdosing and dying.

When she 15, she hung around with another older teenager. "One day, I went into her flat and found her slumped and passed out. And I found out that she had taken heroin and I had to take her to hospital and I had to keep her awake, give her coffee. I didn't know what to do because I was 15, but it was so horrible and so shocking. Since then I've seen lots of people go. That's why I would never have taken heroin."

Hazel's friend died from a drug overdose, which she wrote about this experience in her song "Who Will Care?"

"I just thought people try things when they're young; when everything is kind of cute. Young men who are getting pissed and they're good looking and it's cute, young women like her, slumped out, and maybe it's somehow in your mind, 'Oh, it's youth. It's rebellion'.

"But 40 years on and that's why I wrote this song because I thought, 'You know, in another 10 years it won't be cute, it won't be anything. It'll be like a death sentence'. And so that's what that song was about."

The Coventry-born Hazel—with a father from Galway and mother from Birmingham—has always lived life on the edge. After dropping out of school at 16-years-old, she ran away from home and travelled the world. At one time or other, she lived in an Amsterdam squat, did her driving license in war-torn Beirut, was almost killed by a landmine in North Africa, and was a troupe dancer in Japan.

When asked, she at first said the scariest thing during her five-year long sojourn around the world was witnessing the bombings in Lebanon, but then mid-conversation she goes further by astonishingly confessing to having to endure the horrifying ordeal of being raped—twice.

"When I was 16 and living in Amsterdam I had been raped by a Hari Krishna," she said. (—Coincidentally, she would later go on to marry an ex-member of the cult religion.)

She was also still only 16-years-old when the second sexually assault happened when she met an Algerian man in Marrakesh who invited her to the King's Palace Gardens where he raped her. She didn't resist out of fear and afterwards felt numb and was terrified of becoming pregnant.

How did she deal with these ordeals?

"I don't know. There's certain things that happen and they're so scary and so awful. And I'm maybe so good at moving on quickly, so I don't feel it."

She agreed that it sounds very much like she was running away from her emotions during her formative years. "I mean, it's all going to come to roost one day, isn't it?" she admitted.

On another journey in Algeria, Hazel almost died when she and her then boyfriend Adrian accidentally camped overnight on a minefield.

"The next morning at about six we were woken up with workmen going to work on the main road and they shouted that we were stupid, didn't we know we were in the middle of a minefield that hasn't been dissembled since the civil war?" she recalled.

"I wanted to run away like a coward. I thought, 'We're going to die. We're about to get blown up. If I'm going to go I'll go with my boyfriend', because I really did love him.

"So, our other mate was walking in front of the Land Rover and I sat with my boyfriend ready to die with him. I was lucky but I think that was a scary one too."

After five years of living so dangerously, Hazel was struck down with malaria and returned to England.

"I reached 21 and I really didn't have a clue what I wanted to do because everything I'd done had to do with him [my boyfriend]. And I thought we were going to marry and I was going to have his children and that would have been happiness for me. But he didn't [want that].

"And then I thought, 'Well what makes me happy. What do I want to do with my life?' I just remembered the thing that gave me the greatest joy was singing and playing music with my brother. It did something to me inside that made me feel well. So, I thought, 'I'll do singing'."

After getting away from her drug addict boyfriend, Hazel then started a relationship with a musician who turned out to be violent.

"He hit me twice. I had to lock him out. He was a serious head case. Oh he was horrible," she recalled.

"On the second occasion he hit me, a man from the flats [above] came down and he'd seen everything, he said, 'I saw what you did to her'. And this guy just banged him one and the ex-boyfriend is just going, 'Oh my face, my face.' I said, 'That's it, we're over'."

As an afterthought, she added, "And then I got famous after that," and she then smiled, as if to say that the best revenge is living well.

It was her next step that changed her life—for both good and bad fortune—when she signed up to a small independent record company.

"It was January '78. The record company had nobody to man the telephones because the girl had gone on holiday. I had no rent, so I said, 'Can I do her job for two weeks?' And on the first day they'd all gone out to lunch and this call came through, somebody wanted to talk to the bosses and I said can I help and they said, 'We're looking for this girl called Hazel O'Connor'.

"And I said, 'That's me'. I was amazed that anyone would really know that I existed. They said they were auditioning for this new film and would I like to meet the director tomorrow? And I said, 'Sure yeah'."

Astonishingly, not only was Hazel offered the lead role in the now iconic 1980s film *Breaking Glass*, alongside Jonathan Pryce who went on to star with Robert De Niro in *Brazil* (1985), but she also somehow persuaded the producers to let her—a then totally unknown musician with no track record—to write and perform its entire soundtrack. It included several hit singles, such as the haunting classic 'Will You', and went double platinum, reaching number five in the UK charts where it remained for 28 weeks.

But despite the astonishing proverbial overnight success, Hazel was struggling financially because of the frugal deal she had foolishly signed with the small record company.

The day before she was officially offered the part in the film, the small record label cajoled her into signing a new extended contract.

"The record company got me in their office and said, 'You better sign this long term contract now with us because we've already spent money on you. If you don't sign it now nobody else will want you. We'll get you the best producers'. I was a silly cow, and in the end I signed two contracts.

"They made about £3 or £4 million—never shared a penny of any of the advances that they took. I lost out on a lot of money and wasn't looked after very well at all. I was still on £12,000 a year for the deal I'd done with them and I was paying for the band out of my wages for *Breaking Glass.* And I was on the lowest wage for that, I was on about £250."

She had a fallen out with the record company and they refused to release her from the dubious contract.

"I was down on my uppers after being with the record company and being ripped off, and then they sued me, then I ended up in court cases for years and years. I was very poor," she said. "And being sued in 1982, I couldn't do a new record deal because I was injunctioned against and I got a job for a month singing in a Knightsbridge Supper Club with Clare Hirst [who plays on the new album]."

It wasn't until years later after a long, drawn-out legal battle that Hazel started to get royalties from *Breaking Glass.*

She mightn't have been rolling in it, but Hazel really had the music world at her feet after *Breaking Glass* first came out—with Duran

Duran supporting her on tour, while she performed at the first ever Slane concert with U2 and Thin Lizzy.

However, she was totally uncomfortable with her newfound fame. "It's inhibiting, if you take a girl like me who had been free and had been gypsy-like and suddenly my world becomes super small because I can't get on the bus!" she said.

"It's not about music and it's not about talent, it's about that whole celebrity culture. I found it very, very, very scary and not nice and not suiting to the way I am. I've always been an insecure person."

She told me that the sex symbol label bestowed upon her thanks to the *Breaking Glass* album's and movie's iconic artwork was even worse of a burden.

"How can that be lovely? How can it be unless you're a total egotistical nitwit! It's horrible because it puts you into a trophy status. You become aware that you are a trophy symbol," she said. "And I'm still aware of it. I mean, it's not the same now but I always think about it with regard to relationships."

Hazel's heard some unusual chat up lines at the time, but says the most bizarre was from Prince Charles backstage at a concert.

"He went, 'Ooh, little black dress. Have you got black underwear on to match?' I was really insulted. I thought 'Fuck you!'" she confessed.

"He thought it was a throw away comment to give some little girl a thrill. You know, that was his chat up line. I'm sure he wasn't trying to be insulting but I felt very insulted. I'd been invited to meet the Queen in my early days but I declined because it wasn't really what I stood for or believed in."

At the height of her fame, she dated several celebrities, such as the actor John Finch, Midge Urge, and Hugh Cornwell from The Stranglers.

She laughed when I ask about how she once kissed George

Michael for her music video single, 'Don't Touch Me,' which she describes as "sweet but embarrassing because we were really good pals".

She remembered asking him if the rumours about his sexual orientation were true.

"He never would admit it. We were mates and I would never tread on his toes and say, 'Go on, tell me'. You know, I heard rumours and I had asked him around that time and he said, 'Oh, loads of people ask me that!'" she recalled, laughing.

She was also best mates with Bob Geldof, who would star in a few films himself, and his wife Paula Yates at the time.

"I mean, there's a story! Paula was never a person for any drugs; she just didn't even drink, she went to bed early, got up at six every day," she said. "It's weird isn't it, you see that's what love can do to people."

Speaking of love, Hazel acknowledges that it's bizarre how "then fate had it" that she ended up falling in love with someone who had been in the Hari Krishna, considering her bad memories of being raped by one of the cult religion followers in Amsterdam.

"I hated them with a vengeance, to be honest, for years and years," she stated.

Hazel said she knows her story "sounds like Annie Lennox", who also once married a Hari Krishna and later got a divorce.

"She got a wrong one though! I first met him in the temple because I lived very close to the big Hari Temple just outside London," Hazel said. "I can remember seeing him with his shaved head and I thought, 'Oh, God! He's lovely'."

They didn't meet again until two years later when he'd left the cult religion and the two quickly fell in love and two years later had their lavish wedding ceremony on Venice Beach covered by *Hello* magazine.

The dwarf actor David Rappaport—famed for his role alongside John Cleese in *Time Bandits* (1981)—was Hazel's husband's best man at their nuptials. Tragically, he committed suicide only two years later.

"I knew something was wrong because my phone was clogged with journalists going, 'Could you give me a ring back please?' And I said to Kurt, 'Something's happened, I don't know where or what, but something's happened'," she said.

"Then he'd heard it on the news that David had killed himself—horrible, horrible. I think he shot himself in the heart. He was well off, doing great, but he was down in the dumps, I guess. And I think he'd been down in the dumps for a while."

Like their tragic actor friend, Hazel and Kurt were permanently based in LA during the Eighties, but decided to leave and buy a place in County Wicklow after she was wrongfully diagnosed with skin cancer.

"I thought, 'I don't want to die in Los Angeles. I don't have any affinity with it. I'm going to Ireland'. And we came here and Louis Walsh helped me find a house and get a mortgage. It was Louis that embedded me here, thank God!"

Shortly after arriving here, Hazel received a call from the US hospital with some shocking news.

"I found out I was pregnant when I got here, which was a scary thing for a minute, but then a hospital in America phoned me and said, 'We've got great news for you, we made a mistake in your diagnosis!' They said it was a mistake, but it was a big, big mistake," she said.

"If I was a smarter person in those days I think I would have sued them because it was a big upheaval. But I was glad I was away from America."

Sadly, Hazel had a miscarriage. "I was pregnant and working five/six gigs a week, up and down Ireland. And the husband was driving me. I got some kind of illness, a viral thing, and went to the doctor. The doctor said, 'I can't give you antibiotics because your pregnant'. I said, 'I know, I've got a gig in Cork, what am I going to do?' she said.

"And I went to do the gig because I had to do the gig. You can't just not do a gig. And then about two weeks after doing that gig, I was doing a gig on the Sunday [and] I started to lose the baby. And by this time I was four-and-a-half-months pregnant. So, I lost the baby, the next day, when an ambulance had to come."

It was at that moment, she believed, her marriage started to unravel. "I think that was our undoing. We struggled on till '95. Really, we never recovered from that at all," she said.

They eventually divorced in 2000. When I spoke with Hazel back in 2011, she said she didn't have any room in her heart for a new relationship. "No, I nearly was but when mom was dying [last year from cancer] I didn't have any spare part in me for anybody at all," she explained. "And I don't know whether I'll have a spare part for quite a while, to be honest. I've a lot of grieving to do [for my mom].

"We were touring like only four days after I buried her. I had to because I don't have the luxury of what fame should usually bring which is a healthy bank account. I have to work."

But it was very clear from listening to her speak passionately about music that Hazel still loves performing and recording. Maybe she might even make another film again some day. With Hazel O'Connor, you can't rule anything out.

CHAPTER THIRTEEN:

The Poignant Story Behind Adam & Paul, Mark O'Halloran

It's an eerie line in the deeply moving cult classic film *Adam & Paul*; desperate addict Paul, played by actor Tom Murphy, proclaims: "I'm going to die."

The film was released to much critical acclaim back in 2004. But all these years later, it's still a line that Murphy's co- star, Mark O'Halloran—the award- winning writer of the film—finds incredibly difficult to hear now. For little did they know when making the film that only a few short years later Tom would be telling Mark that he was actually going to die—after being struck down with cancer in his prime at only 39 years of age.

But what makes it all the more painful for Mark is something that fans of the film would never guess—the fact that the two actors were actually lovers in real life for eight years prior to making *Adam & Paul* in 2004. "We had split up about two years before we made the movie and we were still incredibly close. I miss him terribly," Mark revealed publicly for the first time during our interview.

Mark touchingly described Tom as being a soul mate. "I did feel that with him. I felt like I knew him and he knew me. And that's all you want from somebody—that they know you," he said.

Their relationship ended because Tom found himself becoming more and more in demand on Broadway and the West End after he scooped a Tony award for his captivating performance in Martin McDonagh's play, *The Beauty Queen Of Leenane* in 1998.

"We drifted apart because his career went over to America and London," Mark explained. "He was out of Ireland and it became incredibly hard to sustain. So, we drifted apart in that way, but we were still incredibly close."

The split was upsetting despite being amicable. "All break-ups are difficult and it took a while for us to find ground that we could share space with each other. We used to argue all the time anyway," he said, laughing. "We were famous for arguing. Our relationship was an eight-year long argument and so was our friendship—that arguing continued. But we were always laughing at the same time. We never fell out."

Mark first met Tom when he landed his first acting job in a production of *Juno And The Peacock* that toured the UK. "Tom was Johnny Boyle and I was his understudy. So I slept my way to the top!" he joked.

Growing up in Ennis as the third youngest of ten children, Mark had always dreamt of becoming an actor. He couldn't wait to finish school in order to move away from Ennis—not only because he wanted to pursue his dream, but also because he felt oppressed by keeping secret the fact that he was gay. "I suppose it was a secret as much as anything else and you did get the feeling at the time that you're the only gay in the village—little did I know! But you did get that feeling of isolation," he said.

Mark finally came out to his family in his early twenties and he remembers his parents being "lovely" about it.

"It was more of them assuming," he said, laughing about the experience of coming out. Affecting a camp voice, he added: "'I want to be in show business, Ma!' Well, what do you know! But I come from a loving family and they're all incredibly open and fine with it. So in that way I was always saved from the worst excesses."

Mark dropped out of university after only one year after failing his exams and went to work in Amsterdam, doing renovation work on a steel mill. After a year there, he returned home to study at the Gaiety School of Acting.

"My career has always been very slow. When I left drama school I didn't suddenly get discovered and brought to the high heights of recognition. Not that I've ever reached it anyway!" he said.

He was being modest; Mark has a slew of international awards to his name. "Ah, yeah, sure, it's true and I make a living out of it, which is great, but when I left it was like I got three lines in something and then it became four lines and then there might be stretches of unemployment or you might make your own shows," he said.

Adam & Paul is one of my all-time favourite Irish films. Mark also has a blink-and-you'll-miss-it scene in another of my favourite Irish films, *Calvary* (2014).

"I completely forgotten I was in that! Literally I was in it for a second-and-a-half. But people go, 'Was that you?' Some old wag on Twitter said, 'Have things gone so bad?' I was like, 'Yeah!'" he said, laughing.

He also had a blink-and-you'll-miss- him part in *The Guard* (2011), which was also directed by John Michael McDonagh.

"I know John and he gets a kick out of putting me in with a line-and-a-half into a film. *Calvary* is a terrific film and John is a real amazing talent. In a weird way it's lovely having your name attached to something so glorious," he said.

Mark joked that these days he is mostly offered roles as junkies, paedophiles, and idiots. "It is typecasting in a weird way; I generally stay away from romantic leads," he said.

"I did *Pride And Prejudice* but I don't think it was my finest hour by any stretch. I find it difficult—give me junkies, paedophiles, and idiots any day of the week," he quipped.

It was while putting on one on of his shows in Bewley's that serendipity stepped in and he was introduced to film director Lenny Abrahamson, who at the time was working for an ad agency. It was a meeting of minds that would change both their lives with Lenny going on to direct Mark's scripts of *Adam & Paul*, as well as the award-winning *Garage* (2007), which starred Pat Shortt.

At the time of meeting Lenny, Mark was working on the *Adam & Paul* screenplay—an idea that came to him after being shocked by the number of junkies he observed in Dublin's north inner city after he moved into a flat near Mountjoy Square.

Despite their break-up, Mark had written the screenplay with Tom in mind to play one of the lead roles. He only took the other co-starring role himself when another actor pulled out at the last minute.

Tom was a "private person" who didn't like talking about himself and they decided not to capitalise on the fact that they'd been in a relationship when they promoted the film in 2004—even though they knew it would have created acres of additional press for them.

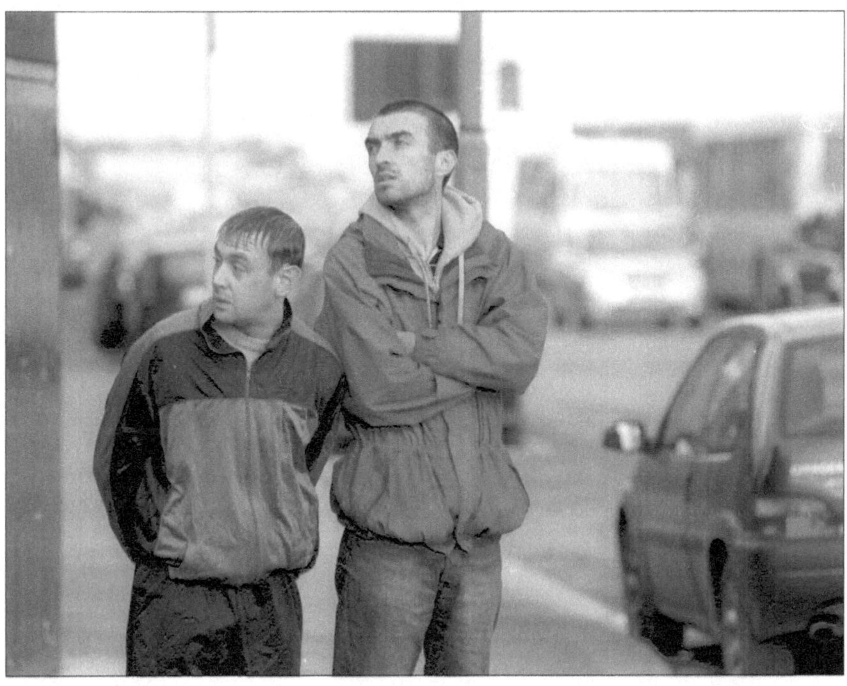

Mark recalled how one of his friend's parents made a humorous joke about it all at the time. "I have a gay friend and his father, who's subsequently passed on, was a very funny man and he loved his son and he didn't mind him being gay. One day he said to his Da, 'You know Adam and Paul are gay!' And his father goes, 'Ah Jaysus! Giving junkies a bad name!' I just think it was brilliant."

It's a film that Mark is justifiably very proud of, but understandably he added: "Although it's somewhat bittersweet to look at it watching Tom."

He continued: "*Adam & Paul* threw us into a whole other experience together because it became quite well-known here in Ireland and we couldn't go anywhere at the time without people going, 'Ah, you junkie bastards!' I still get it. I know when I'm looking pretty rough because people go, 'You're Adam and Paul!' And days I'm looking well I don't tend to get it."

Sadly, Tom was cruelly taken from this world only three years after the film's release. Mark didn't realise right up until the very end that Tom was dying. "I really was not aware that he was in such precipitous decline. And I was annoying him when I used to come visit him in the hospital; he'd be like, 'You never fuck off!'" he recalled, laughing.

"The very last time I physically met him we were in Blanchardstown Hospital (Dublin) and he told me that the chemo hadn't gone so well.

And my way around it was to bluster around it and go, 'You'll be grand'. He was poo-pooing that a little bit and I was going, 'What's going on?' And then he started to cry and I started to cry and this guy comes up to us and goes, 'You are Adam and Paul!' It made us laugh.

"But still at that time I didn't know. I said to him, 'I'm going to go do the Camino to Santiago de Compostela'. He had told me about that back in the day. I said, 'I'm going to do it'. And he thought that it was a great idea.

"The very last text that he sent me—I was two days outside of Santiago—and I still didn't realise he was as ill as he was—but he sent me a text saying, 'Keep going, brave pilgrim'. And then I got to Santiago two days later and I was texting him and I was getting no reply. The day after I flew home to Ireland and at that point he had gone into a coma and a week later he was dead."

He paused and shook his head.

"It was incredibly shocking. I mean, more shocking for his family. It was terrible for me, but for them it was dreadful, they lost their brother," he said.

Mark mourns the loss of Tom not only because he misses his friend and hates to think of a life cut so tragically short, but also because he feels Tom could have contributed so much more to the arts.

"I think he was going to do some cracking performances in his later years. So I think we've all lost something," he said.

It wasn't the first time that Mark had lost someone close to him from cancer—his brother, who was three years older than him, died from the same disease when he was only 24-years-old.

"It was traumatic for us all. It was very tough because I loved him dearly—and I still do. I think anybody who knew him was very affected by his death," he recalled. "He has a daughter who just had a little baby daughter herself lately. It was interesting to watch generations pass on without him. We were all sad but delighted and happy as well that he had become a grandfather without him knowing it."

Yet despite all the heartache in his life, Mark has an incredibly positive and upbeat demeanour.

CHAPTER FOURTEEN:

A Life In Focus, Terry O'Neill

Terry O'Neill, according to the late film director Michael Winner, is as legendary for seducing some of the most beautiful screen sirens as he is for his iconic pictures of them.

The list of Terry's lovers revealed in Michael Winner's autobiography reads like a who's who of Hollywood royalty: Raquel Welch, Ava Gardner, Julia Christie, and Jean Shrimpton. "If I listed them all we'd run to a couple dozen pages," Winner quipped in his book, describing Terry as, "without doubt the greatest seducer in the history of the world."

Ever the gentleman, the world famous photographer—who has the distinction of being the only photographer to work with every Bond actor over a 50-year timeframe—has always declined to divulge the names of his famous lovers . . . until now.

"He says I was with so-and-so and he named some of the girls. They are truthful, yes," Terry sheepishly confessed when we met back in 2013 at a London café.

Let's not forget that there was also, of course, his marriages to Oscar-winner Faye Dunaway and Vera Day, dubbed the British Marilyn Monroe. But the celebrated photographer insisted to me that he'll never resort to penning a sordid kiss-and-tell memoir.

Courtesy of Mirror Images

"I could make a fortune but I don't want to do an honest book. It's all going to stay inside me. I respect the people too much," said the London-Irish photographer, who is very proud of his Emerald Isle roots. "The greatest shame of my life is I was born English. I grew up like a Cockney, but I was conceived in the Bay of Dingle on my mother and father's honeymoon."

But why were some of the most beautiful women in the world attracted to him like moths to a flame?

"People say, 'Why do I only go out with actresses and models?' They were the only people I met, so that's who you end up taking out. Because you take out all these famous actresses people think you are Jack The Lad. But I am not really—if I had met doctors I would have asked doctors out."

Terry, who is clearly more comfortable behind the camera, shunned the limelight for years. He now only does the occasional press for exhibitions of his being held around the world from time-to-time. Notoriously guarded about his fascinating private life, Terry is known for preferring to focus on his work in any rare interview.

But he was clearly in a surprisingly reflective frame of mind when we meet, as he opened up about his tempestuous marriages to Faye Dunaway and Vera Day.

"Vera Day was stunning. She was the English Marilyn Monroe," he recalled nostalgically about the actress, who actually appeared alongside the Hollywood siren he name checks with Laurence Olivier in *The Prince and the Showgirl* (1957).

"I met her because I was taking pictures of her. I unfortunately got married too young. I remember thinking, 'What have I done?' In the '60s if you weren't married by the time you were 21 people thought you were gay!"

It was the lure of working in Hollywood that eventually pulled them apart. "I was off in America for three months at a time and we just grew apart. When you're that young you don't realise the thing about being a father. You just don't understand your responsibilities. I left her. I've all always regretted that, but what can I do?" he said.

It was an acrimonious divorce, but he and Vera "are really good friends now."

Terry's career as a celebrated photography came about by pure accident. His Irish-Catholic mother wanted him to become a priest, but he joined the army with dreams of becoming a jazz musician. Later, he joined the British airline BOAC (now British Airways) as an air steward so he could fly transatlantic routes in order to play at music venues in the US.

But the airline also assigned him to take photographs at the weekend of passengers for the in-flight magazine.

"I had to do pictures of people crying and saying goodbye. I accidentally took a picture of a bloke in the pinstripes suite, who had fallen asleep, surrounded by African chieftains. It turned out the bloke was Rab Butler, the Home Secretary," he remembered.

Terry sold the picture to the *Daily Sketch*, a now defunct national tabloid that was bought by Associated News in 1952, before merging with the *Daily Mail* in 1972. "Brian Fogarty was the *Daily Sketch* star photographer and asked would I work with him and cover for him," he explained.

Tragedy struck soon later when Fogarty was killed in a plane crash. "This was a big shock to me. And I suddenly got offered his job," Terry said.

Terry's initial assignment was to visit Abbey Road Studios to take the first ever press photograph of The Beatles for their first single, *Please Please Me*, in 1963.

"Nobody had ever taken a picture of a pop group before. It was all the singers at the time. The photo editor had said, 'Pop groups are going to be the next big thing'. I just got Ringo holding a cymbal and the guys holding a guitar. It was a very naïve picture," he said.

"It was published and the paper sold out. They thought they'd struck gold, so they said, 'Who else do you like?' I liked The Rolling Stones, so I took them and they were horrified—they thought they were five prehistoric monsters!

"They said, 'We will run them but you've got to get a good-looking group'. I got the Dave Clark Five. They were all great looking guys. They ran it as 'The Beauty and the Beast' in a double page spread. That was the real start of pop in newspapers. Then all the papers started doing it. And that was the start of the pop scene. I started at the top in a way and I never really looked back."

Terry had a good chuckle as he reflected back on how both he and The Beatles were convinced that they pop scene was only ever going to be a short-lived fad.

"We were all convinced that this thing was going to last a couple of years and we would have to get a proper job. Ringo wanted to run a chain of hairdresser's salons! Mick Jagger used to joke about singing at 40. We used to talk about all this being over. We had no idea we were going to change the world," he said, laughing at the memory of it all.

The self-disciplined Terry puts part of his own success down to his astute determination to stay away from drugs. He pointed out, "All I did was try marijuana once and it made me feel so strange I never went near it [again]. I saw the Beatles and the Stones under the influence of drugs and it wasn't a world that I wanted. I had to get up the next day and they didn't."

With an ever-growing reputation, Terry soon found himself being invited to spend time photographing many leading movie stars when Hollywood descended on Europe because of the big tax breaks that made it cheaper to film here.

"I used to go and work on like Paul Newman's movies and spend two weeks shooting him. I did Steve McQueen, Robert Mitchum, Fred Astaire, Frank Sinatra—you name them," he said.

He recounted this story to me about Paul Newman and Lee Marvin: "I remember once I went on a film with Paul Newman and Lee Marvin. I was employed for two days to shoot the film poster so I get to this place and I have to go to Denver. And I go to the set and told, 'Good luck with getting good shots because no one is talking to Lee Marvin and he is not talking to anybody and you will have to go on trying to get this yourself!'

"So, I have two days and I walked straight up to him and he was leaning against the wall and I said, 'Lee, I'm Terry O'Neill and I'm from London, England and I am over here to shoot your film poster'.

"He said, 'You're from London, England? I love the English'. And he shook my hand. I could feel the whole of the set behind me rise up in silent praise because I was the only one to get through to him. So I did all the shots and they were great shots. I mean, all these American stars, you could tell they were natural stars; they were not manufactured or something like that. And they were real men. I think the trouble today is they are all boys. There is no sort of men. I love Mickey Rourke, he is a great character. And he is still a kid. At heart, you know?"

He's not impressed with how things are run nowadays. "Now if you get a photograph of a movie star you have to do it in a hotel and you are controlled—they want one shot here, one shot there—and they want to control the copy. It's a joke now," he said.

Nor is he impressed with modern technology. "What people see now is all retouched. Pictures are about grabbing moments. To get a great picture is what it's about—not using a digital camera and everyone crowds around that machine to see. That is not photography," he said.

When asked to pick one of his most memorable times on a film set, Terry doesn't name an instant classic but rather Frank Sinatra's *Lady in Cement* (1968). Perhaps it's little wonder Terry selects such an unmemorable film as it was on location with Sinatra in San Francisco when he first met the leading co-star Raquel Welch—one of his many lovers, according to Michael Winner's candid memoir.

Terry had blagged his way into Sinatra's inner circle after the singer's ex-wife Ava Gardner—yet another of Terry's many conquests—wrote a letter of introduction for the photographer to the blue-eyed crooner.

"I became friendly with Ava Gardner on a film," is all Terry will coyly say about their relationship. "I said, 'I've got a chance to photograph your ex-husband'. She said, 'I'll write you a letter'. Really, I was more interested in photographing Raquel Welch!"

He said all this in a tone that makes it clear that he was mesmerised with the iconic sex symbol.

"Anyway, I gave this letter to Sinatra and he looks at it and reads it and smiles. And he says, 'You're with me'. And the next three weeks, I went everywhere with him. Every single place. And he was fantastic to me. And then I worked on-and-off with him over the next 30 years," he recalled.

One of Terry's most iconic photographs included in the exhibition in Cork is of Brigitte Bardot smoking a cigar, with the wind blowing her tousled hair over her seductive eyes.

"That was the last frame on the role of film and it turned out to be one of the bestselling shots of all time," he said.

Terry sounded clearly smitten when talking about her, but it also appears that the French beauty was at least one sex symbol that wasn't seduced by his charms.

"She was incredible to work with, although she didn't speak English. She was always in love with somebody or other, so you could never get to talk to her. She would dive off to the trailer with her boyfriend," he told me.

"I always thought she was a little sex symbol, but she was about five foot nine and she had great legs. A stunning looking woman. She could have been a much bigger star than she became."

Did Terry have any regrets about any possible unrequited romances?

"No, not really," he shrugged modestly. "I went out with the girls I wanted to go out with."

It was another one of Terry's iconic photographs that sparked off his most famous relationship: that with Faye Dunaway. Their romance blossomed in 1978 after he took the celebrated image that captures the Hollywood star appearing forlorn as she sits with her Oscar for the film *Network* (1976) at a breakfast table in front of the swimming pool at the Beverly Hills Hotel, with the morning newspapers strewn around her feet.

It may be a great picture, but Terry describes their marriage in 1984 as "a mistake".

Was it love at first sight?

"No, not really. I had met her before but she was married. I took that famous Hollywood picture and it all started from there. She was a great looking woman. I never really wanted to be married to an actress because I don't like that. We were together a long time," he said.

During their time together, the couple had a son, Liam Dunaway O'Neill, born in 1980. Faye publicly stated at the time that she had given birth to their son, but Terry later sensationally contradicted her by stating that their son was adopted.

He explains that Liam was six-years-old before being told the truth. "She was his mother's and that was her decision. She just wanted to protect him. I just went along with her wishes."

Is Terry still in regular contact with his son?

"I talk to him once a week. He lives in LA. He's acting in one of the films she's doing now. I think she wants him to be an actor, which I wouldn't recommend, but he is," he said, laughing.

Terry revealed he left Dunaway after becoming dissatisfied with their Hollywood lifestyle. The couple officially divorced in 1987.

"I really didn't enjoy being married to a movie star. You lose your own personality. You end up being called Mr. Dunaway instead of Mr. O'Neill," he said. "The worst thing is to be surrounded by yes people once you get somewhere. I tried to do it; I produced a film, *Mommie Dearest* (1981) [starring Faye]. It's not a world I really like. It's cutthroat actually.

"And I just thought, 'That's it! I don't want this any more. I don't want to sink into an oblivion; I've got my own career'. I just had it. It just festered."

He continued, "Yes, of course, we had some good times, but I had to get on with my life. I didn't want to live in the shadow of somebody. I was used to being my own boss.

"She didn't want to get divorced and it dragged on, but it was the best thing to do. Actually, I'm not supposed to talk about her because I signed an agreement when I got divorced."

Why was he asked to sign a confidentiality agreement as part of the divorce?

"I think movie stars get paranoid about it. I mean, I don't care; I don't want to talk about it."

So much so that he admits that he can't even think of one nice anecdote about their relationship. "It is all a blank to me now. It is all a blur. I wiped it all out. If something goes wrong I don't really want to remember it. I just cancel it out of my mind. I don't want to get down about anything; I just want to keep a positive attitude during life. All relationships are painful, you know?"

Terry likes to joke that his third marriage about ten years ago to Laraine Ashton—a former model agency executive—is most definitely "my last".

He rarely takes photographs anymore and instead prefers to focus on exhibiting his work around the world. But would he not like to be working with contemporary stars like Colin Farrell and Jude Law?

"They just haven't got it. I'm not really interested in photographing anybody. I haven't photographed anybody who was anybody for nearly 50 years. There is nobody today I really want to photograph. They all look the same to me. All the guys wear black suit and don't really stand out," he said.

"The last person I wanted to photograph was Nelson Mandela, who I did for a week for his 90th birthday. It was a wonderful experience. When he left he gave me a little wave from the car because he's frail and I nearly burst into tears. I realised I was working with a truly great man."

Battling bowel cancer in 2006 had a profound effect on Terry's own outlook on life.

"I only live really for tomorrow. I'm just glad to wake up every morning and have a brand new day now. I don't think about the past because the past is gone. I just look forward to the future. I just want to get into as many countries as I can to sell my photographs and have a great life," he said.

It's a shame Terry isn't tempted to put the unexpurgated version of his remarkable life down on paper—one that sounds like it would easily rival that of Errol Flynn's salacious memoir when it comes to seducing Hollywood starlets.

CHAPTER FIFTEEN:

Hear My Song, Adrian Dunbar

Adrian Dunbar was filled with trepidation. In fact, you could cut the tension with a knife. Word had filtered through that Brian Friel would be making a guest appearance on the opening night of one of his plays that Dunbar was directing at the Millennium Forum theatre in Derry, back in March 2013.

The then 84-year-old playwright, who passed away in 2015, had a special affiliation with the city—it was here that the influential *Translations* made its international debut back in 1980. Indeed, though Friel was born in Tyrone and the play is set in the fictional Donegal town of Baile Beag, the people of Derry like to call the three-act work their own. So it's understandable that despite his appearances in the likes of *My Left Foot*, *Hear My Song* (1991), *The General*, and *The Crying Game* (1992), actor-turned-director Adrian Dunbar was a bundle of nerves when I first met him on the opening night of his play.

By the time the curtain fell for a final time, however, Adrian had received a standing ovation and was visibly relieved to have the first, successful performance under his belt. Backstage, he introduced me to Friel, who was known for his reclusiveness. The writer offered me a warm handshake and praising the production said the show was "fantastic". This clearly made Dunbar smile following frantic weeks of intense rehearsals for the show that will tour Cork, Dublin, and Britain.

Dunbar first worked with the playwright when he staged an updated version of the classic *Philadelphia Here I Come* in London's West End in 2003.

"I don't ring him up and ask for feedback on what I'm doing. I report to him and he asks me a few questions, and from those I understand what I should be doing," said Dunbar, as we sat in a bar across the road from the theatre.

Dunbar struck me as an affable man, but it soon also became clear that he had plenty of opinions and was not one to pull his punches. He admitted that he'd only turned to directing at such a late stage in his career because there was more money to be made in movies and on TV. "It's something that I want to do. And if you're going to do some work, you might as well be lucky enough to do work that's written by Brian Friel, because already you're ahead of the posse," he said.

"I directed some plays in London in the Eighties. So, I had put my toe in the water but I was also aware that directors starting off don't get a pile of money. I stuck to the acting for a while until I earned a few quid. So, I left it a bit late."

The eldest of seven children, Dunbar grew up in a Catholic household in Enniskillen, Fermanagh. As a teenager, he escaped The Troubles by going over to New York for a while. Though that didn't leave him untouched; several friends were murdered, while other contemporaries joined the IRA. He was never tempted to get involved because, as he put it, "I was a bit of a scaredy-cat to tell you the truth, like most people. I couldn't do anything violent, that's not my personality. Everybody knows someone who was killed in The Troubles from here. We were all affected by it somehow."

He eventually left the North for good after winning a place at the Guildhall drama school in London. But the curtain almost came down on his career at the age of 21, when his 50-year-old father died suddenly. "It was a defining moment in our family. Being the oldest boy makes you feel an extra sense of responsibility," he explained.

But his younger brother went home to help their mother put food on the table for their five younger siblings, insisting that Adrian should finish his degree. "I'll be grateful to him for that forever. It was very tough for my mother at the time," Adrian told me.

Soon after leaving acting school, Dunbar was given parts in several TV movies before landing a stand-out role in *My Left Foot*, which brought him to the attention of major producers.

However, he decided to write *Hear My Song* and organise financing for the Josef Locke biopic with his friend Peter Chelsom, who directed.

"It's a lovely film and people still love it. It's a lot of people's favourite film, by the way. It's a great film," he said.

How did it come about?

"We had worked together in a play in Liverpool and Peter [the director] said to me, 'Have you ever done any writing before?' And I said, 'Yeah, I used to write when I was at school and stuff like that'. He said, 'Come over and we'll have a bash and see if we can do something together'. Because he wanted to work with somebody and we ended up spending the next 18 months on-and-off, weekends, and we wrote this script and, you know, it just got done. We had the same sense of humour—that was the main thing."

Dunbar was nominated for a BAFTA for the movie, and he realised he had made it. He actually met his future wife, Australian actress Anna Nygh, who appeared in TV shows like *The Sweeney* and *Minder*, at the BAFTAs. The couple were introduced by Anna's friend, and Val Kilmer's former wife, Joanne Whalley, who later co-starred with Dunbar in the 2005 thriller *Child of Mine*.

"I met Anna backstage at the Royal Court in London. She came to see a play I was in and Joanne wanted us to meet up. I'd seen Anna anyway and started chatting to her backstage. Later Joanne said, 'I'm trying to introduce you to this friend of mine', and I said, 'You're too late. I've met this girl over here'. And Joanne said, 'Oh, that's her'."

Was it love at first sight?

"Yeah, that type of thing," he said, nodding.

What made him think she was the woman for him?

"I like blondes with green eyes. That was the first thing. I just liked her. She's got a great attitude. She sings. And she makes me laugh. So, those were the main things."

Dunbar admitted it was struggle at first to bond with his stepson, who was six at the time. "It's very difficult having a stepchild. It's tough but we're great friends. Ted's doing really well and I'm really proud of him," he confessed.

I presume, particularly since Ted was six at the time, it was difficult for the child to get used to his mother having a new man around?

"Oh, yeah. I think that's always a difficulty thing. It's hard. You have to find a place where you're both happy to accept each other and that just takes a while."

During his 30s, Dunbar became disillusioned with the quality of the television work being offered to him. "You get a bit fed up with it. And I felt the quality of the work had gone down a bit," he said. "But in retrospect that could've been me thinking, 'I need to get out of this and do something else for a while'."

He went through a fallow period in his forties and it was then he decided to stretch himself. "I was getting some work but what it made me do was focus on other things," he said. "So, I went back to music and started a band.

"I was writing a lot, getting more involved in writing things, going back to directing, going back to the theatre. And now I find myself trying to juggle a lot of things. I put a lot of things in train during those fallow years."

He also decided to stop drinking at 40 because he could have been using the valuable time to work on projects. He explains he wasn't an alcoholic—but was the heavy boozing getting him down?

"Well, yeah, it's a depressant. And also it makes you look at the world in a different way. Alcohol is a chemical and it changes the way you think and suddenly the glass was half empty instead of half full," he said.

"I thought, 'I've too much to do and this stuff is getting in the way and I can't be at the party any more. I'm enjoying myself too much'. I was afraid that it was going to interfere with what I wanted to do with my life and I wasn't happy with the space it was taking up. I had to rein it in quite a bit because I was having too much of a good time. I don't have a problem, it's just that I don't want to have a problem."

I tell him I understand exactly what he's saying.

"I'm glad you get me because a lot of people don't get me," he continued. "It seems to me it's very necessary, people are desperate to find out that you're only giving up drink if you have a really a big problem with it, because they know that deep down themselves that they should probably be cutting back on the amount of alcohol they're taking."

Though he's one of Ireland's most successful actors, Dunbar has turned his back on Hollywood. The reason?

His answer surprised me. "The money is not as good," he said. "You get paid in dollars, convert that into real money, take state tax out of it, take the damn IRS, take your agent out of it, take your manager out of it, which you've got to have there, take your publicist out of it, which you've also got to have there—suddenly that money is eaten away.

"There's only a few people who actually make big dough there. You're much more in control of what you do here. I'm having a great time. I'm very happy with the decisions I made. I don't know what I would've missed by going to Los Angeles."

Speaking of Hollywood, Adrian once landed a major role in *Star Wars: The Phantom Menace* (1999) and was even used in the publicity stills to promote it. But director George Lucas cut his scenes at the last minute. Did he confront Lucas over it?

"Oh, I wish I could say I had an argument with George Lucas, but I didn't," he said, well able to afford a laugh at it all now. "I got a call to say, 'George wants to tell you that your character doesn't appear in the film. He thought he did but he's actually fighting in the Clone Wars'. So, that was it."

Dunbar will reject roles if it clashes with his family life. A few years ago he turned down a major film being shot on location in Budapest because his family were at the time moving home in London.

"I could've gone to America, but both the children were quite young at that point. I didn't think I could up sticks and go over," he said. "Also, I'm a bit of a homebird. I like Ireland. I do like the quality of the work that you can do in Ireland.

"You can affect things in Ireland. I know there are some very influential Irish actors in America. For example, Gabriel Byrne is somebody who people greatly respect over there and listen to what he says, and rightly so."

But he remains sanguine about his career. "There are things that I've turned down that have been successful but I'm still happy that I've turned them down," he concluded.

Thinsulate

CHAPTER SIXTEEN:

Throwing it all Away, Alan Devlin

Alan Devlin was once lauded as one of Ireland's finest stage actors after winning a prestigious Olivier award—the English version of a Tony—back in 1983. He was, according to his contemporaries, a better stage actor than Richard Harris. But within a few short years of his triumphant appearance on the West End, Devlin ended up homeless and begging on the streets as his addiction with booze and "dabbling in drugs" almost killed him.

Devlin destroyed his promising career when he famously stormed off stage back in 1987. During that infamous production of Gilbert and Sullivan's *HMS Pinafore*, an inebriated Devlin stunned cast members and audience alike when he announced, "Fuck this for a game of soldiers, I'm going home!"

He then negotiated his way through the orchestra pit and shouted to his onstage colleagues, "Finish it yourself!" as he absconded to the nearest pub for a stiff brandy.

The actor only spoke publicly about the incident once—to myself, about a year or so before his death in 2011. He was initially reluctant to discuss it when we met for his first major interview in decades, at his council flat in Dalkey, South Dublin.

"I'm not a great man for the past, so if you're going to just concentrate on that you're not going to get much out of me. I've moved on," he told me, explaining that the "jumping off", as he puts it, is only going to be "fleetingly referred to" in his planned memoir, which he sadly never finished.

But over the next two hours, Devlin did open up to me about his extraordinary past, including the Gaiety incident. Devlin, who underwent major lifesaving heart surgery six months before our interview, knew that not only was he lucky to still be alive, but also fortunate to be given a chance to tread the boards again. When we met, the Oscar-winning producer Noel Pearson—the very same producer who was behind the aforementioned production of Gilbert and Sullivan's *HMS Pinafore*—actually hired Devlin again to star in a production on the very same stage he had stormed off years previously.

"I didn't think I'd be working in The Gaiety again. I didn't think I'd be in a nice pad; I didn't think I'd have a car. I mean, I slept in a skip for a couple of weeks. I was in a hostel. I've made a remarkable recovery," he said, pouring us both tea before sitting down to commence the interview.

Earlier that week, Devlin was back at the Gaiety for his first read through of the play with the cast. But before signing him up for the production, did Pearson discuss the infamous walk-out with Devlin?

"I don't think we had a talk. We met for a few lunches. I consider him a friend. I'm very fond of him. He may have been sounding me out and seeing 'How well is this guy because he is a fucking lunatic?'

"And then I did a couple of small films and I was straight and even when I wasn't working I was straight. After the death of my father I was straight. He saw I'd given it up rather than I was just off it."

How did he feel when first offered the part, particularly considering the combination of Pearson and the Gaiety?

"I was a bit apprehensive. Just very slightly. For a day or two I got a bit fearful. Then there was the odd wag making the joke: 'There will be a bookie coming to see if you get through the whole lot', you know. And that kind of stuff. I'm sick and tired of it," he said.

"But now the apprehension has turned to anticipation. Keen anticipation because I love Barry McGovern and Gerry McSorley. It's a good cast. We had a read through it and there was no weak link, as far as I could see. Except me probably!"

Did Alan feel he had to prove himself because of all that's happened in the past?

"No. I just go on and do the job as best I can. I was quite a sick person, quite a sick addict."

Devlin's acting career took off when as a young 17-year-old he was encouraged by fellow actor Niall O'Brien to walk into the Abbey Theatre and ask for an audition. But after several years he got fired from the Abbey because he "was missing, drunk" and moved to London, where he quickly picked up work at the Half Moon Theatre. Shortly afterwards, he was given a big role in a BBC mini-series, *The Crezz* and appeared in the likes of *The Irish RM*, *Remington Steele,* and *The Long Good Friday.*

But despite "making a name for myself", Devlin was already showing signs of going off the rails and would "sleep in an abandoned car" when his money ran out, while waiting for the next gig.

"I was in trouble with drink at about 18, but I wouldn't accept it. Everybody knew I was fucking drinking too much, but I didn't see it," he confessed. "I walked off the stage in the West End. Warren Mitchell was in the bed, supposedly having had a stroke, and all he can say is, 'More tea' or something. And once again, I just said, 'This is bollock! I'm going for a drink'."

It was during his time in London that Devlin started experimenting with drugs. He confessed: "I never actually shot anything up, but I used for a while. I experimented with dope in the Sixties, but I never got into it.

"And I did a bit of coke when I was on a big show in the West End and I was moving in these kinds of circles. It was a different type of buzz than drink. It's really sharp. Everything becomes so sharp. But I stopped dabbling in drugs years ago."

Despite the heavy drinking and drug taking, Devlin was bestowed with the West End's highest accolade, an Olivier Award for his critically acclaimed performance in *A Moon for the Misbegotten*.

He was on his way to the big time, but he got "pissed off and came home". But after the infamous Gaiety incident he went completely off the rails with his drinking.

"I was setting up my returning to drink and thinking I'd escape the consequences of sleeping on the roads and begging. Addiction. Pure addiction," he said. "I descended into the hell of fucking full blown alcoholism and everything in rag order and I ended up living on the streets."

Reflecting on the Gaiety episode that is now the stuff of theatre legend, Devlin revealed: "It was Madness. I was out in Sandycove and the show was finished. I did one on Saturday and there was one on the Monday and I got fucking locked over the weekend.

"And I met Gabriel Byrne in the Eagle House because one of his parents had died. And God bless him, he was trying to get me into a taxi. 'Alan, you have a fucking show tonight. Go now before it's too late'.

"But I stopped the taxi at the Punch Bowl and again in Ballsbridge and again in Stephen's Green and I had another large Bloody Mary in each of them. So, I was ramrod stiff drunk going on. I don't know how I even got past the stage door. I got into the costume, beside John Kavanagh, and nobody seemed to cop it.

"But the minute the curtain went up—bang. The bank of lights hit me. I knew I was fucked. I knew there was no way I was going to get out of this. I hadn't got the wherewithal to feign a heart attack. That's what I should have done; just gone, 'Ahhhh, I don't feel well', but instead I just said, 'Bollock to it'."

He paused, shaking his head at the memory of his outrageous actions. "Grandiosity. Not thinking of the consequences at all. And I didn't go off the wings, I went over the musicians. And I remember the orchestra conductor going, 'Fucking hell! What's he up to?'

"I said something like, 'Fuck this for a game of soldiers. Finish it yourselves!' And I went across the road to Sinnotts for a drink."

Dressed in flamboyant admiral's costume with a sword, Devlin causally asked the barman for a large brandy. "And he went, 'Yes, sir', and then he did a double take. He said, 'What the fuck?' I mumbled something like, 'Oh, it's an early interval'. But he knew. But he didn't know what the fuck was going on. But he knew the show was only gone up about 20 minutes.

"I'd forgotten I had a radio mic; a little cigarette packet-sized thing on my belt, under the tailcoat. I had completely forgotten that the stage director could hear all this. 'He's in Sinnotts. No, he's gone, he's moved to Neary's now'. And they came out and disrobed me in the laneway and gave the costume to a guy who had done the part and they somehow struggled through it."

Devlin woke the next morning feeling "fucking awful" and filled with "remorse and guilt". He continued: "I got the 'you'll never work in this town again' line. But everybody forgets that when I jumped off the stage in *Pinafore*, I actually went back," (for the West End Production in the Old Vic).

"Noel asked me back for the London production and said, 'But you'd have to have a minder'. The rule was that the minder stayed in the spare room in the apartment I had in London."

A determined Devlin kept to it and didn't touch a drop of alcohol during the run in the Old Vic, but the Actors' Equity Association refused him permission to work in the Broadway production when Pearson took the show there, demanding that an American actor got the part. Soon afterwards, he was hitting the bottle again.

"The drink took hold of me and I didn't work for ages," he said.

He revealed how his agent Theresa Nolan kept him going by finding him small parts and lending him money. "She kept a roof over my head when I hadn't got a penny. She gave me the rent. I would have been homeless many times except she somehow had faith. I love Theresa, a great friend, much more so than an agent.'

He eventually got a good part in the Irish TV soap *Fair City*, but that also ended in tears.

"I enjoyed it. It was a great job. But I fucked that up as well. They let me go, was the nice word for it. I went in and—I was in bad form or something—and I decided to say, 'This is a load of shite. I could write better myself'. I fucked the script on the ground. The arrogance!" he said.

With an ever-growing reputation for being difficult and unreliable, Devlin found it impossible to get work and was soon on the streets and begging for money to get his next drink.

"Now, I didn't sit with a cup. It was going up to the odd bloke. Not all the time somebody I knew, somebody I vaguely knew. I would follow them into the jacks or something and put the hammer on them," he said.

"I was begging from buskers. I remember in Galway one time stopping a busker and asking him for a few bob, for a can. Not a good place to be at all."

He can't recall the incident himself, but he remembered hearing how he once stopped Noel Pearson's brother to plead for money.

"I heard this second-hand. He said, 'This is going to have to stop'. I was gasping for a drink. And he took out the wallet and had the fiver—and the fiver was like between you and me—and I copped somebody I knew, a fellow actor or neighbour or something, and I couldn't be seen begging on the street, so I snapped the fiver out of your man's hand and waved it in front of him and said, 'Now, listen, this is the last fucking time'. Talk about thinking on your feet," he told me.

I remember I once met Alan in a bar; we didn't know each other, but within seconds of striking up a conversation, he was asking me to buy him a pint, while he cowered in the corner, to avoid the bar staff. The barman later took me to one side and warned me not to buying drink for him.

Alan survived several violent encounters on the mean streets of Dublin and "was seriously beaten up a couple of times. I was hospitalised once or twice". On one terrifying occasion he was almost murdered when he tried to sell his car to buy drink.

"They were known to the police. I met them in a pub and we went back to show them the car. I had forgotten the keys, so I had a naggin in my pocket and I broke the window. It was me and these dodgy characters trying to hotwire a car," he said.

But the Special Branch pounced on them and only allowed them to go when Devlin proved the car was his and lied that he was "was going to let the lads sleep in it".

He continued: "We went back and they said, 'You're a fucking snout, aren't you?' A spy for the cops. I was half-drunk, trying to worm my way out of it. It was a very confined space and I said, 'Lads, come on! I'm an actor'. And the wallop I got and he said to me, 'Who are you calling a nagger?' Alan said.

"And they laid into me. One of them had a wire around my neck and they said, 'Fuck him into the stream'."

Did he think he was going to be murdered?

"I did. Fortunately, one of them got me by scruff of the neck and fucking me out of the wagon and said, 'Consider yourself a lucky man'. I got a couple of yards up the road and I collapsed. A passing taxi driver took me to hospital. I was very lucky. They're the kind of situations I used to end up in," he said.

A couple of years ago, Devlin was told by a doctor he'd be lucky to survive another two years if he didn't stop drinking. Miraculously, he managed to stop for good some 18 months ago now, after vowing at his 96-year-old father's deathbed never to touch alcohol again.

"Thank God I made it up with him before he died. He was heart-broken. He was like a man standing on the shore, watching his eldest son drown. And no matter what he did he didn't seem able to stop it," Alan said.

"But when I went to see him, about two days before he died, he took my hand and he looked at me and said, 'I'm no fool, I know I'm dying. But for God's sake now that you've got hold of it don't blow it again. Don't pour your life down the drain'. That was really the nail that I decided I'm not going to drink again.

"I regret the appalling behaviour toward my family and a lot of friends and girlfriends. Wonderful women who loved me. They begged me to stop drinking and I wouldn't. I left one of them at a doorway once and she said, 'Please come in, don't go out'; and I said, 'I'm going to fucking explode if I don't have a drink'. I left her on her knees, weeping behind the door."

But Devlin is now set for a major comeback when the curtain rises on March 10 with Pearson's production of Brian Friel's play in the Gaiety. The Oscar-winning producer is also planning to bring the play to Broadway and has also offered Devlin a role in his next movie, which will be based on Sebastian Barry's novel, *A Long Long Way*.

He insisted that he is not planning too far ahead.

"I never think like that. Whatever happens, happens. Not at all, I could be dead tomorrow. We all could. The heart surgery taught me that. From my perspective, when you've given it up [drink], I've given it up for today. That's the programme I'm involved in. A day at a time," he said, getting up to make some more tea.

"I slew onto the fast lane on the excitement. Now, I like nothing better than to come home and watch the box and drink tea."

After our interview, Devlin kept in touch with me and was kind enough to send me tickets to one of his plays and bring me backstage to introduce me to his fellow cast members. In return, I set-up a meeting for him with the publisher of Transworld Ireland to discuss his memoir. Sadly, he died before he got to complete the book.

Departm
Arts, Spor
Tourism
IFTN

CHAPTER SEVENTEEN:

About a Girl, Victoria Smurfit

What's in a name? Quite a lot if it happens to be Smurfit. So much so that when actress Victoria Smurfit first trod the boards, she was told she would never make it in Ireland unless she used a stage name.

But the feisty redhead balked at the casting agent's suggestion. "In a town this small, if you put yourself up there someone's going to knock you. I was told I would never work here if I didn't change my surname," she told me. "I wasn't happy about that, so I said, 'I won't work in Ireland'."

Ironically, Victoria's breakthrough roles were in Ireland, albeit for British productions. She may have had the proverbial last laugh by insisting on sticking to her guns, but it irks Victoria when people assume that being the scion of a wealthy dynasty opened doors for her in show business.

"It's quite the opposite," she insisted. "My family works in a completely different business. I came from a successful family, so I didn't want to be the one who got it wrong. But at the same token I had to stay true to myself and do what I wanted to do.

"I always wanted to just stand on my own feet because if you're going to like me or dislike me, do it for what I've done or achieved. I don't want credit for something my dad or uncle has done. And fair play to them and I raise my hat. That was their great success.

"My mum was very pro working out what we wanted to do and to chase it because nobody's going to hand it to us. I'm very lucky. I always wanted to be a working actor and I've managed to do that."

Victoria, or Vicky as she prefers to be called by friends, insisted that she's not as posh as her family dynasty would suggest. "I have a face for the princess or the pauper. My mask when I go out into the public arena is a glamorous look. I really want to do a home-grown film to be divested of this glamorous image," she said.

Growing up in Dalkey, Victoria insisted that she wasn't spoilt by her parents, who instilled in her a real sense of values. She recalled having to clean the car for extra pocket money. "The only difference was the car was a Rolls," she quipped.

Perhaps unusual for such a comfortable upbringing, Victoria maintained that she wasn't lavished with toys as a child, insisting that—just like the majority of Irish children in the gloomy 1980s—she too relied heavily on her inventiveness and imagination.

"You didn't have 'stuff' in Ireland at that time. Now, I bet your kid's got a million plastic multicolour geckos because that's how life is. But back then we'd have a cornflake box and you'd turn it into something," she said.

Or if she hadn't got a cornflake box in hand, Victoria would play for hours with an imaginary friendly ghost in the family's sprawling home.

"My mum's got a great imagination and she sort of fed that to us. And you'd go [upstairs] and chase Charlie the Ghost around. I'm absolutely sure Charlie the Ghost was Mum out the back," said Victoria, pausing to make some howling ghoulish sounds, "but as far as I was concerned it was absolutely real. She was very good at those things."

Does Victoria still believe in ghosts?

"I'm going to sound like such a nut, but, yeah. I hope not, but I'm not a nut, but I believe that it would be arrogant to think that this was it!" she confessed.

I tell her not to feel silly, recounting for her how the former Miss World Rosanna Davison once told me that she believed she might've been married to her father, the musician Chris de Burgh in a previous life!

"OK! I probably won't go there!" Victoria said, pausing to laugh.

Continuing with her thoughts on ghosts, Victoria told me: "I believe there's more than us. I believe when my granny passed she was with us for a while. I entirely believe that, categorically, people choose to stay for a while to keep an eye on their friends until they're ready to move on."

She recalled feeling her grandmother's presence in the house after she died. "I went down to the kitchen on the day and I said to my mam, 'Granny's gone'. And she said, 'I know, she left this morning'. Because mum could also feel that she was there. It's almost as if you still have a cloak of the person around you. I don't even know how you put that in words. . . ."

To illustrate her point, she pressed her hand on my shoulder. "It's almost [like] that. We could be sitting here chatting and you forget that that's there until I did that,' she said, lifting her hand off my shoulder. "And on the eighth day or ninth day she knew that we were all fine and she moved on. I find it comforting. I chat to my grandmother to help me sort things out. It's nice to have somebody. It's nice to have a concept of something bigger and greater than we are. There's got to be more than us, isn't there?"

Victoria's formative years—either in Dalkey or later in boarding school in Ascot—weren't completely idyllic and stress free experiences. During the height of the Troubles, Victoria's parents became alarmed for their children's safety after the supermarket tycoon Ben Dunne was kidnapped for ransom by the IRA back in 1981.

"Mum had said it to us, 'Naughty men had taken away some friends of dad and we just had to be careful'. It was all part of our reality. It was a scary time," she recalled.

"We had to be very aware of it and we just had to be careful of people we didn't know. As a little one, you sort of accept whatever you're told because your reality is whatever it is. We weren't allowed to answer the door if somebody came. You just had to be a little bit security conscious.

"Now, as I look back at it, I'm sure it must have been terribly scary for [my parents] because there was only sort of three or four families at the time who were financially employing a lot of Ireland. It was a tough time at those times.

"As you get older, I was very aware of this strange sense of being liked or disliked for something I had nothing to do with and that would frustrate me greatly. People would be charming to me, overly charming, or overly sniffy with me and, as far I was concerned, I did nothing to warrant that. And, of course, it would be because of the surname and what was going on in the 80s.

"I'm so proud because my family were giving vast amounts of people an income and a livelihood. It makes me enormously proud. I've got a hell of a backdrop to be as good or as nice as because they were fantastic employers from what I hear."

When her father became tired of commuting between his home in Dublin and work in London, Dermot Smurfit moved the family permanently over to the UK in 1987, into a £1.2 million hunting lodge in Windlesham, Surrey.

Victoria was 14 at the time and she hated having to uproot from Dublin. "I was dreading it, but we all did it as a family. I went into a school where everybody was called Camilla and Lucinda and they all said—putting on posh English accent— "'Oh, my God! You're Irish? How lovely. Have you ever seen a bomb? Has your house ever been blown up?' You know, questions like that, which were just born out of not knowing any better and being 14 and living in Surrey.

"I remember the drama teacher who got me involved in drama. We did a play in my last year in school and she came back, as my mum had said, 'Why don't you all come back for tea and sandwiches afterwards after the matinee'. So, my teacher came to my house and she didn't speak to me. And she refused to sit down on the sofa. And I said, 'What's wrong with you?'

"And she replied," continued Victoria, suddenly switching into a perfect working class English accent to mimic her former teacher, "'You've lied to me! I thought you were here on a scholarship! [I thought] You're Irish and you're living in a caravan!' I said, 'That's reverse snobbery. How did you manage to think that?' In her head, I was her touchstone to her world and this sea of nice English girls.

"I had to let her know she was being a bit of an ignorant pig! By telling her, 'You're being an ignorant pig. Don't be ridiculous. I can still be Irish. I've been very lucky. I've been blessed, so it doesn't make [any difference] . . .' I don't know what she imagined."

Growing up, Victoria was a very affable and obedient child, but she recalled having "moments of rebellion" when her parents divorced when she was 16.

"I don't think anybody is able to divorce and for it not to affect the kids, or anybody in that situation. It was heartbreaking at the time. Confusing and bizarre. For us, as kids, it appeared to have come out of nowhere, but obviously my parents were going through their own private hell. And more power to them, they were able to keep us out of that for so long," she said.

Perhaps surprisingly for such a successful actress Victoria says she is not bothered if she doesn't make it big in Hollywood. But she did give Tinsletown a shot. Prior to starting her family, Victoria appeared alongside Chow Yun-Fat and Sean William Scott in the action flick *Bullet Proof Monk* (2003) and she also had a smaller part in *The Beach* (2000), which starred Leonardo DiCaprio. And closer to home she had a decent part in *About a Boy* (2002) with Hugh Grant. Later, she starred with Jonathan Rhys Meyers in the US-UK series *Dracula*, which ran from 2013-2014.

But, Victoria confessed, she found it a lonely existence working on *Bullet Proof Monk*. Speaking about her short time in Hollywood, Victoria explained: "I don't think my heart was in it, particularly. I went over and I met a lot of people and it was all going fine. If I really wanted it I would have chased it. I didn't want to change everything on the never-never when I've got a good solid career in the UK and was living happily here.

"I wanted to have kids and have my kids grow up here and be educated here. So for the last couple of years I've been [based here] and working over in the UK because they were young enough but now Evie is going to school and I'm just in the next life stage. You just have to keep re-evaluating. I just think choosing one path when you're 18 and following it from there on in without veering off the path is a bit naive, you know?"

After over an hour of chatting together, as the interview winded down, Victoria mused: "I'm always re-evaluating. Is it working for me? Individually but, more importantly, is it working for the family as a whole? I feel very lucky that I've got a whole and very chaotic life. Your life sometimes just guides you down a path, really. I didn't want to waste ten years of my life banging on a door that wasn't going to open. It might have opened, I don't know."

Victoria is clearly happy with the path she took. . . .

CHAPTER EIGHTEEN:

An Irish Legend Niall Tóibín

As he confesses himself, Niall Tóibín was "no angel" during his wild years of heavy boozing that almost destroyed his marriage and acting career.

But the legendary actor and comedian, who is now almost 90, once revealed to me that his love for his deceased wife was so strong that he was never once unfaithful during those wild years—even though countless women tried to seduce him when he was at the height of his fame starring on Broadway.

"I did have a lot of American ladies coming onto me. I have all the natural instincts; I'm no angel, but one look and you'd say, 'She's not going to lead me into sin'," he confessed.

And throughout their rock-solid marriage of 45 years, Niall dutifully phoned his wife every night when away working on stage or on a film set—only once ever failing to get through to her and that was because the home phone was temporarily broken.

So, such was their close bond, when his wife passed away from cancer in 2002, the last thing Niall expected was to fall for another woman—but that's exactly what happened. In his mid-70s, Tóibín found happiness again in his twilight years and the couple were together for at least five or six years by the time we spoke.

"I have a partner, but I haven't got permission to tell you anymore," he chuckled, before adding: "I'd rather not go into it at all, but I do have a relationship with a lady who prefers to remain private. I have to be insistent because she does not relish any publicity at all."

But even though he says coming to terms with the death of his beloved wife Judy has gotten easier with time, the father of five children added that there isn't a single day when he doesn't think about their lifetime of memories together.

"She's always there in conversation, if nothing else. She was a wonderful woman," he said. "But she had very bad health for years and she never complained. She was very ill for the last year of her life. It was terrible. She was very brave and she had a great spirit.

"She had the first bout [of cancer] and she recovered completely from it and then ten years later it came back again. She fought it for about a year-and-a-half. She was a fighting baby, I tell you. But she eventually ran out of steam and couldn't fight any longer. I was glad that she was out of pain because it was terrible to watch. That might have been selfish, but it was just like the agony was finished for everybody now, you know?"

How did they first meet?

"I was in digs. One morning, I was shaving and the bathroom door burst open and this girl said, 'Jesus, Mary, and Joseph—get out of my fecking way, I'll be late for work'. And she started doing her things and off she went. I said to the landlady later, 'She has some neck'. She said, 'Oh, I know who that one is—she's mad as a hatter. That was Judy Kenny'.

"She was a fine looking bird, I can tell you. So, that evening, I was having tea in the digs and she came in and said, 'Sorry about that this morning, but I was late for work'. I said, 'I'm going to the dogs in Harold's Cross. Will you come?' She said yes and that was it. We were going out together for a while and then we broke up for a while and then we got together again and we got married."

Born in 1929, Niall was one of seven children raised in an Irish speaking family. He recalled: "My father was an old-fashioned Gaelic Leaguer and we spoke nothing but Irish at home. It could be very amusing at times. You had people with a *cúpla focal* [a couple of words in Irish] striving to communicate with my father, who would look at them with a slight small in his eye, but he still wouldn't talk English to them."

It was his fluency in Irish that helped Niall launch an acting career that would see him go on to star alongside some of Hollywood's biggest names like Tom Cruise, Pierce Brosnan, Peter O'Toole, Julie Christy, Robert Mitchum, and Kurt Russell.

Niall caught the acting bug while in school. "The late Eddie Goulding, who was an Abbey actor, he was a teacher in the North Monastery when I was in second year. I remember we did a Passion Play and Eddie played Christ and when he was up on the cross half of his class were playing the Roman rabble and they really took to the plot with great gusto and they were walloping poor Eddie up on the cross. He could hardly lean down from the cross and tell them to, 'Fuck off!' It was hilarious. I was only eight years old," he recalled, laughing.

After leaving secondary school, Niall was still only 17-years-old when he moved to Dublin to work as a civil servant, while trying to get his foot into the door of acting. 'RTÉ did lots of Irish plays, so because my Irish was good and my acting was also on par, I began to be called in fairly regularly," he said.

Niall got his first big break when he was selected for the lead role in the world premiere of Brian Friel's *Lovers* at The Gate. What happened next, he describes, as a "kick in the hole". The play was picked up for a Broadway run, but the producers decided they needed a big name for Niall's part and replaced him with the American comedian Art Carney, who was nominated for a Tony Award for his performance.

"God closes one door, but he opens another," he said, philosophically.

In a twist of fate, this rejection was actually the making of Niall's subsequent acting career—soon afterwards he received outstanding plaudits and top theatre awards when staring on Broadway in the Tony award-winning production of *The Borstal Boy*, playing Brendan Behan. It's a part that is still very much synonymous with him even to this day, so much so that one national newspaper recently mistakenly printed a front page picture of Niall in an article about Behan.

"I wouldn't have being available to do the Brendan Behan part had I gone with the Friel play. My whole life was really changed and for the better. I played in nine different productions of *Borstal Boy* over the years, including six months on Broadway. That was huge. That's what changed my entire career, really. It was wonderful, but I nearly drank myself to death."

Niall says it wasn't unusual for him to walk onto the Broadway stage, or the Abbey, without spending the better part of the pre-performance day knocking back pints in the pubs.

"I wouldn't be a hell-raiser but I was certainly boisterous. There was almost a kind of a creed in the Abbey that if you didn't drink you couldn't act! I remember going on the stage in The Abbey, with half of the cast maybe, spending the last two hours before the show in the pub and then coming in to do the show. There was a very free and easy attitude about drink. I was an alcoholic. After each show, I'd get home at three o'clock in the morning absolutely pissed. And I had the money to do it. It's amazing that I never got into any real trouble," he confessed.

He remembered going on heavy drinking sessions with the actors Peter O'Toole and Donal McCann, who starred alongside Robert De Niro and Sean Penn in *We're No Angels* (1989), during a production of *Waiting for Godot*.

"We were invited to a university ball in Nottingham. O'Toole was knocking back the brandy. I was having more than a few. But, anyway, we were all pretty well pissed, to be honest with you," he said.

"There was a raffle for a car and O'Toole was asked to draw the ticket. He got out and pulled out the ticket. 'Number 425. Nobody here with that?' And he draws out another ticket and whatever it was 325. And this person with the second ticket came up and he said, 'There you are; you've won the car'.

"And then this lady, who hadn't been there because she was powdering her nose, came back in, someone said, 'What number was your ticket?' Because it struck a bell with them. It was the first ticket. She'd won the raffle and she was still at the dance, so he had no right to go on. I think Mr. O'Toole had to buy her a car!"

Why did he stop drinking?

"I was causing my wife an awful lot of distress and other people were getting pissed off looking at me. I realised that I was breaking up my marriage. My wife Judy—God be good to her—would be asking me, 'You have to stop drinking'. I got to the stage where it was either the drink or a livelihood and I had to pack it in.

"When I stopped Judy never mentioned the matter again. Never again. She obviously was very grateful; but don't ask me how I did it. I didn't go to any treatment, I just stopped. There was no medical road . . . I'm not boasting, but I'm naturally very strong minded and, when I'm very determined to do a thing, I usually stick it out.

"In a way, it was a form of spite. I wouldn't give the satisfaction to people who said, 'Oh, Jesus . . . he won't last long on the drink'. And I decided, 'Fuck 'em, I will [stop]'."

It's forty years since a drop of alcohol last passed his lips. After he pulled himself together, Niall's acting career really took off. He jokingly says that he made a career out of "playing drunks, IRA men, and priests" in TV shows and films, even starring in some Disney productions. Apart from playing Brendan Behan and doing his one-man show, Niall is perhaps most fondly remembered for his roles in *The Irish RM, Ballykissangel,* and *Brideshead Revisited.*

Once or twice, Niall was meant to go out to Hollywood for parts, but the deals always seemed to fall apart at the last minute. But he was always in demand in Ireland and the UK, as well as Broadway, which meant that he could afford to be relatively selective about his roles. To such an extent that Niall even rejected the chance to appear in John Boorman's *Excalibur* because it would've meant wearing a helmet in all his scenes, which he felt was pointless because the audience wouldn't have seen his face even once throughout his time on screen.

Such was the universal appeal of BBC's *Ballykissangel*, Niall has been recognised in some very unusual places. "I brought my sister and her husband for their fiftieth anniversary to New York," he recalled. "We were walking up this hill and there was this big black guy leaning on the railings and he looked over and said, 'Hey, you're the priest!'

"My sister couldn't get over that he recognised me from *Ballykissangel*. I said, 'They have television here too, you know?' People all over the place relate to it. Thank God, it's still being shown all around the world. It was a great series, it was extremely well made." In a clear sideswipe at the Irish national broadcaster, he added: "I don't think RTÉ have ever produced anything of that quality."

Ballykissangel was the launching pad for several young Irish actors, including Victoria Smurfit and Colin Farrell. But an outspoken Niall admitted to being taken aback by how the reformed hell-raiser Farrell became a Hollywood A-list star, as he could personally never see what all the fuss what about with. He confessed: "I can tell you now, you're no more surprised than I am. He certainly didn't show any sign of it then. He was only a kid and he didn't have very much to do in *Ballykissangel*."

He also worked with Tom Cruise, playing his father in *Far and Away* (1992). Speaking about Cruise's accent in the film, Niall admitted: "It was terrible, but I'm sure he's [not] worried," he said, laughing.

"Tom Cruise was actually almost timid. A very nice man, but reserved. He wouldn't be joining in the conversation, telling bawdy yarns; he was very private, but very pleasant."

He's also worked with some of the biggest British actors, both on stage in the National Theatre and in British television productions.

"My great boast, which is complete vanity, is that I worked in a television series about the life of Wagner. At the king's wedding, I was one of the ministers and the other three ministers were John Gielgud, Laurence Olivier, and Ralph Richardson. They were the only three [actors] that had been knighted and it was the first time that all three had appeared in any production together—and they never appeared together again. And the fourth man in the quartet was me, Niall Tóibín from Blackpool, Cork," he said.

In more recent years, Niall appeared on our screens in RTÉ's recently axed hospital drama, *The Clinic*. How did he feel when his character was suddenly killed off?

"I didn't give a bollocks. The producer said, 'That was a great scene today. You've great stuff in the next episode. Very dramatic stuff. As a matter of fact, you're in a car crash and killed'. The fucking eejit. What kind of a man would congratulate one of the cast that he's going to be killed in the next episode? Would you give him another job as a producer?"

Understandably, most actors like to talk about the big roles and ignore any rubbish they might have appeared in. But Niall is refreshingly honest when it comes to discussing the worst films he's ever appeared in. In fact, some of the stuff is so bad that he can't even remember making them, never mind recalling the titles.

"I was in America and I turned on the television at about two o'clock in the morning and there was this girl with her throat slit and I'm bending over her—I thought, 'Oh, Jesus! What the fuck is this?'

"I couldn't remember. It was a vampire film. I had totally forgotten that I was ever in this thing. It was terrible rubbish. I've done so much work, but a lot of it was just run of the mill stuff."

Niall has now retired from stage acting—admitting that he wanted to go out while still at the top of his game and feared ruining his reputation with lesser performances. But he still occasionally does film and TV work. Considering that he's now in his eighties, I wonder if he thinks about death much these days?

"I don't think more about it. I do think there's something beyond, that there is an afterlife. Like everybody else, I don't know. It's an each-way bet, I suppose," he said.

Does he have any regrets?

"I suppose I regret that I didn't treat some people better than I did. Once I stopped drinking I lead a responsible, good life. I tried to play fair by everybody. I'm not conscious of any great sins—except, of course, my vanity; my passions for ladies who won't talk to me; my addiction to drink; my lack of humility—otherwise, I'm a good living man," he said, laughing.

For a man of his age, Niall is considerably fit, has his full wits about him, and even drives himself everywhere still.

"Well, that's not acting. If it was, I'd get the greatest Oscar of all time. Thank God. . . . Both my parents lived to be very old. My mother was 97 when she died. My father was 89. My mother's mind had gone. I went to visit her in hospital when she was nearly 97. She asked, 'Oh, what's your name?' And I said, 'Niall Tóibín'. She said, 'Oh, that's a very well known name'."

CHAPTER NINETEEN:

The Irish Everyman, Simon Delaney

Upbeat but clearly exhausted, Simon Delaney rushed into his agent's office full of apologies for being a couple minutes late as he warmly shook my hand.

"My third son was born two months ago—thus the fact that I look like I haven't had a minute's sleep since Christmas. We have a five-year-old, a three-year old, and a baby. Fuck me! I should've tied a knot in it years ago. You see, there was nothing on telly! These fuckin' power cuts are killing me," he quipped.

Despite being worn-out, Simon was fully animated and in good spirits. He's like the Cheshire Cat enjoying the proverbial milk and who could blame him with both his family life and career flourishing in recent years. It's all the more remarkable a feat considering all the personal tragedies he endured and the hard slog of trying to make ends meet for years as a struggling actor.

Simon knows all about being a starving artist and how it can be a famine or a feast when it comes to picking up gigs. Back in 2011, he was out of work for huge sections of that particular year. But fast forward to 2012 and he not only appeared as Sean Penn's best friend in the critically acclaimed movie *This Must Be The Place*, but he also appeared in Kiefer Sutherland's TV show *Touch*. Then he won rave reviews in *the LA Times* for his guest starring appearance alongside Eddie Izzard in *The Good Wife*, which became the show's most popular episode with a staggering 22 million viewers tuning in Stateside.

The following year, he had parts in *Delivery Man* with Vince Vaughan, *Begin Again,* and BBC's *The Fall* alongside Gillian Anderson of *X-Files* fame, as well as a part in Chris O'Dowd's show *Moone Boy* for Sky TV.

More recently, Simon has appeared in the movies *The Conjuring 2* (2016), *Spiders Trap* (2015), *Don't Go* (2018), and the hugely popular British TV soap, *Coronation Street*.

"The fact that it turned into my living was a fluke," he admitted.

It's clear that Simon is still pinching himself with his recent good fortune. Simon admits that his success tastes all the more sweeter after some persistent attacks from certain downmarket Irish tabloids making fun of everything from his weight to rubbishing him when he spoke about his dream to crack Hollywood.

"It gives you an incentive. It gives you great motivation. But there's no better motivation then the fact that my kids eat food every day," he said, adding that he has a blacklist of certain journalists he plans to name and shame in his acceptance speech if he ever wins an Emmy!

It's certainly been a long and rocky road to Hollywood for the 40-something-year-old actor. He grew in a tough council estate on Dublin's Northside in Coolock, with his father John working as a printer, while his mother stayed at home to raise their four children. "It was Coolock if you were signing on [the dole] and Raheny if you were applying for a job!" he explained.

Shortly before his Leaving Cert, tragedy struck when his mother died at the relatively young age of 50. "She went in to have an operation to have her gallbladder taken out and three weeks later she was dead. They discovered pancreatic cancer when they opened her up," he said.

"After Mammy died you'd often find my Dad sitting starring into the fireplace. He was absolutely broken hearted. That lasted for about six months, but he then looked around and saw he had a 13-year-old daughter and myself and my brother were only going through the Leaving Cert, and my sister was starting work. So, he said to himself, 'I have to get up here and get on with it'. He took retirement from work and he stayed at home and he reared us.

"The year after my Ma died, I had lost my job, my grandmother died six months after that and I thought, 'Jaysus!' I've often said to myself since then, 'If I didn't jump off a cliff at that point, I was never going to do it'. Our lives couldn't have got any lower."

After graduating from secondary school, Simon went to the College of Commerce in Rathmines but dropped out after eight months.

"Could you fucking imagine me as your accountant? You'd be banjaxed! Mind you, with the Mahon Tribunal some of the boys there didn't do a better job than I would've done!" he said.

"I was then a sales rep. I was a van driver for Sam Hire. I sold life insurance, office equipment, advertising, print media, furniture. You name it, I sold it. When I was going for interviews it was quicker for me to tell them who I didn't work for. My fucking CV was like the Golden Pages. I had more fucking jobs."

Seven years after his mother's untimely death, tragedy struck again when Simon's father dropped dead from a heart attack at the age of 69.

"He died out on the 17th green in Ardee Golf Club. He went down to mark a ball and boom—game over. It was a beautiful sunny Saturday morning. I remember he woke me because I was working. He said, 'Come on, get out of bed. The lads are outside, I'm going to play golf'. And then six hours later I got a phone call to say he was gone," Simon told me.

"The seven years we had with him were brilliant. He was amazing. And we became very close. It was really tough when he was taken from us. My little sister was only 13 when my Mam died and she was only 19 when they were both gone. So, it was a rough couple of years. But these are the cards you're dealt. They certainly make you what you are, they form what you are."

Simon tried to find solace in his two passions: football and the local musical society.

"I knew I was never going to fucking play for United at that stage! I was a goalkeeper. The fucking laziest position on the pitch. And I had my cigarettes and my asthma inhaler beside the post. I had to pack in the football because we were doing so many shows; we were rehearsing at the same time as training," he said.

"I only joined the local musical society as a bet! I was about 25 and was going out with a girl, who was in the musical society at the time, who broke my bleeding heart. But it was the worst thing she ever did because the women outnumbered the men ten to one in the musical society. So, to say I enjoyed the social side of it would be putting it mildly!"

Almost two decades ago now, it was while directing a production of *Cabaret* with the Cameron Musical Society that Simon first clapped eyes on his future wife Lisa, who he married seven years ago this June. "She's a dancer and she auditioned and got the part. It took me almost a year then to ask her out," he said.

Did he fancy her straight away?

"I knew she was the one. Oh, Mother of Jesus Christ! She's seven years younger than me. Fit as a butcher's dog. I fancied her straight away. For some reason, I wasn't backwards with ladies, but I just couldn't ask her out. I did a year later. We were mad about each other and we are still mad about each other—we'd want to be with three kids later. We've at least loved each other three times in seven years!" he joked.

"Our eldest son is called Cameron. The papers said we called him after Cameron Mackintosh because I like musicals! Oh, come on! Lads ring me and ask me why, don't just make it up. But he's called Cameron because that's where mammy and dad met."

How did he propose to her?

"Obviously, the *Who Wants to Be A Millionaire* thing happened between us. You're looking at me blankly—you don't remember any of this, do you? It was just before the first series of *Bachelor's Walk* and I entered, as I did every week, *Who Wants To Be A Millionaire* and I got on. I got into the chair to be asked the questions by Gay Byrne. I got to 16 grand and went for the 32 grand question and got it wrong. So, I got a grand.

"While I was on the show, they asked me what I would do with the money if you won it. I said the usual, 'I'd get a holiday, buy a corporate box at Old Trafford, pay off my mortgage, and I'd buy my girlfriend an engagement ring'. So, I said this on the programme and then I lost the money.

"But the day after the show aired the woman who owns a jewellers on Grafton Street rang my agent Lorraine and said, 'We'll give him a ring because they seem like a lovely couple', because Lisa was in the audience and she was heartbroken when I got the question wrong.

"So, they gave us an engagement ring worth seven grand. They brought her into the shop and closed the shop and had champagne and flowers for her and picked out a ring. I booked flights to New York and we got engaged on Valentine's night on the Staten Island ferry. I got down on bended knee. We were due to get married the year after but I ended up in the West End, so we put it off for a year."

Even though he was clearly exhausted from having a new baby at the time of our interview, Simon is a glutton for punishment. "I'd like a big brood. I'd like the whole Walton's things. I'd love a girl, I have to say, because I saw the relationship my sisters had with my dad," he said.

His first big acting break came when he got a part in a short film alongside his uncle Niall Buggy, who starred alongside Richard Gere in *King David* and won a Laurence Olivier Award in the West End. After this, Simon was snapped up by the Lorraine Brennan Management agency.

"Three months later I was on the set with Sally Fields and Michael Richards, who plays Kramer in *Seinfeld*, doing a Hallmark TV version of *David Copperfield*," he said. "I was getting £1,000 a day and I had 18 days in the film and I thought, 'This is a piece of piss'. And then of course I didn't work for six months afterwards. I'd been a real lad and pissed all the money.

"I'm still a sales rep—it's just me I'm selling, I'm not selling photocopiers anymore. The years I had as a sales rep gave me great training as an actor because of the whole rejection thing. I was hearing no 15 times a day as a sales rep selling people shit they didn't want and I knew they didn't want it. So, when I started turning professional and going for auditions and was told, 'No, you didn't get it'. I'd think, 'Fuck it! Go for the next one'."

In the early days, the only job he ever turned down was when he was asked to put on a chicken suit and walk along Dublin's Grafton Street handing out flyers. But I was surprised when he told me how he was financially struggling when he starred in *Bachelor's Walk*, one of the biggest shows on Irish TV at the time—to such an extent that he was forced to take up a part-time job as a postman to make ends meet one Christmas.

"I went up to the Finglas depot and did two or three weeks delivering post up there. I loved it. Baseball cap on and the Walkman on. Anybody who had a dog didn't get post though! I hate dogs. The neighbours got their Christmas cards, or else they went down the fucking shore," he said.

He once stared in a stage show of *The Full Monty*. What was it like stripping off on stage every night?

"We went bollix naked every night. It was fucking terrifying."

Er . . . did any part of him get stage fright?

"Let's just say it was cold in the theatre!" he joked.

Simon came to the attention of Hollywood in 2009 after playing the lead in a small independent comedy called *Zonad*, which was given a five star review in *Variety*.

"I now share an agent with Seth Rogan, which is cool. But he's ten years younger than me and has about $30 million more than me!" he quipped.

During one of his first trips out to Hollywood to do the "meet and great circuit" with directors and casting agents, Simon said one of his highlights was having a pint with Sean Penn. He had gone out drinking with the multi-Oscar winning director Jim Sheridan in the plush Chateau Marmont, which is famous for its A-list clientele.

Picking up the story, he explained: "It was like an episode of *Entourage*. I'm sitting with Jim and he said, 'What are you doing?' I said, 'I'm doing Sean Penn's new movie'. Literally, as the words came out of my mouth, Penn walked into the bar. I went, 'Jaysus! That's mental'. Jim said, 'What?' I replied, 'He's fucking standing there—look!' Jim goes, 'Sean, come here'."

He continued, "It was a good job I wasn't spoofing. He brings him over and says to Sean, 'He's doing you're next film'. He said, 'Wow! Great to meet you man'. He sat down and had a pint. Penn for our generation is the man—six Oscar nominations, two wins. He's the last one of those rock and roll boys—the Dennis Hoppers and Jack Nicholsons.

"Landing that role was great. It's great for your confidence. It's such a great lift for your soul. I was surprised I got it because my character was supposed to be 51 and bald and fat! I'm one out of three!"

He still pinches himself when he thinks about the film's premiere in Cannes. "We got a police escort motorcade down to the cinema and there were banks of photographers all in tuxes. You get out of the car and it's so orchestrated; you're looking down the line and there's Judd Hirsch, David Byrne, Eve Houston, the director Paolo Sorrentino, and I'm going, 'Fucking hell!' I looked like their fucking security!" he said.

"And of course me being me, I walked halfway up and stood in fucking chewing gum. So, I look like I'd just had a fucking hip replacement. It was surreal. And when the movie finished it got a 17-minute standing ovation. I never experienced anything like it. I'm looking around the room and Faye Dunaway looks at me," he said, pretending to be her by clapping his hand and mouthing, "'I loved you in it'.

"I'm going 'Fucking hell!' Sean and Paolo stood and they were taking the applause and then Sean turned around and he looked at me. I thought, 'What's wrong with him. Does he want water or something?' And he pointed at me and said, 'Come here'. And he brings you down and you're standing beside him and Judd Hirsch and David Byrne and you're going, 'This is ridiculous!' It was just amazing."

Those few days in Cannes was actually the first trip he and his wife had on their own since their honeymoon.

"The morning we left Cannes, Lisa was flying to Dublin and I was flying to LA for six weeks," he recounted. "That was rough at the airport. I hate saying goodbye to people. And I'm a home bird. I arrived in LA and I was Skyping Lisa. Lisa said, 'You left a couple of shirts here, I'll post them out to you'. I said, 'Yeah, sure, grand'. She said, 'You left something else here'. I thought it was a laptop charger or something. I said, 'What?' and she held up the pregnancy test. I went, 'My Jaysus!' I didn't see her then for six weeks—it was heartbreaking.

"Lisa is my biggest supporter, she's behind me 100% and she knows I'm doing this to basically feed the family. I'm not going out to America to win an Oscar; I'm not going out to feed my ego; I'm going to work to feed the three kids."

Would he consider moving the family fulltime to America if his career takes off over there?

Without missing a heartbeat, he said, "Yes, I'd love to do that."

Does he feel under pressure to lose weight particularly when you look at how all the Hollywood stars are amazingly slim?

"No. I think that's a fucking myth. The one trump card that you have when you go over there is that you're Irish. This business is all about bringing something different to the table. They love the Irish over there."

I mention how I heard he had spoken publicly about his battle with lactose intolerance.

"Who the fuck told you that? That's bizarre. That's weird."

It's on his Wikipedia page.

"It isn't? You're fucking joking! As long as there's one of two things always in my food—either blood or fresh cream—that will do me. I'm not fucking lactose intolerant. After 14 years, that's a fucking new one on me. Fuck me! What other nuggets have you got there?" he asked, pointing to my list of questions.

That he got his teeth fixed?

"That is true. I got them done for my wedding," he beamed, showing off his shinny white pearls.

Something tells me, Simon will be doing a lot more smiling if this career trajectory continues into a permanent move to Hollywood.

CHAPTER TWENTY:

A Brave heart, John Kavanagh

Anybody eavesdropping mid-conversation could easily be forgiven for jumping to the wrong conclusion. John Kavanagh was sitting at the Abbey Theatre's bar and gushing enthusiastically about a new certain female in his life.

"She looks gorgeous. I think she looks like a cross-between Ava Gardner and Rita Hayward," he told me during a break from rehearsals for the Brian Friel play *Aristocrats* that was about to open later that week at The Abbey.

Beaming from ear to ear, the acclaimed thespian was excitedly talking about the latest arrival to his family—a new granddaughter named Marianne. "She was born a few days ago. Six pounds. She's beautiful. She was a bit premature, a couple of weeks premature. But she looks gorgeous," he said proudly.

He often portrays stern characters on the big screen in the likes of *Braveheart* (1995) and the Colin Farrell flop *Alexander* (2004), but John couldn't be further removed from such onscreen personas—he comes across as much more jovial and laidback in real life, as he talks enthusiastically about Marianne.

Despite being a grandfather, John insisted that he didn't yet feel old—pointing out that he can still do 50 push-ups. But starring as the oldest cast member in the Friel play certainly had him in a reflective mood because he was actually the youngest actor to appear in the first staging of the same play back in 1979!

"I was the young failed solicitor in the first production, and now I'm the old fella. There's the arc of a life. Janey Mack!" he said with a hint of nostalgia.

Growing up as one of four siblings in South Dublin's Middletown, John had no aspirations to be an actor. Instead, he dreamt about being a cop in the US, but decided against the idea when the Vietnam War broke out. John fell into acting by accident—he only ended up attending acting school because he thought it would help him get his foot into the film business as a cinematographer.

John worked an assortment of jobs: everything from a clerk in wholesale grocers, to working at an advertising agency, to being a cinema manager at the Ambassador and the old Capitol beside the GPO—before finally getting his big break when he was taken on fulltime by The Abbey in 1967.

As John's career flourished in acting, so too did his older sister Anne Bushnell's singing career. During her career, she performed with the likes of Ronnie Drew and Joe Dolan, and had her own TV show on national Irish telly.

Anne, who once appeared on stage with her brother John, also performed as a backing singer for Johnny Logan when he won the Eurovision with *What's Another Year* in 1980.

Sadly, Anne died from bone cancer in 2011 at the age of 72.

"Terrible," he said shaking his head. "Sometimes I think it's hard to believe she was ever here, you know? It's funny. Weird."

The conversation moved onto happier memories. It was through The Abbey that John met his wife Anne back in 1968.

"It was across a crowded room—literally. She was about 18 and I was 21, something like that. There was a guy that used to work here [in The Abbey] and he used to have parties every Saturday night in his house in Rathgar and there'd be a massive big pot of stew, and everyone would be waiting outside to get in. They were fantastic parties," he recalled.

"And that's where I met her—across a crowded room. I think she was going out with somebody else at the time, but it didn't bother me—I asked her out anyway."

John confessed that he was "surprised she turned up" for their first date. "I didn't think she'd see anything in me. I'd very low self-esteem, I'm afraid, at the time. But I kind of grew in confidence," he said, laughing.

The couple married five years later in 1973 and have lived in Terenure, Dublin, ever since. When the couple were expecting their first child, John made the brave decision to quit the security of a regular pay check at The Abbey for the precarious life of freelance actor—but it was a gamble that quickly paid off.

Unlike many of his contemporaries, John—despite having appeared in several Hollywood and UK movies—never emigrated for the simple reason that he was "too busy here" in Ireland and the UK.

Also unlike many of his contemporaries, John never succumbed to the curse of alcoholism that ruined many promising careers. John made a conscious decision to stay away from heavy boozing because he "saw how people ended up".

He explained, "No drinking before a show or anything like that. I always kind of drink very little, moderately—particularly when the show's running. You've got to be fit for this game—mentally and physically. It catches you eventually. You're not going to get away with that."

John was once horrified to find himself standing on stage when the late Alan Devlin was so inebriated that he marched off stage. During an infamous production of Gilbert and Sullivan's *HMS Pinafore* at the Gaiety, Devlin stunned cast members and audience alike when he announced, "Fuck this for a game of soldiers, I'm going home." He then negotiated his way through the orchestra pit and shouted to his onstage colleagues, "Finish it yourself!"—and absconded to the nearest pub for a stiff brandy.

A twist in the tale that nobody knows is that John's brother-in-law met Devlin outside the theatre and leant the actor a fiver to buy his drink.

"The one thing that annoyed me really—apart from him walking off that time—was that the way that it was written up in a lot of papers," he recalled.

"There was some paper with a headline thanking Alan, praising him for the courage of his convictions! I thought, 'How dare you! Do you realise what we went through when he left that stage?'

"There was 15 minutes—the scene would've gone on for 15 minutes. Nobody knew what to do. A lot of these guys were singers, not actors. There was one guy playing the captain of the ship and he was literally struck dumb—his mouth was hanging open. He couldn't believe what had happened—your man walking up the centre aisle."

With everybody dumfounded on stage, John decided to start ad-libbing.

"This is Saturday night and the place is packed. I don't know where it came from—you rack your brain, you go into overdrive—it's like when something happens on stage you can think of two things at the same time practically; you can be speaking something and thinking of something else," he said.

"And I came up with this line and I don't know where it came from—and it was a cue for one of the leads, which was word cue that then became a music cue. So, one thing led to another and we kept going."

Another embarrassing moment for John was when a picture of

him naked being whipped by Joanna Lumley for a scene in an 1997 version of *Sweeney Todd* ended up being splashed across the front pages of some tabloids.

"She had her clothes on—I didn't! It was closed set supposedly but somebody got a still and put it on the front of the paper. I think my daughter saw it when she was a kid—I had to try and say it was a body double! I had to tell her it was a body double. It was my head but a body double superimposed!" he said, shaking his head laughing.

But the most surreal experience has to be when John discovered that both he and Oscar winning actress Hilary Swank both felt the presence of a ghost when working together on the film *The Black Dahlia* in 1997. The film—which was directed by Brian De Palma and also starred Scarlett Johansson and Josh Hartnett—is based on the true story of the gruesome murder of Elizabeth Short in 1947.

"I had weird dreams. I felt this ghost was in the room or in the bed. I was checking with Hilary and she said, 'I had weird dreams because of this'. Weird dreams," he said.

"So, I think there was something in the ether. I don't know what it was, it's like the spirit of the girl we depicted in the film who was murdered. She was severed. It was a shocking, weird business. No one was ever got for it."

John said the only regrets he has in his career is how he was forced to turn down parts in a film by Swedish director Ingmar Bergman and Terence Malick's *The Tree of Life* (2011), starring Sean Penn and Brad Pitt.

"There's two things that I'd love to have done," he said, explaining that he was unavailable because he was under contract for other projects on both occasions.

John is probably best known for his role in Mel Gibson's *Braveheart*. John laughs when he recounts how the *Lethal Weapon* star carried around a book entitled 'How To Direct An Epic', which was made up as a joke by the props department.

"The way I got the part was extraordinary. I never even auditioned for him. He came to see *Juno and the Peacock*—myself and Brendan Gleeson were doing it at The Gaiety—and he was after Brendan to play his buddy in the film.

"My agent sent me to see him after a matinee one day. I went to see him at The Four Seasons; I went up to his bedroom and I was knackered and he was knackered.

"And the casting director said to us, 'Do you two went to get into bed, you're so tired!' He gave me the script and then he came to see the show on the Friday night. He said, 'Did you read it?' I said, 'Yeah'. He said, 'What do you think of the part?' I said, 'I think it's terrific'. He said, 'Well, it's yours if you want it!' That was it."

As the interview winds down, I mentioned how on his IMBD webpage—the Bible for Hollywood insiders—John is described as "one of Ireland's underrated character actors. Little detail is given on him, yet he has appeared in many well-known films and television series . . ." Does John—who vows that he will never retire—feel underappreciated?

Roaring laughing, he said: "I never think about myself. Somebody told me that once. I thought to myself, 'Here! Who writes these things? Underrated, overrated—who cares? Well, the opposite of that is to be overrated! More to come. Watch this space!"

CHAPTER TWENTY-ONE:

Raise the Titanic, Jason Barry

Back in 2011, for Jason Barry, stepping out of the limo onto the red carpet to be met by flashing cameras and receive an emotional hug from Kate Winslet at the premiere of the 3D version of *Titanic* in London made him reflect on how he was once tipped for stardom after playing Leo DiCaprio's Irish sidekick.

It was also an all too painful remainder of the "dark days" that almost made him walk away from acting because he was finding himself unable to live up to the hype after his 15 minutes of fame in one of the biggest box office hits in movie history.

But after slipping out of the limelight, the future is now looking bright once again for the new, leaner Jason—after shedding five stone, which is clearly helping rejuvenate his career.

Our paths first crossed in 2012 when Jason was back in Ireland to work as the new leading villain in the third season of *Love/Hate*, which was the most successful Irish-made TV series in donkey's years and has even been favourably compared to *The Sopranos*. Apart from acting, Jason is also writing scripts and directing himself now.

"I'm in a really good place mentally and physically," he told me over a pint in one of my favourite Dublin pubs, the H'Penny Bar, after a day's filming. "If the second chance comes around I'll grab it and it seems to be coming around right now. *Love/Hate* is the icing on the cake."

With such a huge weight loss, it'll be quite understandable if *Titanic* fans fail to recognise the now 40-something Dubliner—as even Kate Winslet didn't know who he was at first when they met at the Royal Albert Hall for the *Titanic* reunion.

"I had not seen Kate in about 12 years and she stopped an interview mid-sentence at the premiere and pulled me aside, saying she couldn't believe how different I looked. She also said jokingly, 'Where have you gone?' She was genuinely shocked," he said, laughing.

"I see Billy Zane a lot now in LA, but the first time he saw me after many years he did not recognise me. Neither did Bill Paxton. I bumped into James Cameron about two months ago and chatted to him. I felt he did not recognise me and then after about two minutes he said, 'Jason, you got be kidding me! I thought you were someone else'."

Originally from Artane in North Dublin, Jason was still studying acting in Trinity when he was offered the lead role in a BBC film *O Mary This London* (1994). He then landed parts in *Circle of Friends* (1995) and played Jared Leto's best friend in *The Last of the High Kings* (1996).

"The summer of '95 was an absolutely scorching summer, so the film looked so beautiful because the light for those eight weeks was absolutely stunning.

"It was great: we had Catherine, Emily, Lorraine, Colm Meaney, and Stephen Rea. A really good cast," he recalled. You get a bunch of people together on a nice summer and we all became very close and we socialised a lot. I actually watched it in America recently, it's called *Summer Fling* over there."

It was a role that brought him to the attention of *Titanic* director James Cameron.

"At first, they put people on tape and sent them over to him and then they dwindled it down and he came over and I spent about 45 minutes with him," he recalled. "I did some improvisation and then we chatted for about a half an hour.

"I kind of knew walking out that I had a serious chance, because you can usually tell if you've got a really good chance of getting the job. If you're looking somebody in the eye you get things from them that tell you if you've got the job. I remember I really felt that when I finished that audition.

"I was doing okay for a young Irish actor and he would've seen that at least I had worked a couple of times and that I wouldn't be overawed by the experience.

"And then about three weeks after I met him I got a call and they said, 'Do you want to go to Mexico for six months?'"

He didn't have to be asked twice. Jason remembers it being a "wonderful experience" staying in a plush hotel in Mexico for six months while making *Titanic* and bounding with Leo DiCaprio and Kate Winslet.

"Myself and Leo hung out a lot. We played a lot of video games during our downtime and he once brought me for dinner with my mum and granny when they visited the set.

"Kate's a real sweetheart. Kate called me after she saw the first rough cut to tell me how much she enjoyed what I did. I was surprised as I had just moved so I don't know how she got my number," Jason said.

From the moment he met Leo, Jason knew that here was a guy who was going to be a superstar.

"With Leo, I saw *Romeo + Juliet* (1996) when we were shooting *Titanic* and I just felt, 'This guy is going to be a movie star', he told me. "I'd seen Kate in *Sense and Sensibility* (1995) and *Heavenly Creatures* (1994) and I think she got Oscar nominated for both of those movies. She was just definitely somebody who was going to be the Kate Winslet she's become.

"When you're an actor like me and you work with your Jared Letos, or your Leos and your Kates, you kind of see who's going to go off and do very well and you can see who's not. Definitely Kate and Leo were going to go off and fly irrespective of whether *Titanic* would've been what it was."

Did the cast get up to much mischief on the set of *Titanic*?

"We were in this golf course hotel in the middle of nowhere and by nature actors like to enjoy themselves and have a good time and get up to shenanigans. The odd morning a golf cart or two would've been seen being dragged out of the lake!

"The locals who worked at the hotel invited us out a lot. We went to a wedding one time and the bride really fancied an actor, which almost caused dangerous mayhem with the male locals—some of whom may have worked on the other side of the law!"

Did he have any flings during his time in Mexico?

"No, I didn't. They happen more often than not [on film sets]. On that particular job I don't think I got up to any friskiness with anyone!"

The one thing that irks him in hindsight about *Titanic* was the contract he signed up to.

"The only downside with *Titanic* is that because we shot it in Mexico, it was a non Screen Actors Guild of America (SAG)," he explained. "Now, if you're a member of SAG you make a lot of money because, let's say, you're supposed to get a 10 or a 12 hour turnaround [work notice] and they call you in early you get $1,000 per hour. If you're lunch is late you get $500 every 15 minutes or something like that.

"But because we shot in Mexico I wasn't entitled to any of those rights. So, I had my flat fee, no overtime. I was too young to even question the money. It would've been around 60 grand. Hindsight's a wonderful thing, but I would never let it happen again.

"The biggest bummer out of all it is that I didn't make any residuals. I've had multiple emails and texts from Billy Zane over the years telling me he got another residual cheque. But the bottom line is I genuinely would've done that movie for free."

He sheepishly admits that he found women flirting with him after *Titanic* became a smash hit.

"I was a chunkier guy then so I didn't necessarily have the women throwing themselves at me, but you're a young guy and you're in the public eye and people find them attractive if they see them on TV or movies," he confessed. "You can look like the back of a bus and people are still going to find you attractive!"

Titanic led to Jason getting starring roles in films such as *MirrorMask* (2005), which was made by *The Muppet Show* creator Jim Henson, and in the Australian film *Muggers* (2000). While Down Under, Jason—despite being the "chunky guy"—managed to woo his future wife Nicola Charles, who was back then on *FHM Magazine*'s list of the top 100 sexiest women. She was on the cover of *FHM* when they were shooting *Muggers* together. They were together for about 10 years and have two daughters. Jason has since remarried Kristin Alayna, who is an actress, singer, and producer.

Prior to getting hitched again, Jason shared an apartment in LA with his younger brother Glen, who is also an actor and has starred in the US comedy *Van Wilder 2* (2006) and alongside Julie Walters in *The Return* (2003).

Together, they have formed a film production company and Jason drew on the experiences of his marriage break-up for their first short film entitled *100 Degrees* (2012), in which he stars and directs.

"It's about the consequences of the breakdown of a marriage. Write about what you know! We hope it's something that can showcase our talent. I'm going to finish my editing my short and then go back to meet with Jim Cameron who wants to look at it."

They are now working on putting together a feature-length comedy entitled *Marathon Man* to be filmed in Dublin, which draws on Jason's experience of becoming a long distance runner.

"I have to give my ex-wife fair dues on this: about seven years ago she looked at me and said, 'Jason, you just look ridiculous. You've got to do something about it'," he told me back in 2012.

"The next day I went out for a run and I ran for about five minutes and I nearly killed myself. I kept at it. I stopped smoking when I started running. I started to get addicted to it. It's a very important part of my life now. I'll run eight or nine miles a day, six days a week. What I love about running is that it's just time to me and I can think about what I need to sort out in my head. I do six-minute miles. I ran the London marathon in 2 hours 48 minutes."

Does he believe his weight held him back from getting big parts after *Titanic* launched him?

"I think definitely for the kind of work I wanted to do. I didn't help the agent because my physique didn't lend itself to a lot of work. There was a big part in *Saving Private Ryan* (1998) that I nearly got and I was very disappointed when I didn't get it. My physicality worked for the role in *Titanic*. But was I going to become a movie star from these roles? No, of course not."

He also believes other factors played a role in holding back his acting career during the Late Noughties. He explained, "I don't know if it was a lack of maturity. I think I lost focus. I lost sight of the craft. I had a good life, a few bob in the back pocket. Do you take the foot off the gas a little? Maybe, for me.

"It's something I think about a lot because you're always going to look back at the 'what ifs?' I've been trying in my head to think what it is that I lacked that made me not go to places that I could've in my career."

He added, "I genuinely lacked a maturity to understand what was happening and where I was going and where I could go. It affected me in the way that I made some bad decisions. I mean,[after meeting Nicola] I ended up living in Australia for a year when I probably shouldn't have done that.

"I was ill advised, but in fairness to my management, they would be screaming at me to come back. It was a lack of experience and a lack of maturity and I didn't have anybody guiding me. I didn't have somebody helping me when they saw pitfalls that I was falling into.

"I floundered for many years and then frustration creeps in a little bit when you can see it moving away from you. You see your peers doing really well. And then the panic sets in a little bit."

He admits that he frequently thought about walking away from acting.

"You have your dark days. You look in the mirror and think, 'What's the point of it?' It's a great industry when it's good and it's a terrible industry when it's bad. There's nothing worse—it's such a lonely business," he said.

"The hardest part is when you've tasted some great work and worked with some great people and tasted a great lifestyle and travelled the world. When it all dries up you just sit there and you get frustrated.

"I was frustrated at myself for making mistakes. It was a case of knowing that I had some chances that didn't roll my way or I didn't help facilitate roll my way. I made some mistakes and I'm rectifying that now. I'm sure *Love/Hate* will change that. I had no idea how big that show was before I came here. I'm a much more confident man now. The second chance is coming around and I'll grab it."

Photo by Suzan Ni Tuatha

CHAPTER TWENTY-TWO:

Commander in Chief, Martin Sheen

Martin Sheen has starred in some cinematic masterpieces like *Apocalypse Now* and *Badlands*. He is one of America's most prolific actors but, unfortunately, there is a downside to this: Martin admits to making more than his fair share of turkeys.

"I am proud of just a handful of films. I would say 90% of it was basically trash. I did it for the money, and most of the stuff I did was a great source of embarrassment to me," Martin confesses when we first meet at the aptly named Presidential Suite in The Westbury Hotel, Dublin, for this interview. The 67-year-old Ohio-born actor, who has played the President of America four times, points to the suite's title and light-heartedly says: "Perhaps they should call it: The Former Acting President's suite!"

Martin describes *Apocalypse Now* as being "both a career-changing experience as well as a personal voyage" because it helped him to face his own "darkness and inhumanity". After suffering the near-death experience of a heart attack on set in the Philippines, Martin gave up his excessive drinking and returned to his Catholic faith. "I had to come clean of that. I had to find myself. That was a long and very painful journey, which accumulated in my return to Catholicism," he explains.

Apocalypse Now took up 15 months of Martin's life and, after it finished, he spent the next four years focusing on inner contemplation. Eventually, Martin emerged re-invigorated by his new-found belief in religion, and determined to have a positive influence on society, particularly with human rights issues. When he's not making films or television shows, Martin can be found campaigning on a wide variety of social, political, and humanitarian issues. He has set up a foundation to help the poor in Third World countries, and he frequently visits deprived areas to help "shine the press light" on horrible conditions. In fact, Martin has been arrested 65 times for his involvement in many radical campaigns in America, including stances against nuclear weapons and the invasion of Iraq.

The *West Wing* star shocked the show-business world when he decided, earlier this year, to move to Ireland and become a student. He regretted never undertaking a third-level education, and decided to live out his "romantic fantasy" of returning to his mother's homeland to study at the National University of Ireland, Galway. Since arriving in Ireland, Martin has repeatedly turned down requests for interviews, insisting that he wants to keep a "low profile". This was his first and only interview with the Irish print media during his stay in Ireland.

O'TOOLE: Instead of studying here in Ireland, you could be off in Hollywood acting today . . .

SHEEN: I don't know about that! I don't get big pictures these days.

O'TOOLE: Why did you decide to come to study in Galway?

SHEEN: I guess it is a romantic fantasy. I guess that's the best way to describe going to school in Ireland. It has been on my mind for many years. I kept putting it off and, finally, when the *West Wing* series ended, I thought I had a window of opportunity. I don't know how much time I have left [*laughs*], but I am truly enjoying it. As I say, it is a great adventure. I come here a lot. I have been coming here since 1973. My mother's from here, I've lots of Irish relatives and I adore all of them. I see them quite often. I'm captivated by the country—the spirit of the country, the people. I have never had a bad day in Ireland. It just awakens a sense in me that [*pauses*] . . . it nourishes me in ways that no other country does.

O'TOOLE: How are you finding student life?

SHEEN: I'm not an ideal student. It's a great adventure and I'm enjoying it. The only regret I have is that I didn't do this 50 years ago. But it's really great, and the people in Galway and at the university have been very supportive. I feel right at home—in fact, I am at home.

O'TOOLE : What subjects are you studying?

SHEEN: I'm studying Philosophy, English, Earth and Ocean Science, and Computers because I never worked with computers before. So I have a full schedule and I'm enjoying it immensely. I have no background in science at all—in fact, I haven't been to school since I finished high school nearly 50 years ago. The old brain is being cranked up and it's not on full throttle yet. I'm very grateful that the National University of Ireland allowed me to come study. I'm not a great student, unfortunately, but I'm inspired. I know now why people go to school when they are young—the energy and the focus is so enormous. I came because I work for a lot of environmental organisations in the States—I do a lot of documentaries, a lot of voice-overs. I try to expose a lot of the destruction of the environment, in the hope that people will begin to wake up and help repair it. I thought it would be a good idea if I knew something about what was happening with global warming, so that's what inspired me to do it. Almost two years ago I visited NUI and toured the Ryan Institute, which is doing a great deal of research, and they invited me to come back.

O'TOOLE: You are quoted as saying, 'I love being Spanish as much as I love being Irish—and I really love being Irish'. Does that really sum up your identity?

SHEEN: I do really love being Irish. When you have parents from two different cultures, you're bound to carry both equally. You might favour one over the other at one time or another but, basically, you have to be balanced with them. That was simple in my case because they are both so much alike: they are both Celtic tribes. I visited my father's place in 1969 and I visited my mother's village in 1973 for the first time, and they were both very similar in their structure, their colour, their people, their character. The cultures were very, very close. Land was very important, family was very important and you had all the personalities in a community integrated. Both cultures had such similar basic accommodation. They were family-orientated, they were peasant-orientated, they were land-orientated, they were Celtic people and their personalities were such that you could switch one for the other. They are very easy to identify with. I'm comfortable with both cultures.

O'TOOLE: You took your stage surname from the Rev. Fulton J. Sheen. You obviously had a lot of admiration for the man?

SHEEN: No, I had a fascination with him when I was a boy. He had a prime-time, half-hour television series every Tuesday night. He would appear and give a lecture on television. He was the first televangelist, basically. He was the Auxiliary Bishop of New York and he was on television for years and years. He was a very powerful, very popular figure. He was also somewhat conservative but I didn't have a clue, at the time, about what his politics were.

I just thought of him as being this great actor. He was this great figure on television and I just thought, 'Oh, my God! This guy is really powerful'. I thought of him as an actor giving a performance. So when I decided to use his name—and I met him as a result—I felt it suited me, you know. I took Martin from a guy I'd known when I first came to New York who was very helpful to me, Robert Dale Martin. And I took Sheen partly because it sounded Irish, and partly because this guy had inspired me as an actor—not as a churchman.

O'TOOLE: Apart from being so prolific as an actor, you spend a lot of time working on human rights issues. How do you have time for a personal life? It seems to take up a lot of your energy.

SHEEN: It does. Anyone gets tired, you can only do so much, but I really don't separate the human rights work from any other part of my life.

O'TOOLE: What initially sparked you to get involved with charitable work?

SHEEN: I came from a very large immigrant family. My mother, as you know, was Irish and my dad was Spanish. They were very poor. I had to start working when I was very young. I was nine-years-old when I started caddying at a local golf club, a very exclusive club. I saw the effects of racism, and I felt the barriers between rich and poor.

I would work for people who were pillars of the community; you know, the doctors, the lawyers, the politicians—the powerful ones. There were no blacks or women amongst them. And they were not heroic people, it's sad to say.

So, I learned much from them about what not to do. I didn't aspire to be anything like them. I respected them as human beings, but I felt sure that was not what I wanted to become: wealthy or privileged in any way because I knew that was the death of the soul. Instinctively, I knew that and most of the kids I grew up with knew that. They didn't want to become those guys they worked for. There was nothing about them that was inspiring.

O'TOOLE: Caddying must have been a strenuous job for a child?

SHEEN: When I was about 13, I organised a strike and formed a caddy union because the wages were very low and the work was very hard. We were children. Today, it would be called child labour. We were all kids, and we were working for these wealthy people. Those bags were heavy. If you were big enough, strong enough, skilled enough, you would carry two of them and make $4.25. This was in the mid-1950s.

I knew a love of work. I struggled to make a living. All of us did—all my brothers, nine boys and one girl. All of the boys in front of me had caddied and it was just a natural progression. When I became strong enough to carry a golf bag, I joined the ranks of the caddies. I became, basically, a professional caddy, and I did it until the age of 17, when I left home. I had other little jobs, but that was the steady one.

From early spring to late fall, that was what we did. We would save our money, in the summer particularly, and it would help our dad with the tuition. We went to an all-boys Catholic high school. We needed books, you had to wear a tie, and we had to dress a little more snappy. So that all helped him. He was a factory worker and he didn't make a lot of money, so we all had to pitch in. That was my upbringing.

O'TOOLE: I read you have been arrested 70 times?

SHEEN: No. I have only been arrested 65 times. I am almost up to my age [*laughs*].

O'TOOLE: What motivates you to participate in humanitarian work?

SHEEN: Well, the Gospel, primarily, motivates my human rights activities. The command of the Gospel is to feed the hungry, to clothe the naked, house the homeless, to visit the imprisoned, to do justice, and to love, and to walk humbly. That's the command of all the Gospels. And I think that the only way you come to know yourself is by serving others. I don't know a better way, otherwise it is self-service, service to a company for profit.

So much growth happens within you when you're involved in peace and social justice work, because it takes you into areas that you would not normally go. And you touch people that you would not normally touch: the marginalized and the poor and the disenfranchised. You're dealing with people who suffer on a daily basis, and who are left out. They have no voice, so you have to be a voice for the voiceless.

But you grow in so many ways, if you're willing to take the risk. It is risky, it is going to cost you something, and you've got to take it personally. If it's not personal, it's impersonal, and if it's impersonal, who cares? You can't idly stand by, you can't elect not to do it once you are informed about what's going on. You have to take a stand, otherwise you become part of the problem.

My whole adult life, I've been involved in various peace and social justice issues, and I wouldn't have it any other way. The only regret I have is that I didn't get involved earlier. I was never arrested for anything involved with social justice until I was nearly 45.

O'TOOLE: Why so late?

SHEEN: I keep asking myself that question. It is just basically fear. You don't want to suffer the consequences.

O'TOOLE: Can you remember your first time being arrested?

SHEEN: Yes. We were fighting against the establishment of Star Wars, which was an effort by the Reagan administration to place nuclear weapons in outer space. We placed our bodies at the doors so the employees on the project couldn't get through, and I remember being terribly frightened by what was going to happen.

The police captain came and I remember Fr. Bergin offering the New York police to come and join us in our protest. They said, 'No. You have three minutes to get out of here'. And I thought, 'Gee, what's coming down now?' It was the scariest moment of my life, and the happiest was when it was over because I had done everything I possibly could. I'd done it non-violently, I'd even done it joyfully—and now I had to pay the consequences, which was a little while in jail and personal humiliation.

Martin Sheen with Fr Shay Cullen in the Philippines.

It turned out that I met one of my heroes in the paddy wagon—if you will pardon the expression, that's what we call them in New York. This young fellow was arrested with us. When we got to the police station he was collecting everyone's summons, and he came to me and offered to represent us in court. I asked him how he planned to do so, and he explained that he was a criminal attorney. 'Oh', I said, 'but you were arrested with us'. But he said he believed in the cause. That was a very risky venture, because lawyers have to be careful of their criminal records. And he did represent me, and we became very close friends. He's like a brother really.

O'TOOLE: You have been arrested while protesting against The School of the Americas, which is a military base that trains Latin-American soldiers. You have been involved in demonstrations against the base since 1998. Can you explain a little about this?

SHEEN: Fr. Rory Brogues founded the SOA Watch (The School of The Americas Watch). He is a priest who has served in Central and South America, and saw first-hand the effects, in those Third World countries, of the militaries that were trained at Fort Benning, and how those tactics—including death squads—were used on their own people. He awakened us to that reality, and focused on getting attention on that programme at the base.

So, we would gather there every late November around Thanksgiving, and protest, and try to break into the base—trespass, to be arrested and thrown off. So, yeah, I went there several times and was arrested there. It's now been re-named the Western Hemisphere Institute For Security Co-operation.

O'TOOLE: You have been very vocal in your criticism of American foreign policy, particular with the invasion of Iraq. Not many American celebrities have been as outspoken as you. Why do you think this is?

SHEEN: Anybody courageous enough to speak out against the war was publicly humiliated and, sometimes, punished. It was very costly and still is. Now the country is finally waking up, and they are comparing it to Vietnam. The Administration refuses to acknowledge that they've provoked a vicious civil war, and it is going to cost them in the mid-term elections. It has also cost 2,800 American lives, 600,000 Iraqi lives and countless others in Afghanistan. We saw it coming.

There is the old adage, 'Choose your enemies well, for he is what you will become'. It's just common sense. I think all war, all violence, is a reflection of despair, and we have showed a tremendous amount of arrogance and ignorance. I believe that arrogance is ignorance matured. This became obvious to all of us about this administration—they didn't listen to anybody, they had no set true form of diplomacy, it was always force.

O'TOOLE: Have you ever considered running for public office?

SHEEN: No, no, no, thank God. I've never had any interest in entering political life. I am happy being an actor. I'm very lucky to have made my living—all my adult life—as an actor. I hope to continue with acting but, right now, I'm a student and I'm able to do it because I made my living out of acting. I have a great interest in public service, but no interest in politics per se, and I think there's a big difference. We have people who are very interested in political power, but have very little understanding of true public service. That's what's been lacking in our country over the past five years.

O'TOOLE: You must have a very supportive family, particularly your wife, Janet. You have been married since 1961, which is very unusual for a Hollywood actor.

SHEEN: Well, we weren't married in Hollywood! We were married in New York [*laughs*]. I never thought of myself as a Hollywood actor per se. I'm just an actor, you know? I never identified with one coast or another really, it was just what I did, whether I was on stage or film or TV, it didn't matter.

O'TOOLE: You have done a lot of political documentaries, particularly about the former Yugoslav states and Third World countries, so it really does seem that the film projects you choose are politically motivated. Is this a fair assessment?

SHEEN: I would do those types of parts exclusively if I could. If all the roles had some human rights or social justice theme, I'd be more than happy to get involved. We hoped that we could raise some awareness with these films.

O'TOOLE: Is it true that you donated your fee from *Gandhi* to Mother Theresa?

SHEEN: Not all to her. I split it up three ways. A third apiece to Mother Theresa, to the American Service Friends Committee—who are the Quakers, they are anti-war—and to Concern, which started here in Ireland.

O'TOOLE: Did you get to meet Mother Teresa?

SHEEN: Yes, I did. I met her a couple of times. The first time was during the height of the first Gulf War, when my attorney called me up during the war and said, 'I am going on a peace mission to Rome to meet Mother Teresa'. And his idea was that he wanted to take the case of the war to The Hague and get a ruling on it there, but you can't go as an individual. You have to go as a nation, and the only nation that unilaterally opposed the war, and offered both sides mediation, was the Vatican, which is actually a nation. The Pope is the head of a nation, so his idea was that he would represent the Vatican against the war at The Hague pro bono. He thought this was the way to get the message out about war not being a good idea. John Paul II was the only internationally-recognised government leader who really opposed the war and offered to mitigate.

So, off we went to meet Mother Teresa, and it was a profound incident in my life. A sister brought us in and told us to sit down. We were sitting there in the church, and suddenly a door burst open and there she was. She had the dimensions of a child, she was tiny, and you could look over the top of her head. I felt uneasy, like I had to get smaller. I thought she was ten feet tall, didn't you? I broke into tears when I saw her.

O'TOOLE: You actually cried?

SHEEN: Oh, God, everybody does. To see her is to realise, 'My God! It's for real'. You can see it. You can see the light. You can feel the power. We spent about an hour and a half with her talking. Joe explained his mission and she said she'd never heard of the World Court. This is Mother Theresa!

And he said, 'Oh, yes, Ma'am. It has been around for a while and they litigate between countries'. And she looked off wistfully and asked how The Hague could enforce its judgment. And Joe said, 'No, they couldn't. It would be a moral victory. They have no power of enforcement'. She was captivated by the idea and she said yes, she would take it to the Holy Father. That was a Wednesday and she took it to the Vatican on Thursday, and she asked us to come to the early mass on Friday. When we arrived to meet her, the news greeted us that the war had ended in the Gulf that day. It was February 1 to 2, 1991.

O'TOOLE: You have described Martin Luther King as being an inspirational figure for you. Did you ever have the opportunity to meet him?

SHEEN: I helped organise a benefit for Martin Luther King back in '65. It turned into such a huge event because Sammy Davis Junior got involved and made sure it was going to happen, and invited everyone on Broadway to get involved and participate. There were people like Barbara Streisand.

It was this huge night on Broadway, I think it was the Majestic Theatre, and Reverend King came. I was backstage—I wasn't performing, I was just helping people get chairs to sit down and wait their turn to go on—and King was standing right beside me. I was stunned by how small he was. He must have been 5ft 5, no bigger. I couldn't believe he wasn't 10ft tall.

My consciousness started to get to me: 'Go and get the blessing! Go shake his hand. This is a man you love. He is your hero. Go and talk to him'. But then I thought, 'No. Don't bother the man. He doesn't want to be bothered. He's tired. He's just waiting for Sammy to come off stage to say goodnight, and then he'll go out the backstage door'. I was torn. There was nobody between us, there were no bodyguards, and I'm looking at him and I'm torn: 'Go. No. Go. Don't bother the man. Yes, bother the man'. And I didn't. I regret that. I wanted to shake his hand, but I didn't want to bother him, so I let it pass.

O'TOOLE: You helped set up a charitable foundation, the St. Carlos Foundation, in 1984, which primarily sends volunteers to Hispanic

Third World countries. But, after meeting an Irish priest in 1991, you decided to branch out into the Philippines to help the homeless. How did this come about?

SHEEN: I have always found that wherever I went in the Third World, I would go to the darkest and most depressed area, and I would find an Irish man or an Irish woman doing the work of the Gospel. Feeding the hungry, clothing the naked, housing the homeless, visiting the imprisoned. Those NGO's called me and asked would I tour the Philippines, to shine the press light on the terrible living conditions people were forced to endure.

Fr. Shay Cullen, a Dublin Columbian missionary, took me to the Payatas garbage dump, where I witnessed the plight of 5,000 families searching the garbage for scraps to live on. It was totally unimaginable. I had noticed over the years the introduction of disposable diapers, and they add an extra, horrible danger to the people who live in these garbage heaps. The stench alone is enough to make you retch. It is so heartbreaking to see these people living in these horrible conditions.

O'TOOLE: It sounds like a living hell.

SHEEN: This is right out of Dante's Inferno. I think you have to taste and feel poverty up close, otherwise you can't imagine what it's like. After this tour I thought to myself, 'If I lived here, what would I want at the end of the day?'

Naturally, it would be a bath. I appealed to the board of St. Carlos to build a house of refuge—a water centre, a bathhouse. It has now become a community centre, not just a bathhouse. They serve one full meal a day, and they also buy school equipment [and] uniforms for the children, so they can go to school.

I can come and go, but Fr. Shay has been there for over 30 years. Fr. Shay runs PREDA, this organisation that rescues young people primarily from the jails, from the sex trade, and helps to rehabilitate them. He has saved the lives of thousands of these poor children, and he's helped jail some of the world's most evil paedophiles. What he's achieved is nothing short of a miracle.

O'TOOLE: Do you feel *Apocalypse Now* portrays an accurate depiction of the Vietnam War?

SHEEN: Yes, I do. Most of the critics panned *Apocalypse Now* when it was originally released. It really struggled to find an audience, until the Vietnam veterans passed the word on about how good the film was. For them it was, at that time, the only Vietnam film that came close to the real thing—which was insanity. And it was their support of the film that brought people back for a second look. When you ask an American how many people were killed in Vietnam, they would probably estimate about 55,000—they think of the war as this thing that happened to America. They don't think about the two and a half million North Vietnamese, South Vietnamese, Cambodians, and Laotians—as well as Australians and some Koreans—who died in the Vietnam War.

O'TOOLE: What would be your favourite Martin Sheen movie?

SHEEN: It would have to be *Badlands*. I remember reading the script and thinking, 'This is—without doubt—the best script I have ever read'. I had reservations about doing the movie because the protagonist, Kit, was only 19 years old, and I was 31! They looked at 10 or 15 different actors for the part. Eventually, I got a phone call from Malick [the director] and he offered me the part and it suddenly dawned on me that I was being offered the role of my life. I actually wept with joy when I got that part. It had a profound effect on me because it was a realisation of a dream—a dream that I never thought would happen to me.

O'TOOLE: What type of music do you listen to?

SHEEN: I adore Frank Sinatra. I would know the lyrics to most of his songs. He would be my favourite crooner. I love the classics, stuff like Dylan and Kris Kristofferson. I would listen to Dylan a lot, probably most days of the week. I actually like U2 too.

O'TOOLE: What are your future plans?

SHEEN: I have no plans. I am going to finish the semester in NUI and, hopefully, go home by Christmas. I need to get back into the family and get caught back up in things. When I came here I just shut down the shop, left home [*laughs*], and I'm not doing anything. I have no projects lined up. Not a single thing.

Courtesy of Mirror Images

CHAPTER TWENTY-THREE:

One of the last surviving stars from Golden Age of Hollywood, Maureen O'Hara

Shortly after her nonagenarian milestone, Maureen O'Hara adamantly told me that she intended to be around for at least another dozen years.

"I plan to live to 102!" she told me with steely determination.

The actress dubbed "The Queen of Technicolor" explained that the reason she had picked this particular age was because the mother of her late, third husband Charlie Blair—a decorated war veteran who tragically died in a plane crash—had herself lived until 102.

"Charlie Blair's mother lived to be one-hundred-and-two. She was the boss. She was a fabulous woman. She was from Donegal," she told me.

Sadly, Maureen's vow to reach this elusive centenarian milestone was one determined plan that the famously feisty, larger-than-life character was unable to keep after passing away at the age of 95 in October 2015.

Prior to her returning to America in 2012, I had the privilege of being granted a rare personal audience with the Hollywood icon, which transpired to be the last major in-depth newspaper interview that she conducted in her beloved Ireland. It's also possibly the last interview she granted with any print journalist, considering that she rarely, if ever, granted interviews in her twilight years.

As we sat down, Maureen's assistant presented me with a beautiful black and white photograph of the actress in her formative years.

"Do you have any kids?" Maureen asked me, as she took the photograph off me to sign it.

I told her I had a young daughter named Marianne, who was only three-and-a-half-years-old at the time.

"Ah, she's just a wee baby."

Maureen insisted on mentioning my daughter in the inscription, as her assistant remarked, "You're very lucky because she doesn't normally write that much on autographs."

After Maureen handed it back to me, she said: "I don't know if you can read it."

"Yes," I told her, "I can easily make out every single letter of your elegant handwriting."

The framed photograph now hangs proudly on my study wall. As I type up all this, I can glance up and make out the exact wording: "For Jason, it was good to meet you. Good luck and may Marianne love you always. Love from me too! Maureen O'Hara."

The ink has not faded yet. But even if all begins to vanish like snow before the summer sun, I'll always have this transcript of our taped conversation.

O'TOOLE: You were still only 19 when you moved to America to become a star. . . .

O'HARA: I didn't *move* to America: I was taken to America by Charles Laughton and Eric Palmer. Eric Palmer was the great movie producer from Germany. One of the most famous in the world and a charming, brilliant man. He formed a company with Charles Laughton and I think I was practically the first—and only person—that they signed. They signed me to a seven-year contract and they took me to America. So, that was it.

O'TOOLE: Do you ever wonder where you career might have been if you hadn't met Charles Laughton?

O'HARA: No, I think I'd be exactly where I am. Maybe a little further.

O'TOOLE: Do you wish you kept your surname? They wanted you to change your name; they suggested O'Mara or O'Hara, but you didn't like O'Mara. . . .

O'HARA: I tried to. But that was Charles Laughton who changed my name. He said, 'Oh, no, that would be horrible up on a marquee—Maureen Fitzsimons. We're going to change it to O'Hara'. And I said, 'Oh, no. I'd like my own name'. And that was it—take it or leave it. But Laughton was a wonderful person to work with, believe me. They were all very pro-Irish. Alec Guinness was too. We made *Our Man in Havana* (1959) together.

O'TOOLE: They then sold your contract on to RKO. . . .

O'HARA: They'd sell bits of you in those days. I don't know what they do today. But then they sold [me] first to RKO, then part of me to Twentieth Century Fox for *How Green Was My Valley*, one of the greatest movies ever made. Oh, it really was.

O'TOOLE: I watched it again last night.

O'HARA: You did? Wasn't it a fabulous movie?

O'TOOLE: Yes. John Ford was a fantastic director.

O'HARA: The best. You can't get any better than that.

O'TOOLE: And you were very good in it; so was Roddy McDowall.

O'HARA: Roddy's people were all from the County Meath area in Ireland. And a little bit of Scotland.

O'TOOLE: I read in your memoir that you were not that enthusiastic about becoming an actress. But yet you became one of the biggest in the world. So some part of you obviously must have really wanted to be big a movie star—otherwise, why do it?

O'HARA: Oh, no. I wanted to be an opera star. I wanted to be an opera singer. An actress in theatre and movies are two different things. Or, at least, you think they are two different things. I don't know now—acting is acting.

O'TOOLE: What's your fondest memory of your Hollywood career?

O'HARA: Oh, God. You didn't give me a chance! If I'd know you were going to ask that I'd have sat down and thought. Oh God! When you make 63 or 64 movies, which memory from which movie, you know, you think? God, you're now going to start me thinking.

I loved *The Hunchback of Notre Dame*. I loved *How Green Was My Valley*. I loved *Sentimental Journey*, which was very, very, very sad. And it was number one, as I told you, in China. And there was a section of the movie were I died. My husband didn't know I was dead, it was John Payne, who was another charmer. A wonderful person to work with. Tough.

And the end of the movie, I'm dead and the audience knows I'm dead, and he's looking for his wife and he comes into the place where she is lying dead in the bed and walks through looking for her. And the music the studio put in under the scene was *I'm Going to take a*

Sentimental Journey, which was a great, big hit song. I don't know if you ever knew it, if you're not interested in music, you won't know it. But that was one of the big hits. It was a number one hit in the world.

All they did was play the music and he walked through and the audience sobbed out load in New York. And in the big magazine—*Time*, *Life* was it? It was the one [that's] all pictures. *Life* magazine. They had in it the next day that the people came out crying. Men sobbed at the movie. But, anyway, the men sobbed out loud in the theatre and it hit the newspapers the next day. And they said that the men in the movie sobbed, not because of the super sadness of the movie but because they couldn't get their money back!

I didn't know if you ever saw it? Oh, no, find it. *Sentimental Journey* with John Payne and Maureen O'Hara. I don't know if they have it here.

O'TOOLE: I'm sure there's some movies you'd rather forget too.

O'HARA: Oh, God, yeah! You'd be surprised at movies you thought were fabulous and they just made there way. And then something that you thought, 'Oh, good God did I really do that?' And it'd be a smash hit, you know? It's amazing what the public falls for.

O'TOOLE: *Mr. Hobbs Takes a Vacation* was on TV the other day . . .

O'HARA: That was a big hit. That's one, thank God, touch wood, I had wonderful leading men. Jimmy Stewart, John Payne, John Wayne. All of them. And all wonderful. And Cornel Wilde was a fine fencer. And I was a damn good fencer. We made *At Sword's Point* together. You had to fight for roles. You couldn't sit back and hope it's going to come and jump in your lap. But not be rude or hurtful with anybody, no way.

O'TOOLE: You enjoyed a special bond with many iconic actors and directors, but it appears to me that your closest bond was with John Wayne. . . .

O'HARA: Oh, yeah. He was a wonderful person. And a wonderful person to work it. We were proud of our work and proud of ourselves. And he had a wonderful family and wonderful kids and a wonderful wife and they were all for each other, supporting each other. And you were a member of a gang and it was wonderful. And a gang that you knew, if there was ever a problem or trouble, that support you. That they'd be there.

O'TOOLE: Who else were you close with?

O'HARA: John Ford.

O'TOOLE: John Ford was born in America but he really wanted to be perceived as Irish. . . .

O'HARA: Well, he was. You know where he was from? His real name was Sean Aloysius O'Fearna [*John Martin Feeney in English – JOT*]. That was his name. And he was from Spiddal. He was very proud of it. And, of course, they all liked to boast that they had Irish blood—actors. I don't know why. Maybe Irish were hams. You know what a ham is? An 'over actor'. If you're a ham, you over act. What do you call it? Hamming it up.

O'TOOLE: Who else did you enjoy working with?

O'HARA: There were other wonderful people like Jimmy Stewart and Brian Keith and Anthony Quinn, who was very proud of the fact that, though he was born in Mexico, he had an Irish name! He was very pleased. Laughton was excellent. Laughton was a Catholic.

And you'd be surprised of how many of them were Catholics. Alfred Hitchcock was a fine, fine, fine director, and another Catholic. His mother was Irish. And another one was Alec Guinness. And a very strong Catholic. And if you were one minute late for mass, he made you go to another one. Oh, yes [*laughs*].

O'TOOLE: You had a tough, feisty persona on screen. But deep down, is there a softer side to Maureen O'Hara?

O'HARA: If it has anything to do with family. Kids and family.

O'TOOLE: Were you always tough?

O'HARA: Yeah. I had two tough brothers. There were six of us: four girls and two boys. And the two boys saw to it that all the girls in the family were tough. And we were. My older sister Peg, she was an Irish Sister of Charity. She became a nun. But she was also a wonderful person; she won a scholarship as a soprano. And gave it up to be a nun. So, in the family, we had all of that.

My brother Charlie was a barrister in the Gaelic language and he won the gold debate medal of Europe. And my brother, Jimmy, the other boy, he won the Leinster 500, which is the motorcycle race from the North down into Dublin.

So, the whole family, we were tough. We were all number one at no matter what we touched. We didn't brag about it. We were proud of it. We were so proud of the fact that we made our mother and father proud of us.

O'TOOLE: I suppose *The Quiet Man* must be one of your all-time favourite films?

O'HARA: Oh, gosh, yes. You'd be surprised at how many years it took to try to raise the money to make *The Quiet Man*. It was a long, long, long time. Republic Studios [eventually] put up the money. But [before this] we could never get the money anywhere. They'd laugh. They'd say, 'Poor Irish!' And you wouldn't get anything. And we made a movie just before we made *The Quiet Man* called *Rio Grande* (1950). And when that was shown to the theatre men, Ford [suddenly] said, 'Stop, stop, stop . . . cut'. And they said, 'We want to see it all'. And they created such a hullabaloo that they put the movie back on and let them see the whole movie. And it was then the head of this Republic Studios, when he heard all of that fuss and, you know, support going on, he agreed to finance the movie.

It was wonderful. With the script, my brother sat with John Ford and he said, 'Tell me so and so. Describe so and so'. My brother Charlie Jr. produced a whole lot. He did all of the Batman [1966 movie] and all of those. We were thrilled. And, of course, my mother and father were in Hollywood then and John Ford talked to my Dad.

I have a list of my films. I should've brought the list. I could get it for you or get it copied; I made 60-something movies and there's a whole list and it's done not to boast or anything, but it's done to have it so if somebody asks you a question you could check it. It's the movie, then it's the year, then who the director was and who the producer was and who the actors were and each one done like that. There are many times when I have to check: 'God, what did I do after so and so?' And I just look at that list and there it is.

O'TOOLE: I have the list here. . . .

O'HARA: But I don't think the list is like my list. Do you have everything? Ah, mother of God. There were some wonderful ones. Naturally, you love the first big break, which was *The Hunchback of Notre Dame*. And then, of course, you love ones like *How Green Was My Valley*, *A Miracle on 34th Street*, *Spencer's Mountain*, *The Long Great Line*, and then there was one very sad one, *Sentimental Journey*, which became number one in China.

O'TOOLE: You came out of retirement to make *Only the Lonely* with John Candy, which was released in 1991. He sadly died from a heart attack in 1994, at the relatively young age of 43.

O'HARA: He was a charmer. And he was coming here to play in my golf tournament and he had to go down into Southern California to do a certain thing and he died. So, he didn't [get to] come. But boy we were looking forward to him coming. Can you imagine if we had John Candy out on that golf course? God! He was a very, very nice person; a very strong Catholic. We used to meet after mass on Sunday, his wife and his kids and me and all of my relatives. We'd all meet outside of the church and we'd yakety yakety yak. We were all chatters, you know? And it was wonderful.

O'TOOLE: Was it difficult for them to talk you into acting again to make *Only The Lonely*?

O'HARA: No, no, no. I gave up because it was John Wayne who nagged me. And he was playing chess with Charlie Blair. The two of them were great pals. And he said, 'Well, don't you think it's about time you quit?' And they were playing a game of chess and I went out to see if they wanted something to eat. And Duke said that to me. And I said, 'Okay, I quit. Right now'. And I did.

O'TOOLE: You gave it up for love?

O'HARA: Yep. Yeah. I said, 'I've done it—right now'. That's true. Oh, if you met Charlie Blair you'd say, 'What a wise decision you made'.

O'TOOLE: You never once missed it?

O'HARA: Never. Well, I was so involved with the airline business, you know? They even say that I was the only woman who was the head of an airline company.

O'TOOLE: Hollywood has dramatically changed since your era. There's more media intrusion these days.

O'HARA: Well, there was never any really privacy—you were always a subject to the public's opinion of you. And it had to be up to you to see that it never became a bad opinion, [that] it was always a good opinion. And that they appreciated you and liked you and liked the kind of work you were doing. You had to stand up for yourself. It wasn't much different than being in school.

O'TOOLE: You weren't really on the receiving end of much criticism, but it must've hurt when it ever did pop up?

O'HARA: Oh, there was plenty of criticism. And jealousy. It did hurt. It hurt if anybody was jealous of you or of anybody tried to talk against you, or criticise you. It's the same as anybody would feel in any career, you know, a footballer, a writer, anybody, if you're severely criticised it's tough to take and stand up under it.

O'TOOLE: Your acting came across very natural on screen.

O'HARA: I was taught here in Dublin. One of the best schools we had for acting was the Ena Mary Burke School [of Drama and Elocution] on Kildare Street, across from the hotel, the Shelbourne.

O'TOOLE: Do you regret that you never got to trod the boards as a leading lady in our national theatre, the Abbey?

O'HARA: No. I worked [there]. Well, in the movies, you call it as an extra. I did act and I did help clean the stage after a show finished. We had to carry the stuff off the stage and put it in the storage rooms, where everything was supposed to be, and to see that everything was packed and put away properly for the night. We got to do that. And I was well thought of.

To work in The Abbey, you had to take an audition. And when you took the audition, the judge, or the man who was going to judge you, sat in the theatre and you went out on the stage and he told you what he wanted and you had to do it. And then he judged you on the basis of what he felt you were going to be able to do to benefit and help The Abbey Theatre. So, he either recommended you or didn't recommend you to be hired by The Abbey. And when I did my interview, he recommended that I be hired. So, I was hired by The Abbey. We used to get like ten shillings or a pound a week, you know? But you were thrilled; you were proud of yourself.

O'TOOLE: I heard you liked to do your own stunts.

O'HARA: The first time I fenced in a movie, *At Sword's Point*, and the director [Lewis Allen] was saying, 'Oh, no! Not fencing in the scene!' And they—the front office—were saying, 'Oh, no, no, no. We want that scene'.

So, I was trained by the fencing master from the Belgian army and he was wonderful. All the fencers who worked in the movies, and all the big scenes, pirates fencing and you had 20, 30, 40 fencers, were trained by this same master who trained me and they kept nagging, 'Keep your mouth shut. Keep your mouth shut. Quiet. Do what your told. Do what you're told'.

And I'm hearing these nasty remarks by the director, which I can't say I blamed him because at that time women didn't do stunts. I had to step out of a coach and immediately start fencing because I was attacked. And so the guys were saying to me, Get out there and do it. Don't do that. Remember what you're taught'.

I was ready to panic and run away. And finally they said, 'Alright'. And the director was sneering, worse than sneering. He was belittling the idea of a woman fencing. He was against it. The studio wanted it. And I jumped out of the coach and, boy, I fenced their arses off!

The director said, 'Cut! Cut! Print! Print!' You know, the whole place fell apart laughing and screaming and applauding. They were so thrilled. Because it belittled—well, not belittled. It did what to the director? It made him look like a fool.

When I did *The Quiet Man*, I did all those things: working with the men, stunts, and actions. I did so many pictures that involved fencing, fighting, punching, boxing, jumping off buildings, and everything.

There was one picture, *McLintock!*, with The Duke where I had to climb a ladder to the second story and then fall backwards into a water trough—and it was very dangerous. Actually, I could have killed myself. If I had fallen long, I'd have hit my head off the top of the water trough and I'd have broken my . . . I'd have been dead! If I fell short, I'd have broken my legs.

The stuntman said, 'Get off you damn fool; you're going to kill yourself'. And I said, 'Why the hell didn't you tell me that a couple of weeks ago? Or even a couple of minutes ago?' But I didn't say a couple of minutes ago. 'When I agreed to do the bloody stunt? If I'd known . . .'

Well, I didn't *know* that it was dangerous. And, so, I did it. When it was over, I fell into the water trough and got almost drowned and I had to get out and face Duke. Watch him, next time that you see that movie.

And Duke looked at me and he said, 'You didn't get your hair wet!' Oh, really! [*Laughs.*] That was his way of saying, 'Good girl'. No, really. It was his way of cutting the drama and making everybody laugh.

O'TOOLE: Was there anything you couldn't do?

O'HARA: The only stuff I didn't do was on a horse, properly. I couldn't look professional on a horse. And there was a girl and she went everywhere with me. But if I had to be on a horse, she did it. She was wonderful. Oh, boy. I'll never forget it. I was really frightened. I really was. But I did it all. But that stunt in *McLintock* was the one thing that frightened me because I thought, 'God, I may be dead in five minutes'.

O'TOOLE: You're justifiably described as iconic and beautiful—yet you appear to always keep your feet on the ground. You strike me as being very modest, despite all the attention. How did you manage to keep your ego in check?

O'HARA: I had a fabulous mother and father and five brothers and sisters and they wouldn't ever permit you to get more important than you thought you were. You know. And I won most of the fèis [Irish dancing competitions]; I won the Rathmines Fèis; the Father Mathew fèis; the Dublin fèis. I won them all. I was just delighted that I won them.

I won the competition and the next day in the paper, the judge, who was a lady, said in the paper the next day that if she could have given me more than 100pc she would have. I had the page and I lost it. I don't have it anymore, so I can't tell you what the competition was. It was in Dublin city. But I'd love that page out of it. It was a big fèis, but anyway I was thrilled when won that.

You had to sit there and then you were called up on the stage and then the judge would question you, and then you did whatever you were going to do, and then you waited for the votes to be . . . come through. But, I hate to tell you, I won them all. I was proud of it but I wasn't egotistical about it. I was just thrilled that I was winning.

O'TOOLE: You're clearly very proud of Irish culture and your roots.

O'HARA: You've got to remember one thing that's so important—when you're Irish, you're Irish. And nobody is better than you or there is nowhere better than the country you came from. It sounds almost silly, but it's true. It's amazing. You go anywhere in the world and people say, 'Where you from?' And you say, 'Well, I'm Irish'. And they say, 'Oh, you are? You're Irish? Oh, oh'. And they are thrilled to meet you because you're Irish.

We, as a nation, should be very proud of that—that we earned that reputation in the whole world, that being Irish was something special. I don't know if you all realise it, but I've been everywhere in the world—Australia, France, Germany, Italy, Africa—and all you say is, 'I'm Irish'. It's really wonderful. To think that all of the people earned . . . the Irish people that travelled in the world, seeking a job, seeking work, just travelling, just enjoying it, they earned in the world that reputation. It wasn't given to us. We earned it.

This is the country I was born in, I grew up in. It gave me the talent, you know, that gave me the position in the world that I have. And, thank God, still have.

O'TOOLE: Why did you pick here in Glengariff, County Cork to live?

O'HARA: It's beautiful. We were looking for a house in Ireland because the houses that we had were sold long ago when we moved to America. We came here, Charlie Blair and I, because I wanted to do something in Ireland. We came here and we went looking for a house. We drove down to Glengariff. I had never been in Glengariff. And we saw this house and Charlie Blair looked out at it and he said, 'Oh, my God! This is a perfect place to land a seaplane. We're going to buy the house'. I said, 'Wait a minute! Let's look at the house first before we decide on the basis of a seaplane'. And we fell in love with house and we bought the house.

And, yes, we did land the seaplane. Did you ever meet anybody that was here when the seaplane came in? Oh, God. There's a photograph at home. Charlie flew flights up to the Aran Islands. You'd be surprised at the people who'd come along and take a ride on the plane. And the young boys, they would just stand and look at the plane. And it was a beautiful plane. It was a plane that crossed from the United State to Ireland, over the Atlantic. Beautiful plane.

O'TOOLE: You never lost your faith in God?

O'HARA: No, I never questioned my faith. I believed in God and I still believe in God. But I did feel it was a terrible thing to happen to me. It was absolutely awful. And he was a wonderful man. And if you could meet some of the old people that he knew here: young boys and kids, just [to] touch his hand would thrill them because he was a very brave man and part of the military, as you know.

He was a general in the air force, but then he was in commercial too. He was the senior pilot of Pan Am. He flew the first flight across the Atlantic to land in Ireland. He flew the first flight over the Pole—militarily, that was very important. He flew the first flight to land in Portugal. He flew all over the world. The first flight in Africa. He did the first everywhere in the world. And he was not egotistical. And young boys: just to touch the bottom of his coat, they were so thrilled. And he was so kind and good to them. It was wonderful to watch him handle young boys, you know?

O'TOOLE: I'm sure you still miss your husband every day.

O'HARA: Oh, God, yes.

O'TOOLE: It sounds like he was your true soul mate.

O'HARA: Oh, boy, yes. Everybody that knew him here, he's their soul mate too, you know? Particularly one of the lads here called Patrick Carey. Ah, they worshipped him.

O'TOOLE: But does time make it easier for you?

O'HARA: No. No. No. You wouldn't expect it to? I don't.

O'TOOLE: You're now 90 and still going strong. What's your secret to such longevity?

O'HARA: That's your gift from your parents. You inherit that. But then, of course, you can damage it. But if you appreciate what God's gift has given to you through your parents then you should do what you're destined to do. You really should.

I guess I was always tough. I always intended to do great things. I didn't do all of the things I wanted to do. I wanted to sing; I wanted to be an opera singer. And I wanted to write beautiful poetry, which I think I did, but it's all gone. I don't know where it is, or who has it, or what happened to it, I don't know where it is.

There's a couple of things that I don't do: I don't have whiskey. Oh, I don't smoke. Always in bed early. Food: plenty of vegetables; some good meat. And then as a special, special treat I have what's known—and you'll have to find somebody to explain it to you—a Rock Bun [cake] with my cup of tea. Oh, they're gorgeous. A nice hot cup of tea with a Rock Bun. Oh, God! You can't have anything better than that [*laughs*].

You know what they say about old age? Old age is a terrible thing, particularly when it strikes you when you're so young. You never heard that? I think that's a Dublin remark.

There's so many wonderful remarks and sayings as kids and most of them are gone. That's what we are going to do, is a book. We're working on it. Every time I think of something, we'd write it down, old sayings. Here's another one: Love is a thing shaped like a quiver, runs through the heart.

They're wonderful, but they're all forgotten. When I was in school we had those sayings. When we were kids, they had all those wonderful poems and sayings and silly songs and, you know, a couple of kind of nasty things that kids shouldn't be saying. But we did. We didn't know that they were actually that bad.

O'TOOLE: You said that you want to grow old to be a wonderful, eccentric, tough old lady. . . .

O'HARA: I'm doing it right now [*roars laughing*]. And I'm going to do it. Oh, God! I've brought my cane. Here it is [*She waves the cane in the air*].

O'TOOLE: You once told Larry King that you planned to live to 102. What made you pick that age?

O'HARA: Charlie Blair's mother [who was from Ireland] lived to be one hundred and two. And she was also head of all the girl scouts of the area she lived in. She was the boss. And she was a fabulous woman. And, believe me, all of the enthusiasm and ambition of Charlie Blair, he got from his mother. She was a terrific woman. And she was from Southern Donegal. McGonegal. Well, you know, you try to mix with the Irish; you don't try to be involved with strange people.

O'TOOLE: I suppose the negative thing about living to 90 is that you're constantly bidding farewell to friends and relatives who don't live as long. It must be really tough.

O'HARA: Yes, it is. But, at the same time, you always say to them that, 'You know, when you get there help and tell them not to cast me aside! To let me come too'. And you mean heaven. But you do. You really do. I often think about how I am going to handle it. You know, when I get there. And thank God I've never doubted. I never thought I was going to go down—I was always going to go up. But you do think about, 'What am I going to do? Who am I going to watch over? Who am I going to help? Who am I going to talk to God about?' You know, you really do. It's amazing.

O'TOOLE: What is heaven going to be like for Maureen O'Hara?

O'HARA: I hope all my wonderful relatives will be there. And I'll be able to watch a couple of soccer games. It was very hard on me in America as there were no soccer games on TV. The TV is well used now for the games. Really, soccer was my favourite sport.

I wanted to play soccer. I did play camogie. But I always felt we needed a mask in camogie because the swing of the club and in those days there wasn't. And now there is. And it's wonderful to see and to know that has come about. And I think it's a great game and we should keep supporting it and saying too, 'We don't [want to] lose any of the great things that are Irish'. Nobody [else] in the world has hurling or camogie for girls. Camogie makes the girl tough. And today in this world—and the world since the beginning of time—a woman has to be tough.

O'TOOLE: Do you still go regularly to mass?

O'HARA: Oh, what do you think?

O'TOOLE: How do you want to be best remembered?

O'HARA: Me? [*short pause.*] I don't know. As an Irishwoman who made a success in the world; never let Ireland down. I'm very proud of being Irish. No, I am. I think Ireland is one of the great countries of the world and we have sent people out to every country in the world and they've done famous things and become famous people. And it's amazing that there are people who want to be Irish, but they're not, but they want to be.

O'TOOLE: Do you have any regrets in life?

O'HARA: Oh! Maybe that I didn't fight harder for certain roles that I would've loved to have played. I don't know. To do a thousand things. I could never satisfy myself by doing a little bit of this, or a little bit of that. I always wanted to do something important and big, be a great representative of Ireland. I don't know. Not everything. I'd like to have sung.

Notes

Chapter One: a shorter 2,000 word version of the Maureen O'Hara interview originally appeared in the Irish Daily Mail, *October 2010. I was fortunate enough to spend an entire weekend with Martin Sheen, which gave me enough material for three published in-depth interviews with him for* Empire, Hot Press *and the* Irish Mail on Sunday. *The vast majority of chapter two originally appeared in* Empire *magazine, April 2009, but has been slightly updated for this book. Chapter Three first appeared as a two-part feature in the* Irish Mail on Sunday *on 9 September 2012 and then in the* Irish Daily Mail *on 10 September 2012. Large sections of the chapter about Saoirse Ronan originally appeared in* Hot Press *in January 2008 and the* Irish Mail on Sunday *in October 2009. Chapter Five: A shorter version of this interview was first published in the* Sunday Times *in January 2017 and* Hot Press, *March 2007. Chapter Six: A slightly shorter version of this interview was first published in the* Irish Mail on Sunday, *December 2010. The John Boorman chapter appeared in* Hot Press, *March 2017. Various parts of Chapter Eight about Brenda Fricker have appeared in different versions, with the first interview being published in the* Irish Daily Mail *in February 2012, while a second version was published in London's* Daily Mail *in May 2012, and, finally, the interview, along with fresh correspondence with the actress, was used for the basis of a feature published* Hot Press *in October 2016. Chapter Nine: Johnny B Goode, Jonathan Rhys Meyers, was first published in* Hot

Press, *December 2007. Chapter Ten: A Survivor's Tale, Peter Sheridan was first published in the* Irish Mail on Sunday, *January 2013. The Hazel O'Connor interview first appeared in its entirety in the* Irish Mail on Sunday, *September 2011. Chapter Thirteen: The poignant story behind Adam & Paul, Mark O'Halloran was published in June 2013 in the* Irish Daily Mail. *A considerably shorter version of chapter fourteen, A Life In Focus, Terry O'Neill was published in 2017 in the* Irish Daily Mirror. *A large excerpt from Chapter Fifteen: Hear My Song, Adrian Dunbar was originally published on 23 March 2013 in the* Irish Daily Mail. *Chapter Sixteen: Throwing It All Away, Alan Devlin was first published on 13 April, 2010 in the* Irish Daily Mail. *With regards Chapter Seventeen: About a Girl, Victoria Smurfit, this interview with was conducted in October 2009 but, despite being commissioned, was never published. Chapter Eighteen: An Irish Legend Niall Tóibín originally appeared in the* Irish Daily Mail *on 29 May, 2010. Chapter Nineteen: The Irish Everyman, Simon Delaney first appeared on 15 April, 2012 in the* Irish Mail on Sunday. *Chapter Twenty: A Brave heart, John Kavanagh first appeared in the* Irish Daily Mail, *June 2014. Chapter-Twenty-One: Raise the Titanic, Jason Barry was first published on 16 April, 2012 in the* Irish Daily Mail. *Chapter Twenty-Two: Commander in chef, Martin Sheen was first published in* Hot Press, *November 2006. This last piece was, coincidentally enough, my first commission for* Hot Press. *The last chapter is the complete transcript of my interview with Maureen O'Hara, published here for the first time in full.*

Acknowledgements

I'd like to thank the following for their support and encouragement: John Drennan, Rosaleen O'Toole, Jackie Hayden, Noel Taylor, Mick McNiffe, John 'Jumbo' Keirans, Pat Flanagan, Demelza de Burca, Sylvia Pownall, Zoe Watson, Francis Callaghan, Francis Veale, Trevor O'Rourke, Linda Langton, Vincent Smith, George Plummer, Keith O'Toole, Stephen Browne, Declan Cassidy, Eric Bailey, John Lee, Amy O'Toole, Lorraine O'Toole, Marianne O'Toole, Lee Dunne, Linda Maher, Valerie Hanley, Fr Shay Cullen, Caridad Prat, Jesús Elices, Olga Prat, Juana Prat, Fernando Prat, Ascension Gonzalez, Gary Walsh, Frank Tighe, María Teresa Sevilla Maté, Jose Álvarez, Niall Stokes, Darlene Swanson. I would like to thank my good friend Darren Kinsella for providing many of the photographs used in Hollywood Irish, as it wouldn't have been visually as good a book without the use of some of his wonderful portraits. I'd also like to express thanks to Ben Ohmart, Daniel Swanson, and all at BearManor Media for their stellar work on this book project.

Finally, I'd like to pay tribute to my father Gerry O'Toole and my mentor Paul Drury, who both sadly left the party too early. I'll be eternally grateful to them for going out of their way to help me on countless occasions. They're deeply missed.

Index

Numbers in **bold** indicate photographs

www.ingramcontent.com/pod-product-compliance
Lightning Source LLC
Chambersburg PA
CBHW020839020726
47497CB00005B/1179

* 9 7 8 1 6 2 9 3 3 4 1 8 9 *